GW01377027

Care and Coronavirus

A necessary book for indeterminate times. Viewing childhood through the prism of Covid, these interdisciplinary and international contributors marry research and experience to provide intimate views of how existing health inequalities are not only brought into relief – but can be effectively addressed – to better serve young people, families, and communities in pandemic eras. Informative, provocative, and grounding for those charged with caring about the very future of care.
—*Rachael Stryker*, **Professor, Department of Human Development and Women's Studies, California State University, East Bay, USA**

EMERALD STUDIES IN CHILD CENTRED PRACTICE

Series Editor: Sam Frankel, Western University, Canada

Emerald Studies in Child Centred Practice: Voice, Collaboration and Change seeks to reposition the place of childhood studies as a discipline, highlighting its social value. This series explores the application of theories from childhood studies in practice. It highlights the place, purpose and power of these theories to inform practice and seek to shape a child-centred approach across the settings within which children live and experience their everyday lives – schools, families, the law and the care system. Uniquely, books in the series will not only draw on academic insight but also include the perspectives of both practitioners and children. The series makes the case for the need for a shared dialogue as a foundation for re-imagining practice.

This new series offers a new and valuable dimension to childhood studies with relevance for how wider society comes to engage with it. Indeed, it offers a chance for childhood studies to increase its presence in society – to demonstrate how an awareness of children's agency and the constructed nature of society can positively influence discourse and debate – with the hope that this can increasingly shape policy and practice and add value to children's everyday experiences. Proposals are welcome for the series that align to this goal and help us to develop and grow childhood studies. The series is particularly keen to explore multi-faceted aspects of children's lives, such as schooling, home lives, children's rights, child protection, activism and more.

Published Titles

Children as Change Makers: A Resource to Enhance Child Centred Practice and Extend Active Learning Opportunities by Sam Frankel & Daniella Bendo

Learning Allowed: Children, Communities and Lifelong Learning in a Changing World by Sam Frankel & Caroline E. Whalley

Participatory Research on Child Maltreatment with Children and Adult Survivors: Concepts, Ethics, and Methods edited by Maria Roth, Ravit Alfandari & Gemma Crous

Establishing Child Centred Practice in a Changing World, Part B edited by Sam Frankel

Establishing Child Centred Practice in a Changing World, Part A edited by Sam Frankel

Care and Coronavirus: Perspectives on Childhood, Youth and Family

EDITED BY

TOM DISNEY
Northumbria University, UK

AND

LUCY GRIMSHAW
Northumbria University, UK

emerald PUBLISHING

United Kingdom – North America – Japan – India – Malaysia – China

Emerald Publishing Limited
Emerald Publishing, Floor 5, Northspring, 21-23 Wellington Street, Leeds LS1 4DL

First edition 2025

Editorial matter and selection © 2025 Tom Disney and Lucy Grimshaw.
Individual chapters © 2025 The authors.
Published under exclusive licence by Emerald Publishing Limited.

Reprints and permissions service
Contact: www.copyright.com

No part of this book may be reproduced, stored in a retrieval system, transmitted in any form or by any means electronic, mechanical, photocopying, recording or otherwise without either the prior written permission of the publisher or a licence permitting restricted copying issued in the UK by The Copyright Licensing Agency and in the USA by The Copyright Clearance Center. Any opinions expressed in the chapters are those of the authors. Whilst Emerald makes every effort to ensure the quality and accuracy of its content, Emerald makes no representation implied or otherwise, as to the chapters' suitability and application and disclaims any warranties, express or implied, to their use.

British Library Cataloguing in Publication Data
A catalogue record for this book is available from the British Library

ISBN: 978-1-83797-311-8 (Print)
ISBN: 978-1-83797-310-1 (Online)
ISBN: 978-1-83797-312-5 (Epub)

Printed and bound by CPI Group (UK) Ltd, Croydon, CR0 4YY

INVESTOR IN PEOPLE

For our families

Contents

About the Editors *xiii*

About the Contributors *xv*

Acknowledgements *xxiii*

Chapter 1   Introduction: Care, Childhood, Youth and Family in the Context of Coronavirus *1*
Tom Disney and Lucy Grimshaw

Section 1: Early Systems of Care

Chapter 2   Children's and Parents' Experiences of Care During the Pandemic: An International Review *19*
Fabio Dovigo

Chapter 3   Childcare, Responses to Poverty in Preschool and a 'New Normal' After COVID-19 Pandemic? *39*
Donald Simpson and Sandra Lyndon

Chapter 4   COVID-19 Anxiety and Early Childhood Development: Reflections From Practitioners in Early Years Settings *55*
Charmaine Agius Ferrante and Elaine Chaplin

Section 2: Children and Young People's Health and Wellbeing

Chapter 5   Experiences of Vulnerable Girls From an Informal Settlement in South Africa During COVID-19 Lockdowns *65*
Lucy Currie, Sibusisiwe Tendai Sibanda and Athenkosi Mtumtum

Chapter 6 Children's Care for Public Health and Politically Expedient Care for Children in Aotearoa New Zealand's COVID-19 Pandemic 81
Julie Spray

Chapter 7 We Were the Only Ones Still Seeing Families, We Just had to Be Creative About How! A Reflection on Health Visiting Practice During the COVID-19 Pandemic 97
Frances Gunn

Section 3: Parents as Subjects and Recipients of Care

Chapter 8 A Simple Life? Parents' Early Narratives of Babies Raised During the COVID-19 Pandemic 105
Laura Bellussi and Siân Lucas

Chapter 9 'I Don't Have a Lot of Choice ... My Boss He Still Likes to Go to the Office Everyday Pretty Much' – Exploring the Impact of COVID-19 on Parents' Decision-Making When Planning Care During Their Child's First Year 121
Clare Matysova

Chapter 10 Family Life, Covid and Care: A Conversation Between Parent and Child 137
Fiona Ranson and Cuong Nguyen

Section 4: Schooling as Care

Chapter 11 Caring and Schooling in the Time of COVID-19 145
Tom Disney, Lucy Grimshaw and Judy Thomas

Chapter 12 'Take Care Everyone!' Care Ethics at Work Whilst Homeschooling and Caring for Children During the COVID-19 Pandemic 163
Lucy Grimshaw, Kay Heslop, Kirstin Mulholland, Vikki Park, Jill Duncan, Jaden Allan, Cathryn Meredith and Christopher Warnock

Chapter 13 Teaching During Lockdowns *181*
Linzi Brown

Chapter 14 Precarious Schooling and COVID-19 *185*
Jason Burg

Section 5: Young People Navigating Care and Control Beyond the School

Chapter 15 Virtual Hearings and Their Impact on Children's Participation in Decisions About Their Care and Protection *191*
Catherine Nixon, Kirsty Deacon, Andrew James, Ciara Waugh, Zodie and Sarah McGarrol

Chapter 16 Everyday Life, Informal Care and Grassroots Sports Clubs *209*
Stephen Crossley

Chapter 17 Youth Work During Covid Lockdowns *225*
Alison Ní Charraighe, Kelly Coates, Shannon Devine and Elisha Sanchez

Final Commentary

Chapter 18 Childhood and Care in the Time of Coronavirus, A Commentary *233*
Rachel Rosen

Index *243*

About the Editors

Tom Disney is a Social Geographer and an Associate Professor of Childhood Studies at Northumbria University, in the Department of Social Work, Education and Community Wellbeing. His research centres on families and children experiencing interventions of the state, exploring how these interventions break or facilitate marginalisation. He has conducted research on residential care settings for children and young people, child protection practice and participatory arts-based research to improve local authority Early Help systems.

Lucy Grimshaw, PhD, is an Assistant Professor of Social Policy at Northumbria University in the Department of Social Work, Education and Community Wellbeing. Lucy is a Social Scientist whose research examines intersectional inequalities in urban spaces, communities and institutions underpinned by feminist critical pedagogy and employing participatory methods. Recent research projects have focused on children's sense of place in relation to local heritage and inequalities among staff and students in higher education institutions.

About the Contributors

Jaden Allan is an Assistant Professor of Nurse education at Northumbria University in the Department of Nursing, Midwifery and Health. Jaden's research and scholarly activity include peer humanistic support and development in higher education and healthcare, along with simulation-based education (SBE). Jaden also develops and delivers nursing transnational education programmes globally and is an executive board member for the International Family Nursing Association (IFNA) UK and Ireland Chapter.

Laura Bellussi has a background in psychology, and her research interests include adults' and children's mental health, domestic abuse, discrimination and social equality. Her work entails evaluating innovations and adaptations in children and families' social care using qualitative, creative, and mixed methods.

Linzi Brown has always had a passion for the early years and pursued this by training and working as a practitioner in Early Years and health settings, supporting children and families. She then continued her education and graduated from Northumbria University after studying BA Joint Honours in Childcare and Education/Early Years and Childhood Studies. Linzi studied on the Graduate Teacher Programme (GTP) at the school she currently teaches in led by Northumbria University. Linzi has worked in a Further Education college and three secondary schools in the North East of England over the past 17 years. She has held positions in teaching and learning, pastoral and now, alongside continuing to teach, leads a Faculty of Health and Wellbeing in a large secondary school in Northumberland.

Dr Jason Burg is a historian who completed a PhD entitled 'Remember where you are!: The use of English Cathedrals as sites theatrical performance, 1928–2015' in 2017 at the University of Birmingham. He worked for several years in academia before retraining to teach history at secondary school, completing his PGCE teaching qualification in 2020. He now works at a large rural secondary school in the North East of England teaching History and Politics.

Elaine Chaplin, a dedicated advocate for the well-being of young minds, intertwines her passion for early years and mental health in her impactful work. With a background in early years education, she creates narratives that delve into the delicate nuances of early childhood development and its profound connection to mental wellness. Elaine's commitment to fostering resilience and nurturing the emotional growth of children is evident in her works. As an educator, and mental health ambassador, Elaine Chaplin leaves a memorable mark on the intersection of early childhood and mental well-being.

Alison Ní Charraighe is an Assistant Professor of Childhood and Youth Studies at Northumbria University. She has a professional background in Youth Work and Community Development work, having worked for 17 as a youth worker and manager in the North East of England. She has recently completed her training as a Counsellor, specialising in working with young people.

Kelly Coates, Shannon Devine and Elisha Sanchez are practitioners are from Projects4Change a youth work project based in Newcastle upon Tyne.

Stephen Crossley is an Assistant Professor in Sociology at Durham University. He rejoined the university in June 2020, having previously worked at Northumbria University. He completed an ESRC funded PhD at Durham in 2017, examining the UK Government's Troubled Families Programme. Prior to entering academia, Stephen worked in a number of public sector and voluntary sector roles in the North East of England, working on issues such as estate-based youth work, community cohesion, tenant participation, health inequalities, and child poverty. He has published extensively on issues relating to 'troubled families', child poverty and social justice and his research interests revolve around policy responses to social disadvantage and inequality and the symbolic power of social policies.

Dr Lucy Currie is an Assistant Professor at Northumbria University, Newcastle. With an education career that started in Secondary Schools in Zimbabwe and Botswana, Dr Currie has worked in Higher Education in the United Kingdom since 2003, mainly in Special Education and Inclusion, Work Based Learning and Professional Learning. Dr Currie's interests are in educational equity, inclusive practice, widening participation and professional development. As such, her research interests focus on examining the relationship between culture, heritage and learners' educational experiences and outcomes.

Dr Kirsty Deacon was a Research Officer at the Scottish Children's Reporter Administration while carrying out the piece of research contained within this book. Her background is in criminal justice and her research interests focus on imprisonment, particularly in the context of families and relationships.

Fabio Dovigo, PhD, is a Professor of Education at the Social Work, Education and Community Wellbeing Department of Northumbria University, UK. He has held the UNESCO Chair in 'Supporting Early Years Care and Education'. His research interests lie in the fields of Early Childhood Education and Care and inclusive education. He is a convenor of the Special Interest Group Sustainability in ECEC of the European Early Childhood Research Education Association. He has coordinated several EU International Research Projects, including 'Building High-Quality Early Childhood Education Systems Supported by International Evidence' and 'Enhancing Quality in Family Day Care'. His recent publications include 'Educator identity in a neoliberal context: Recognising and supporting early childhood education and care educators' (EECERJ, 2020), 'Early Childhood Care and Education teaching staff and educators: Challenges and Opportunities, WCECCE Global Thematic Report' (UNESCO, 2024), and 'Promoting transformative practices for sustainability in Early Childhood Education and Care' (EECERA Praxis Series, Routledge, 2024).

Jill Duncan is an Assistant Professor of Education at Northumbria University, former Teacher and Leader across different school settings including international activity. Jill's research and scholarly activity focuses upon an ethic of care, specifically focusing on holistic provision for postgraduate trainees within initial teacher education (ITE). She works in close collaboration with local partners such as The Baltic Centre for Contemporary Art and is a member of national organisations such as the British Educational Research Association (BERA).

Charmaine Agius Ferrante, PhD, Senior Lecturer in Education, Children and Young People, Northumbria University. She is currently the Director of Education for Undergraduate Programmes in the Department of Social work, Education and Community Wellbeing. She is Senior Teaching Fellow HEA and the Programme Lead for BA Childhood and Early Years Studies. She is also a consultant Developmental Educationist and has advised policy around inclusive education in Malta where she was involved in supporting the development and provision of inclusive practice. Her research interests are the politics, policy and practices of inclusive education with respect to the education of disabled children. Research themes include developmental education, early intervention, early years teaching and learning, creating spaces and places for all children, sexuality and relationships in young disabled people, the relationship between disability theory and the local and global disability movements together with the possible connections between inclusive education and disability studies. She is a committed advocate for inclusive education, assisting parents, individuals, schools and communities to work towards building inclusive communities of practice.

Lucy Grimshaw is an Assistant Professor of Social Policy at Northumbria University in the Department of Social Work, Education and Community Wellbeing. Lucy is a Social Scientist whose research examines intersectional inequalities in urban spaces, communities and institutions underpinned by feminist critical pedagogy and employing participatory methods. Recent research projects have focused on children's sense of place in relation to local heritage and inequalities amongst staff and students in higher education institutions.

Frances Gunn works in a Health and Social Care Partnership in Scotland as a Service Manager with responsibility for Health Visiting. Prior to this, Frances was a Child Protection Health Advisor, Health Visitor and Midwife. Frances is also an Associate Tutor and a PhD student in the Centre for Child Wellbeing and Protection, University of Stirling. Frances's doctoral research study title is 'An exploration of professionals and families understanding of child neglect using an ecological framework perspective, with data from Ayrshire & Arran providing a geographic case study'.

About the Contributors

Kay Heslop is the Department Head of Education within the Department of Social Work, Education and Community Wellbeing at Northumbria University. Kay has worked with people of all ages in her professional roles over four decades. She has endeavoured to develop inclusive, authentic and motivational educational activities which meet personal interests and build upon current skills. As a Researcher, Kay favours a participatory approach which has an impact on practice and for people.

Andrew James, Ciara Waugh and Zodie are Board Members of Our Hearings, Our Voice; an independent children and young people's Board for the Children's Hearings System. It exists to ensure that the voices of children and young people are included in decisions about meaningful change within the Children's Hearings System and to ensure that any proposed changes are implemented in a way that does not disadvantage the Rights and participation of children and young people. Since becoming Board Members Andrew, Ciara and Zodie have played an active role in trying to improve the experiences of children and young people coming to Hearings. Information about the range of work that Andrew, Ciara and Zodie are involved in can be found at www.ohov.co.uk

Dr Siân Lucas is a registered social worker and has research interests in perinatal support, migration, linguistic discrimination and social justice. She has worked on various research projects to explore dimensions of well-being and service delivery using creative, qualitative, visual and participatory research methods.

Dr Sandra Lyndon is a reader in Childhood and Social Policy at the University of Chichester, UK. Sandra is the programme coordinator for the BA Hons Early Childhood Studies Level 6 top up and teaches across a range of Childhood programmes within the Institute of Education and Social Sciences. She is the Childhood Research Champion and takes a lead on research within the team. Sandra has many years' experience working with children in a variety of settings; she is a qualified Teacher and an Educational Psychologist. She completed her doctoral studies at the University of Sussex and her research interests include poverty, homelessness, intergenerational practice and narrative methodologies.

Clare Matysova, University of Leeds, UK – Clare Matysova is a PhD Researcher at the University of Leeds focusing on gender equality and exploring the impact of the United Kingdom's shared parental leave policy from the perspective of couples' decision-making. She also works as an Equality, Diversity and Inclusion practitioner in Higher Education, currently at the University of Aberdeen, previously Head of Equity, Diversity and Inclusion at the London School of Hygiene and Tropical Medicine.

Cathryn Meredith has practised and taught mental health social work for 25 years, and none of this prepared her for parenting through the pandemic. She leads Northumbria University's Approved Mental Health Professional (AMHP) and Best Interests Assessor (BIA) provision within the Department of Social Work, Education and Community Wellbeing. Her scholarly interests lie in social approaches to mental distress and the emerging discipline of Mad Studies. She collaborates with people with lived experience to undertake ethnographic, naturalistic enquiries.

Athenkosi Mtumtum is a HPCSA Registered Counsellor and Co-Founder of Sizakala Wellness Counsellors in South Africa. Her passion for philanthropy has its origins in the belief of the innate resilient spirit we all possess. She believes that the act of empathy shown in our interactions with others serves as a subtle reminder to people in need of their resilience. This reminds them that even though they may be victims of circumstances, the will and power to overcome their challenges rests within them. Since her B-Psych Honours (2012) completion Athenkosi has acquired a BA Honours in Community and Health Psychology (2017).

Kirstin Mulholland is an Assistant Professor of Education at Northumbria University and former Primary Teacher and School Leader. Alongside her role at Northumbria, Kirstin is a Senior Associate for the Education Endowment Foundation and also collaborates closely with a number of national organisations, including the Maths Hub Network and Research Schools Network. Her research interests centre on educators' professional learning, including the use of research evidence to inform professional practice.

Dr Sarah McGarrol is a Senior Research Fellow with the NIHR funded Aberdeen Health Determinants Research Collaboration, based at Aberdeen City Council. Her research interests include social and geographical inequalities in health, ethics of care, the impact of adverse childhood experiences for children in conflict with the law and critical reflections on health inequalities fieldwork.

Dr Catherine Nixon is the Research Manager at the Scottish Children's Reporter Administration. Her research interests focus upon the lived experiences of children and young people who are care- and/or hearings-experienced. She is particularly interested in how changes in practice and policy affect the Rights and participation of children and young people.

Cuong Nguyen was living with Fiona Ranson when COVID first appeared in the United Kingdom; he is Fiona's foster son and was a care leaver, still living with her at the time. In this chapter he reflects on how COVID impacted on his time at home. Cuong was attending college and had a part time job, which both came to a halt during COVID. He recalls monitoring responses from elsewhere in the world and comparing these to what was happening in the UK, which made him more anxious about Covid. Later he returned to work, where there were robust COVID measures in place.

Vikki Park is an Assistant Professor of Interprofessional Education and Collaborative Practice (IPECP) at Northumbria University in the Department of Nursing, Midwifery & Health. Vikki's research and scholarly work explore collaboration and interprofessional learning between health and social care professions within educational and practice environments. She has an established national and international profile in the field of IPECP, and recent projects relate to IPECP in the pandemic and strategy and policy development within UK universities, national and international organisations.

Fiona Ranson fostered young people who were unaccompanied and seeking asylum in the United Kingdom (known as UASC). The young people were in her care and remained in her care as 'care leavers' during COVID. Having previously worked as an education improvement adviser with responsibility for the achievement and provision of ethnic minority children in schools, including those seeking asylum in the UK; Fiona undertook her PhD in Northumbria University where she examined experiences of care of UASC, via participatory arts based research with carers and carried out a policy review.

Rachel Rosen is a Professor of Sociology at the UCL Social Research Institute. Her research focuses on unequal childhoods, stratified social reproduction and migration in neoliberal border regimes. Methodologically, she is interested in the ethics and politics of ethnography and participatory research with children and other marginalised social groups and is committed to change-orientated research for social justice. Rachel is the co-author of *Negotiating Adult-Child Relationships in Early Childhood Research* (2014, Routledge) and the co-editor of *Reimagining Childhood Studies* (2019, Bloomsbury Academic), *Feminism and the Politics of Childhood: Friends or Foes?* (2018, UCL Press), *Childhood, parenting culture, and adult-child relations in global perspectives* (2020, FRS) and *Crisis for Whom? Critical global perspectives on childhood, care, and migration* (2023, UCL Press).

Ms Sibusisiwe Tendai Sibanda is a qualified Counsellor, Co-founder and CEO of Sizakala Wellness Counsellors in South Africa. Her journey into mental health began after watching her grandmother battle with dementia. Her need to understand mental health issues drove her to pursue a B-Psych degree at Midrand Graduate Institute. After obtaining her degree in 2012 and through her voluntary work, Sibusisiwe realised that there was a crucial need for the provision of affordable mental health care services in disadvantaged areas. That is when Sizakala Wellness Counsellors was created: An organisation dedicated to providing vulnerable and disadvantaged individuals with free psycho-social support.

Dr Donald Simpson is a former Primary School Teacher with an early years specialism. He is now a Senior Lecturer in Education at Teesside University (UK) where he has taught early childhood studies for many years. Donald has conducted several research projects with an early years focus. His work has explored professionalisation of the early years workforce as well as preschools' responses to poverty across England and the United States. He has published many research articles with an early years focus including contributions to several respected international journals. These include: *Journal of Early Childhood Research, European Early Childhood Research Journal, Early Years* and *International Journal of Early Years Education*.

Julie Spray, University of Galway, Ireland, is an interdisciplinary Medical and Childhood Anthropologist who researches children's perspectives on health and illness, public health policy and interventions and health inequalities. Integrating biosocial, ethnographic and visual arts-based methods, her work advocates for greater inclusion in health policy of those marginalised by dominant social structures and values, particularly children, young people, and racially or economically disadvantaged communities. Her research has been based in Aotearoa New Zealand, the United States and Ireland with analyses focusing on intersecting issues of rheumatic fever, asthma, stress, infrastructure, nutrition, self-harm, mental health, COVID-19 and health policy. She is the author of *The Children in Child Health: Negotiating Young Lives and Health in New Zealand* (Rutgers Series in Childhood Studies, 2020).

Judy Thomas completed her practice-based PhD at Northumbria University, with her area of study concentrating on the Artist Facilitator role and collaborative practice within the context of artist-led learning programmes. She is the current Head of Department at Teesside University for the School of Arts and the Creative Industries. She has worked in academia since 2010; her previous roles include Learning Manager at Creativity, Culture and Education (CCE), Learning Manager at Waygood and Programme Manager for Learning and Inclusion at Liverpool Biennial. Before this, she was Acting Head of Education and Public Programmes for Baltic Centre for Contemporary Art, Gateshead.

Christopher Warnock is an Assistant Professor of Education at Northumbria University in the Department of Social Work, Education and Community Wellbeing. Chris works predominantly across Post-Graduate Certificate in Academic Practice and Initial Teacher Education programmes, supporting colleagues in achieving HEA professional recognition and students in their journey towards QTS. His research interests focus primarily on the professional identity of the teacher as an academic and the academic as an educator, utilising narrative methodologies to explore the perceived tensions and dilemmas experienced during transition between these established roles.

Acknowledgements

We would like to acknowledge and thank the participants and presenters at our conference 'Childhood Care and Coronavirus' held in December 2022 at Northumbria University, UK, from where the idea for this book and some of the chapters originated.

Thanks also to the Social Policy Association (https://social-policy.org.uk/) which awarded us an Opportunity Grant to fund the conference.

We would like to thank the team at Emerald for their support and the anonymous reviewers for their comments on the book proposal.

We would also like to thank our colleagues Dr Stephen Crossley, Dr Lewis Mates, Prof Liz Holt and Prof Tim Rapley.

Final thanks go to all the authors for their contributions to this book and their patience during the process.

Chapter 1

Introduction: Care, Childhood, Youth and Family in the Context of Coronavirus

Tom Disney and Lucy Grimshaw

Northumbria University, UK

Abstract

This introductory chapter provides the context for this edited collection: Care and Coronavirus: Perspectives on Children, Youth and Families which aims to understand care in the context of COVID-19, the practices, experiences and potential futures of it for children, young people and families. In this chapter, the authors begin by exploring COVID-19 and its implications for children, young people and families. This includes a consideration of how particular discourses of childhood and youth often led to the marginalisation of children in care policy and practice during the lockdown periods. The authors then discuss interdisciplinary literature on care to identify directions in policy, practice and research, drawing attention to the political nature of care and the need for scholars of childhood, youth and family to engage with these critical and political approaches to care. The authors argue that developments in the field of Childhood Studies can be brought into productive dialogue with care to forge new ways of thinking through care and childhood. The final part of the chapter provides an overview of the ensuing chapters and concludes with the implications of this work for future research, policy and practice. The authors argue that COVID-19 heightened the attention paid to care and the ways in which care is vital for the maintenance of ourselves and the world around us, while also cautioning about the inequalities and the commodification of care that was revealed in these times. The authors end with a call for reflection on the failures and successes of caring during the pandemic and in its aftermath so we might plan a more caring, hopeful future.

Keywords: Childhood; care; COVID-19; family; politics of care; young people

Introduction

On 3rd January 2020, the BBC reported on a 'mysterious viral pneumonia' and concerns that this infection might resemble the flu-like SARS virus, which killed 700 people in 2002–2003 across the globe (BBC, 2020). Within a month, the situation had changed dramatically, and the World Health Organisation (WHO) had declared the outbreak a global emergency. By 20th March, there had been 10,000 recorded deaths, with unofficial figures likely much higher; many countries began to lockdown borders and officially limit social contact between their citizens. What we now know of as COVID-19 is, according to the WHO (2024), officially connected to an excess mortality of at least three million people globally. We use the term 'connected' deliberately because as Horton (2020: 874) notes, COVID-19 did not act in isolation but was made particularly deadly through its interaction with a range of non-communicable diseases that clustered in particular social groups 'according to particular patterns of inequality deeply embedded in our societies.' This avoidable context of social and economic inequality that allowed COVID-19 to particularly ravage certain communities underscores the political nature of the pandemic. A common refrain during these uncertain times was 'we are all in this together!' yet when examining the impacts of the virus, exposure was deeply stratified across racialised and gendered lines with certain groups essentially positioned as 'surplus populations' (Tyner, 2013) pointing to the biopolitical nature of this pandemic. In addition, forms of state withdrawal and erosion of formal care services exacerbated community vulnerability to the virus. In the UK, for instance, a preceding decade of unrelenting and cynical austerity policies withered the state's infrastructure and ability to protect its citizens. As Raghuram (2021: 865) argues these outcomes can be read as the 'inheritance of uncaring economies and states.' The necessity of care and the failure of its provision was starkly felt across the world. In amongst the horrors that were experienced throughout the pandemic, this period was also marked by hope; there was optimism that the intense shock of such a phenomenon might finally herald a change to the dominant capitalist system and precipitate a kinder, more caring form of governance (Mazzucato, 2020).

Today, it can feel like the possibility of radical alternative futures that prioritise care has diminished, as countries across the world have now largely reoriented themselves back to business as normal; lockdowns have now ended, the virus has cemented itself into everyday life, having become endemic, and capitalism has retained its hegemonic position. If anything, the virus itself has now become a new means of accumulation, co-opted by capitalism, reflecting its tendency to cannibalise seemingly everything (Fraser, 2022). Despite this, there were moments, practices and experiences during the height of the pandemic, where care, and its potential, offered a glimpse into what might be or what could be if we were brave enough to radically alter our state of being and approach to care. It is this premise which is the inspiration for this edited collection to understand care in the context of COVID-19, the practices, experiences and potential futures of it for children, young people and families. We argue that

COVID-19 has fundamentally challenged perspectives on childhood and care, opening up important new possibilities for Childhood Studies.

This collection draws on the perspectives of academics from a wide range of disciplinary backgrounds, including geography, sociology, art, child development, education, social policy and public health; insights from practitioners working during the lockdown periods, in fields such as early years, education, youth work and public health; and finally, also the voices of those who lived during these periods, including young people. In doing so, it provides unique insights into experiences of children, young people, families and practitioners during the peak of the pandemic across the globe but also indicates future avenues for care policy, practice and conceptual understandings within this area.

In this introductory chapter, we begin by providing an initial commentary on COVID-19 and its implications for children, young people and families to contextualise and situate this collection. In particular, we reflect on the ways in which children were often marginalised in care policy and practice during the lockdown periods, shaped by particular discourses of childhood and youth. Next, we draw inspiration from interdisciplinary literature on care through which we seek to forge future directions in policy, practice and research. There have been critical engagements with the pandemic in care literature that highlight the political nature of care, and we argue this is important for scholars of childhood, youth and family to reflect upon. We also take time to reflect on developments in the field of Childhood Studies, which we argue can be brought into productive dialogue with care to forge new ways of thinking through care and childhood. Finally, we provide an overview of a rich collection of chapters and conclude with the implications of this work for future research, policy and practice.

COVID-19 and Children, Young People and Families

In 2020, the virus spread across every country in the world, but there were differentiated policy responses; some countries introduced lockdowns with strict rules rendering some people housebound, while in other contexts there was the opportunity to leave the house for time limited periods for specific purposes. In contrast, some locations, such as some US states, resisted the imposition of state controls entirely and left people to regulate themselves. Regardless of lockdown measures, the spread of COVID-19 across the globe radically reshaped the lives of children, young people and families. Alongside direct impacts of the virus, such as illness and death, families were impacted by a range of indirect implications of lockdowns, such as income precarity, (un)employment, isolation and mental ill health (Lebow, 2020). In contexts where lockdowns occurred, there were concerns about the long-term developmental impacts upon children (see for example European Commission (2021) report on Denmark, Spain, Greece, Ireland, Germany and France). This period was also marked by diverse and heterogeneous experiences; for example, studies of family well-being across a range of countries during this time noted both heightened levels of familial stress due to prolonged proximity but also enhanced levels of closeness and resilience (see for example Shah et al. (2021) for UK, Italy, Lebanon and Singapore; Gadermann et al. (2021) for Canada and Lee and Ward (2020) for US).

Childhood and youth, as social constructions that are constituted by and enmeshed in wider systems of power, were unavoidably impacted by the social and economic inequalities that contributed to COVID-19's rapid and deadly spread through certain communities (Khan, 2022). The closing of schooling spaces, for instance, has been noted as having a significant impact upon children and young people; 188 countries closed schools and educational spaces (Cortes-Morales et al., 2022), with an estimated 91% of the world student population affected (UNESCO, 2020a). But significantly, the impact of this is not even, and it is girls who are predicted to be most greatly impacted by the closures (UNESCO, 2020b). Similarly, while certain children and young people were able to draw on family units to facilitate resilience, certain childhoods were also particularly vulnerable. For example, the implementation of social distancing legislation led to the invisibilisation of children at risk of serious harm through the disruption of in person child protection practice (see Katz et al., 2022 for a review of Australia, Brazil, US, Colombia, England, Germany, Israel, Japan, Canada and South Africa). The confinement to family also put LGBTQ+ children and young people at risk of violence or discrimination (Shah et al., 2021). Not all children necessarily resided in families either; children and young people entangled in the criminal justice system, in particular those institutionalised in detention settings, were particularly marginalised during this time (Khan and Boswell, 2022: 18). Writing about the US, Khan (2022) illustrates the intersectional impacts of COVID-19 on children and young people, with Black and Hispanic children more at risk of economic precarity.

Whilst research on the material, health and educational impacts of COVID-19 and lockdowns on children, families and young people is well-established, the role of discourses of childhood and youth, which heavily permeated societal engagements with children and young people at this time are perhaps less acknowledged or understood. In many Global North countries, social constructions of childhood as a period of 'innocence' and 'in need of protection' led to the imposition of policies that emphasised children's vulnerability; for example, many universities at this time prohibited research with children as a 'high risk group' (Cortes-Morales et al., 2022). While the intention was to protect, the outcome is a silencing of a particular group in society. Where it suited governments, childhood 'innocence' could be mobilised in public health messaging as a form of affect management to achieve behaviour change. This was particularly apparent in then New Zealand's Prime Minister Jacinda Arden's seemingly child orientated speeches, which were lauded across the globe, yet as Spray (2025) notes New Zealand's own public health measures largely ignored children's voices and failed to address children as meaningful subjects. At the same time, children and young people were also considered 'risky' as potential vectors of disease and inherent rule breakers, indicated by the closure of schools to limit their mobility to family homes, but also through direct messaging such as in the UK where young people were warned to stay away from elderly relatives with statements such as 'Don't kill grandma!' (Walker and Pidd, 2020). In some contexts, the notion of young people as reckless vectors of disease was notably stigmatising and resulted in stricter lockdowns, as Cortes-Morales et al. (2022) note in relation to Columbia and Chile. The unevenness of childhood experience during these times point to the important role of Childhood Studies in unearthing the distinctive construction of childhood and its variations across the globe. What is common to both the conceptualisation of children and young people as either in need of protection or vectors of disease is the erasure of their own subjectivity. Children and young people were largely sidelined during the height of the pandemic and treated as objects of public health intervention, yet they were central actors in caregiving in many contexts across the globe. Children and young people are conscious and sensitive to economic inequality and the impacts of poverty (Ridge, 2013), and the pandemic was no different (Shah et al., 2021), indeed if anything this awareness was heightened and demonstrated by their own caregiving activities.

Care and Childhood

COVID-19 and the lockdowns became a defining moment when the essential nature of 'care' and the very word itself came to the fore in all societies in the world (Fine and Tronto, 2020); how could states enact care for their populations and protect them from infection? Who should be prioritised? How best to care for those who had become ill? Not only were there diverging opinions about what form this care should take, there were also intense and heated debates about whether or not caring policies had gone too far or not far enough to protect human life. These different approaches and debates are indicative of the complicated and multifaceted nature of 'care.'

Care has been understood as a relational process and the work of Fisher and Tronto (1990) has often been central. They define care as

> [...] a species activity that includes everything that we do to maintain, continue and repair our 'world' so that we can live in it as well as possible. That world includes our bodies, ourselves and our environment, all of which we seek to interweave in a complete, life-sustaining web. (Fisher and Tronto, 1990: 40).

Academic scholarship has often separated care into two strands: caring *about* and caring *for* (Tronto, 1989), the latter encompassing care practice (both formal and informal) and the former focused on the emotional and affective dynamics of care. While it is often associated with being proximate, care is not limited to close physical contact; transnational care has been enacted in the form of remittances sent between countries to support families divided by borders (Carling, 2014). As Milligan and Wiles (2010) note, and hinted at in Fisher and Tronto's definition, care extends to whole networks of relations and is multidirectional and weblike; analysis of care should encompass a focus beyond the individual and simplistic interpersonal relationships. Care and care giving is complex, extending additionally beyond human actors; the wider environment and natural world, and its interconnected entities such as the soil, can be understood as a caregiver that sustains life rather than a resource for human consumption (Puig de La Bellacasa, 2017).

Care is also interlinked with social reproduction, and the inequalities inherent in care work have been of particular interest within feminist and Marxist thought (Schwiter and Steiner, 2020), pointing to the contested and political nature of care. It is this political and expanded notion of care that is of interest to us in this edited collection. Given the deeply unequal impacts of the pandemic, an attention to the political nature of care is thus unavoidable in our minds. Equally important, is that while proclamations such as 'we are all in this together' may have rung hollow, neoliberalism's valorisation of individualism was undeniably undermined given how survival during these times was premised on collective action, and so care must be understood as deeply intertwined in the wider world beyond the individual, including the human and non-human. This points to a need to consider care as a form of radical interdependency, and recent developments thinking through care during the pandemic help to make sense of this. This is articulated particularly effectively in the Care Manifesto (Chatzidakis et al., 2020) in which the authors argue that predominance of neoliberalism and its fetishisation of individualism has led to societies that see little value in care, this in turn hastened the damage wrought by COVID-19. It is important, however, to note that neoliberalism is not a feature of all places; not all countries will have experienced this specific devaluation of care, and this reflects concerns that care literature studies are often Western-centric (Raghuram, 2021).

In a recent contribution on COVID-19 and care, Neely and Lopez (2022: 2) similarly argue to push 'against neoliberal frameworks of individualism and autonomy, recognizing interrelatedness both as material fact and as ground through which to imagine worlds otherwise.' However, they argue that during COVID-19, care across the globe has been impacted primarily by the role of racial capitalism rather than neoliberalism and highlight the concept of 'othermothering,' drawing on Black feminist care ethics. Othermothering originates within African American communities during and beyond slavery, where practices of education and socialisation took place outside of the nuclear family, involving wider networks of people in caring (Guiffrida, 2005). It challenges Western conceptualisations of care and family, resisting neoliberal individualism, the privatisation of care and the resulting exploitation within capitalist care relations. The attention to the Black Feminist care ethics and intersectional experiences of care necessarily emphasises the political nature of care and the fight against social oppression (Neely and Lopez, 2022). Both the Care Manifesto and Neely and Lopez's use of othermothering are important and critical interventions within care literature to make sense of pandemic times. Both point to our interdependencies and the politics of care which inform this edited collection; we also aim to extend these debates in care by incorporating children's own subjectivities during the pandemic.

Children are often obscured within caring processes and practices, with assumptions about their inherent vulnerability often positioning them necessarily as simple recipients of care. Children feature primarily as objects of care, and how the care they necessitate may be stratified by inequalities. Rarely, are they meaningful subjects within care literature; Horton and Pyer (2017: 13) note that research '*with* - rather than *about* – children and young people in relation to care seems to be, problematically, rather marginalised; certainly it is relatively rare to encounter children and young people's *own* voices, experiences, issues, practices, politics and ethics represented within the very rich body of work on care.' While children and young people certainly are recipients of care, often within families or designated spaces of care, this does not mean that they are not also sophisticated and meaningful caring agents. Childhood scholars have been at the forefront of exploring children's caring agency and responsibilities within both the Global South (Evans, 2010) and the Global North (Disney, 2015). We argue that there is much of value in literature exploring care during pandemic times, but they should be brought together with recent developments within Childhood Studies to think through the complexities of care during the pandemic.

Critical Childhood Studies

The current vibrant and expanding interdisciplinary field of Childhood Studies, often drawing from the sociological New Social Studies of Childhood (James and Prout, 1997) has pioneered more sophisticated engagements with the social and cultural contexts of childhood (Wyness, 2012) and has endeavoured to treat children as subjects and participants in social research (Wells, 2017). Central to much scholarship within Childhood Studies is that children are social agents and not passive recipients of adult culture, rather they are meaningful rights bearers and beings with the capacity to remake and reshape the social world (Corsaro, 2015). The social construction of childhood and children's agentic capacity are now very much foundational aspects of Childhood Studies (Wells, 2017). With this rich scholarship has come limitations, however; the discipline has been argued to have remained largely preoccupied with the micro-scale of childhood and children's everyday lives, despite now longstanding calls to reflect on macro-scale processes which shape and produce childhoods (Ansell, 2009). Additionally, the discipline has been argued to be 'complicit in valorizing children's agency to the point of fetish' (Spyrou et al., 2019: 3). There are political consequences to the conceptual dominance of agency in Childhood Studies scholarship as Spyrou et al. (2019) caution; such approaches that celebrate individual action risk reflecting and supporting neoliberal and late capitalist agendas that have often had negative consequences for many children across the world, exacerbating poverty and inequality. The preoccupation with children's agency in the discipline has furthermore restricted the discipline from other ways of knowing childhood and children's everyday lives, resulting in more partial views and understandings. Psychological and developmental approaches are often perceived with wariness (Tatlow-Golden and Montgomery, 2021), and a focus on the micro-scale agency of children has neglected more structural approaches (Spyrou et al., 2019).

In an important recent conceptual intervention, Spyrou et al. (2019: 6) suggest reorientating our attention to 'the relational and interdependent aspects of children's lives as well as the ethics and politics that characterise them.' They employ a relational ontology to understand childhood subjectivities, embedding them within the wider political and structural contexts in which they live and thus move Childhood Studies beyond a fascination with the individual agentic child. Ultimately, what matters, they argue, is 'not what [children] are but how they affect and are affected in the event assemblages they find themselves in' (Spyrou et al., 2019: 8). Notably, their approach is implicitly underpinned by care ethics; they caution childhood scholars to question which child is brought into view by our research activities. This points to the important synergies between recent developments in care literature and Childhood Studies; a focus beyond the individual and a call for attention to the political nature of our interdependencies embedded in socio-structural scalar processes. Childhood scholars could find much of value in recent care scholarship that decentres the individual and radically embeds us within the world around us, acknowledging human and non-human subjectivities. Similarly, critical childhood scholarship has much to offer care literature – in questioning who we bring into view with our research and resisting the prioritisation of adult voice and the marginalisation of children's subjectivities. We suggest such an approach is vital in order to help understand childhood, youth and family and for conceptualising and developing future caring practices in the wake of COVID-19.

Structure and Contributions of the Book

The book is organised into five sections which explore the COVID-19's incursion into the everyday lives of children, young people and families across the globe. These sections comprise 'Early Systems of Care,' 'Children and Young People's Health and Well-being,' 'Parents as Subjects and Recipients of Care,' 'Schooling as Care' and 'Young People Navigating Care and Control Beyond the School.' Within each section authors present research on diverse topics across various contexts with a central guiding theme of how care was enacted, experienced or denied during these times. Each section ends with a reflection from practitioners and those who lived through the pandemic voicing their experiences of the lockdowns, providing rich and moving accounts that remind us how these times were felt.

The first section examines experiences and practices of care within systems of early childhood during the lockdown periods. In Chapter 2, Fabio Dovigo notes there has been surprisingly limited research focused on exploring the implications of the pandemic upon children's development and their socialisation within early childhood settings. This is mirrored, he argues, by a similar dearth of insights into the impacts of the lockdowns upon parents. His chapter provides an important reference point, addressing these lacunae through a systematic literature review of international literature to explore the experiences of children and their carers during the pandemic. He points to the need for interventions to address lost learning and socialisation but with a clear focus on supporting parents and carers in this. With an international focus, this chapter provides an important macro-scale perspective on the impacts of COVID-19 on childhood and care.

In Chapter 3, Donald Simpson and Sandra Lydon argue that despite the importance afforded to early childhood, the role of care has been gradually eroded in these settings for some time. In earlier research with early years practitioners in England and America, they noted the circulation of deficit discourses when working with children in poverty and an overall prioritisation of education rather than care. As they explain, the circulation of particular discourses of the importance of care during the pandemic offered an opportunity for a reset and to deconstruct deficit approaches, echoing the aims of this collection to explore what might have been from the pandemic. While practitioners did exhibit increased poverty sensitivity and focus on care, it is notable that this quickly succumbed to pre-pandemic ideals of 'school-readiness' and the relegation of care to secondary importance in these settings. The result of this was again that children in poverty experienced unequal provision, highlighting a significant lost opportunity. Despite this, they argue that there will be 'small places' where caring adaptations will persist, and while much of what we see today may suggest a return to the 'normal' of pre-pandemic times, it is important to excavate these moments of care and emphasise them to help develop a kinder, more caring society.

This section on early childhood systems of care ends with a reflection from practice provided in Chapter 4 by Charmaine Agius Ferrante and Elaine Chaplin. In their conversations with early year practitioners, Ferrante and Chaplin's contribution highlights the strain that practitioners were under to provide care under during the pandemic, the adaptations they have implemented to support child development and how this has remained unspoken and unacknowledged. Ferrante and Chaplin's intervention and Dovigo's highlight the importance of sufficiently resourcing and supporting early childhood systems of care in order to safeguard the well-being of children. Their contribution, as with Dovigo's, emphasises the developmental impacts of the pandemic and are situated within these literature studies and perspectives. Significantly, these contributions thus root the collection in a more holistic approach to Childhood Studies, resisting Childhood Studies' traditional scepticism of developmental ways of knowing.

In the second section, the chapters explore children and young people's health during the pandemic. While the notion that children are biologically and developmentally vulnerable is common in societal discourses, policy and practice, it was perceived that children generally experienced milder symptoms of COVID-19 (Roluto and Palma, 2023). Despite this apparent resilience, children and young people were not free from negative impacts upon their physical and mental health during the pandemic. In Chapter 5 Lucy Currie, Sibusisiwe Tendai Sibanda and Athenkosi Mtumtum explore the impacts of lockdowns on young girls living in a South African settlement in a collaborative piece between academia and practice. They demonstrate the precarity of care through a situation marked by state abandonment and where the family might be thought to constitute a safe space this was not always the case, with significant implications for their mental health. Despite this, the girls in their chapter demonstrated resilience in these informal settlements during the pandemic, engaging in care for their communities, their families and friends, and themselves. Currie, Tendai Sibanda and Mtumtum caution, however, that this resilience persisted despite many of the structures that should have been there to support these girls. Such insights underscore the importance of not reproducing neoliberal logics of individualistic coping, and to look at where resilience could have been fostered by the state, within settlements. To focus solely on how these girls coped is to absolve other actors of responsibility to have provided care; this lesson is starkly relayed in their chapter and has a powerful message of the need to prioritise care for all, so that no one is abandoned by state inaction (Davies et al., 2017). In the same section, Julie Spray in Chapter 6 provides powerful insights into the manipulation of public affects through the mobilisation of childhood as a public health tool. Drawing upon an innovative method of co-making comics with children and an extensive review of government transcripts of the time period, Spray examines how children and their perspectives were represented. She argues that during New Zealand's lockdowns, childhood was coopted for the purposes of public health protection. The result of this was that children's own subjectivities were largely erased, and their voices ignored. This underscores children's widespread systematic exclusion from meaningful engagement in political processes and highlights their minority status. Spray's contribution highlights how despite intentions, care can be extractive and exploitative, which should lead us all to question where children's voices are in policy and how they are accurately represented.

In Chapter 7, Frances Gunn a Service Manager with responsibility for a Health Visiting service in Scotland reflects on her experiences. She explores the role of health visitors as a vital early care service for infants and parents, and how this was enacted during and between lockdowns. Despite the severity of Scottish lockdowns, health visitors adapted and engaged in creative practice to make sure they were able to see families with newborn children. Gunn's contribution highlights the precarity of certain people during this period, in particular women and girls at risk of abuse and underscores the importance of health visiting as a technique to facilitate safety for these families.

In the third section, the authors explore experiences of parenting during the pandemic. Through the contributions within this section, the gendered impacts of care are powerfully illustrated. In Chapter 8, Laura Bellusi and Sian Lucas analyse gendered experiences of new mothers, finding that the enforced isolation exacerbated the 'impression management' that new mothers engage in. The emotional and physical labour that new mothers had to engage in during this time increased, as did the anxieties about needing to be 'good enough' and feel knowledgeable about child health and development whilst they were physically distanced from child professionals and their normal support networks were restricted. The amplified pressure on mothers at this time again highlights the multifaceted nature of care, where caring can be debilitating and unequal. Despite this, Bellusi and Lucas identify moments of hope with mothers able to resist these societal discourses and practice care for one another. With an allied focus, in Chapter 9 Claire Matysova explores the implementation and experience of 'shared parental leave' during the pandemic. Drawing inspiration from feminist ethics of care literature, she examines the potential disruption of gendered norms during this time and considers the possible hopeful reimagining of shared parental care through the closure of schools and nurseries and the resourcing of childcare to the family home. While Matysova finds hope in the possible future flexibility, she notes that dominant masculinist working cultures impede this advancement and cautions that the responsibility for greater cultural shifts must be placed on wider society rather than parents themselves.

Completing this section is Chapter 10 – a powerful reflection from Fiona Ranson and Cuong Nguyen on their experiences of being a parent and child, respectively, during this time. Their contribution takes the form of a conversation, tracing the implementation of the lockdown period, the spread of the virus and the implications for the mutual care they shared during this time. Ranson and Nguyen's recollections highlight the corrosive role of racism during the pandemic, and the protective caring measures enacted to defend against it. Critically, their reflection is emblematic of the multidirectionality of care, with child providing care for parent as well as being a recipient of care.

The fourth section focuses on schooling as an often central facet of children and young people's everyday lives. In Chapter 11, Tom Disney, Lucy Grimshaw and Judy Thomas draw upon arts-based participatory methods to explore the experiences of teenage secondary school girls in England who found their schooling disrupted by the pandemic and implementation of lockdowns. They draw on Katz (2008) to argue that children and young people experience ever increasing pressure to act as redemptive future agents and thus sites of capital accumulation. Despite this, they argue there were important moments, practices and experiences of care during the lockdown periods that can be harnessed to help resist the capitalist logics that exert such pressures upon current school children. The girls in their study were able to point to many positive experiences of schooling during this time, in contrast to the negative media discourses about COVID-19 and home learning that have become common place. Their findings point to the potentialities of care and the hope that can be excavated from this time and importantly that these young girls were also sophisticated and important caring agents, despite a lack of societal acknowledgement. In Chapter 12, Lucy Grimshaw, Kay Heslop, Kirstin Mulholland, Vikki Park, Jill Duncan, Jaden Allen, Cathryn Meredith and Christopher Warnock examine the experiences of an online peer support group comprising academics caring for children and homeschooling whilst working. They present innovative research based on analysis of the group's digital chats (which form a contemporaneous historical diary) during the pandemic and lockdown periods. They demonstrate how the group was underpinned by an ethic of care, based on reciprocal relationships of care across multiple caring roles which enabled them to cope with homeschooling periods. They demonstrate the strength and benefits of caring collectively whilst adapting to challenging and stressful home, school and work routines. Whilst acknowledging gendered inequalities in care provision and workplaces, the group illustrates the possibility of developing a caring and inclusive peer support group (including mothers, fathers and grandparents) which sought to influence and enhance caring cultures within the workplace.

This section finishes with contributions from two secondary school teachers in England, both of whom were active practitioners during the pandemic, although within different contexts and with different experiences. In Chapter 13, Linzi Brown reflects on the struggles of trying to continue to provide education in a time of significant disruption. Motivated by care, she articulates a number of interventions she implemented to keep students engaged and connected. This came at a personal cost, reminding us that practitioners working through the pandemic were often in a precarious position. This is also powerfully illustrated by Jason Burg in Chapter 14 where he traces his precarity as an early career teacher and then hourly paid teaching assistant working among students during the pandemic. His reflection draws attention to the political nature of the pandemic, whereby those often most at risk of infection were in positions of low pay with little protection despite fulfilling vital caring roles for children; such interventions underscore the societal devaluation of care and thus its own precarious nature.

In fifth section, the contributors reflect on the experiences of young people, who were often positioned at the sharp end of narratives of risk and being considered 'out of place' during lockdown periods in contrast to the notion of early childhood 'innocence.' In Chapter 15, Catherine Nixon, Kirsty Deacon, Andrew James, Ciara Waugh, Zodie and Sarah McGarrol provide an examination of the Children's Hearings System, a Scottish welfare-based tribunal-based system. This system is particular to Scotland and is central to caring for children in need of protection but also those who come into conflict with the law. Critically, their contribution involves young people who have experience of this system as authors and meaningful contributors, providing unique insight into young people's perspectives. The pandemic resulted in hearings being conducted virtually with implications for the young people attending them. Their chapter underscores the complexity of care during these times; the experiences were multifaceted, with some finding their sense of safety and control eroded by virtual hearings, whereas others argued that avoiding the Hearings centres meant that they avoided re-traumatisation through visiting a place that was associated with a lack of safety and control. The authors argue that the system could learn from this period to address potential re-traumatisation and how attending hearings from a safe place may alleviate anxiety, ultimately creating a more caring system. The role of the state in promoting care for young people is further explored in Chapter 16 by Stephen Crossley. He provides a discussion of grassroots sports clubs and traces their importance to formal and informal caring practices for young people. He argues these spaces have been neglected and undervalued in their importance in the UK compared to other countries, not least following a decade of austerity policies and a prioritisation of elite sport during lockdowns. Drawing on Tronto (2015), he notes that care needs to, and does, take place in the everyday among the multiplicity of relations and connections we have. These sports clubs are often embedded in local communities forming links, for example, between and within families, and provide meaningful moments of connection and care. This was particularly felt as they became incrementally available as lockdowns eased in England. He calls for future research to meaningfully examine the role of these spaces in facilitating care for young people.

In the final practitioner reflection, in Chapter 17, Alison Ní Charraighe, Kelly Coates, Shannon Devine and Elisha Sanchez discuss their experience of the role of

Youth Work during the lockdowns. They argue that Youth Work was overlooked in many respects as a profession, with priority status given to other professions that worked with children and young people, such as child protection social work. Their chapter is delivered as a conversation piece between Ní Charraighe (an academic and Youth Worker) and three current Youth Workers in the North East of England. They argue that the lack of priority given to Youth Work during the lockdowns reflects the devaluation and decimation of this service through austerity policies and consequently a neglect of young people who do receive support from a service which is intertwined with care, or what Hooks (1994) terms 'professional love.'

In Chapter 18, Rachel Rosen provides the final commentary 'Childhood and Care in the Time of Coronavirus.' She draws our attention to the global impacts and inequalities of COVID-19 for children and young people. Noting the unevenness of childhood globally, she traces the ways in which familiar tropes of child at risk and risky child have been deployed to control rather than care for children. She challenges us to think beyond these and consider children as potential carers themselves. In doing so, she challenges readers to consider the implications for children's subjectivities, relations and worlds and the caring practices that are brought into being through this.

Conclusion

This collection of chapters marks an important contribution to understanding the role and nature of care for and by children, young people and families during unprecedented times and for the future. Central to the collection's significance is its diversity; the collection is grounded in interdisciplinary scholarship, with insights from sociology, geography, social policy, art, anthropology, education and developmental approaches to understanding childhood, youth and family. It is vital that academics resist disciplinary silos, which limit our insights and potential contributions to the world. Furthermore, this significance is evidenced through a range of methodological approaches that provide multifaceted insights into the experiences and practices of care during the pandemic. These range from arts-based participatory methods revealing rich examples of lived experience to quantitative methods that draw our attention to the socio-scalar implications of COVID-19 for care.

Many of the chapters demonstrate the sophisticated caring agency that children and young people displayed for themselves and others, both human and non-human, and the complex and political nature of care within families, communities, organisations and societies. This collection highlights the important role and experiences of children and young people in care and caring. The sophisticated relational caring agency exhibited calls for academics, practitioners and policy makers to consider new ways of thinking through the care that took place during the Coronavirus pandemic without erasing children's subjectivities.

Too often those who are the focus of academic work are only partially represented in academic texts and an important contribution of this collection is the inclusion of the practitioner reflections and the young people who have co-authored chapters. Rich narratives from practitioners and participants in the various studies highlight the challenges of providing care during those uncertain times but also the joys of caring. The nature of care in everyday lives is revealed as multidirectional, relational and reciprocal, but also sometimes through small, overlooked acts of 'being there' (Askins, 2015).

This collection tells us much about care and caring in our world, highlighting important lessons from the lockdowns. COVID-19 remains a hugely significant global phenomenon with macro-scale implications for us all. The attention to the scalar complexities of the pandemic within this volume highlight the political nature of care; in many chapters, caring took place despite the withdrawal or failure of formal caring policies and processes during and preceding the pandemic. It has underscored the centrality of care to our world – a return to a pre-pandemic 'normal' is not possible nor desirable. Care is not a commodity to facilitate capitalist modes of being, but a vital means by which we sustain ourselves and our world, which is demonstrated again and again in this collection. Yet, it is also clear from this collection that care is fragile and may be destabilised by crises such as COVID-19 but also by its devaluation through austerity policies informed by neoliberalism. It is important the COVID-19 does not mask the fragilities of care that preceded it, where it has been cannibalised by capitalism to facilitate greater profit making (Fraser, 2022).

Ultimately, this collection calls for us all to confront the legacy of COVID-19. To examine the failures and successes of care, inequalities and the impacts on children, young people and families preceding the pandemic emergence and its aftermath. This book provides an opportunity to reflect on and resist the ways in which care has been so systematically eroded and devalued in our societies; that we might recognise our mutual vulnerabilities and interdependencies and plan for a more caring future.

References

Ansell, N. 2009. Childhood and politics of scale: descaling children's geographies? *Progress in Human Geography*, 33(2), 190–209.
Askins, K. 2015. Being together: everyday geographies and the quiet politics of belonging. *ACME: An International Journal for Critical Geographies*, 14(2), 470–478.
BBC 2020. China pneumonia outbreak: mystery virus probed. Available at: https://www.bbc.co.uk/news/world-asia-china-50984025. (Accessed 29 January 2024).
Carling, J. 2014. Scripting remittances: making sense of money transfers in transnational relationships. *International Migration Review*, 48(1), 218–262.
Chatzidakis, A., Hakim, J., Littler, J., Rottenberg, C. and Segal, L. 2020. *The Care Manifesto – the Politics of Interdependence*, Verso Books.
Corsaro, W. 2015. *The sociology of childhood*, 4th ed, Los Angeles, Sage.
Cortes-Morales, S., Holt, L., Acevedo-Rincon, J., Aitken, S., Ladru, D., Joelsson, T., Kraftl, P., Murray, L. and Tebet, G. 2022. Children living in pandemic times: a geographical, transnational and situated view. *Children's Geographies*, 20(4), 381–391.
Davies, T., Isakjee, A. and Dhesi, S. 2017. Violent inaction: the necropolitical experience of refugees in Europe. *Antipode*, 49(5), 1263–1284.
Disney, T. 2015. Complex spaces of orphan care: a Russian therapeutic children's community. *Children's Geographies*, 13(1), 30–43.

European Commission. Directorate General for Education, Youth, Sport and Culture 2021. *Early Childhood Education and Care and the Covid-19 Pandemic: Understanding and Managing the Impact of the Crisis on the Sector.* Available at: https://data.europa.eu/doi/10.2766/60724. (Accessed 05 May 2024)

Evans, R. 2010. Children's caring roles and responsibilities within the family in Africa. *Geography Compass*, 4, 1477–1496.

Fine, M. and Tronto, J. 2020. Care goes viral: care theory and research confront the global COVID-19 pandemic. *International Journal of Care and Caring*, 4(3), 301–309.

Fisher, B. and Tronto, J. 1990. Toward a feminist theory of caring, In *Circles of Care*, Eds E. Abel, M. Nelson, pp. 36–54, Albany, NYSUNY Press.

Fraser, N. 2022. *Cannibal Capitalism: How Are System Is Devouring Democracy, Care, and the Planet – and What We Can Do about it*, New York, NY, Verso.

Gadermann, A.C., Thomson, K.C., Richardson, C.G., Gagné, M., McAuliffe, C., Hirani, S. and Jenkin, E. 2021. Examining the impacts of the COVID-19 pandemic on family mental health in Canada: findings from a national cross-sectional study. *BMJ Open*, 11, e042871.

Guiffrida, D. 2005. Othermothering as a framework for understanding African American students' definitions of student-centred faculty. *The Journal of Higher Education*, 76(6), 701–723.

Hooks, B. 1994. *Teaching to Transgress*, New York, Routledge.

Horton, R. 2020. Offline: Covid-19 is not a pandemic. *The Lancet*, 396, 874.

Horton, J. and Pyer, M. 2017. Introduction: children, young people and 'care'. In *Children, Young People and Care*, Eds J. Horton, M. Pyer, London, Routledge.

James, A. and Prout, A. 1997. *Constructing and Reconstructing Childhood: Contemporary Issues in the Sociological Study of Childhood*, Washington DC, Falmer Press.

Katz, C. 2008. Childhood as spectacle: relays of anxiety and the reconfiguration of the child. *Cultural Geographies*, 15(1), 5–17.

Katz, I., Priolo-Filho, S, Katz, C, Andresen, S, Bérubé, A, Cohen, N, Connell, CM, Collin-Vézina, D, Fallon, B, Fouche, A and Fujiwara, T. 2022. One year into COVID-19: what have we learned about child maltreatment reports and child protective service responses? *Child Abuse & Neglect*, 130(1), 105473.

Khan, N. 2022. Introduction - unmasking childhood inequality. In *Covid-19 and Childhood Inequality*, Ed N. Khan, pp. 1–12, London, Routledge.

Khan, N. and Boswell, A. 2022. Pandemic eugenics. In *Covid-19 and Childhood Inequality*, Ed N. Khan, pp. 13–34, London, Routledge.

Lebow, J. 2020. Family in the age of COVID-19. *Family Process*, 59(2), 309–312.

Lee, S.J. and Ward, K.P. 2020. *Research Brief: Stress and Parenting during the Coronavirus Pandemic*. Ann Arbor, MI, University of Michigan Parenting in Context Research Lab, WPRN-517152. Available at: https://wprn.org/item/517152

Mazzucato, M. 2020. The Covid-19 crisis is a chance to do capitalism differently. *The Guardian*. Available at: https://www.theguardian.com/commentisfree/2020/mar/18/the-covid-19-crisis-is-a-chance-to-do-capitalism-differently. (Accessed 29 January 2024)

Milligan, C. and Wiles, J. 2010. Landscapes of care. *Progress in Human Geography*, 34(6), 736–754.

Neely, A. and Lopez, P. 2022. Toward healthier futures in post-pandemic times: political ecology, racial capitalism, and black feminist approaches to care. *Geography Compass*, 16(2), e12609.

Puig de La Bellacasa, M. 2017. *Matters of Care: Speculative Ethics in More than Human Worlds*, Minneapolis, MN, University of Minnesota Press.
Raghuram, P. 2021. Caring for the *Manifesto* – steps toward making it an achievable dream. *Social Politics*, 28(4), 865–873.
Ridge, T. 2013. We are all in this together'? The hidden costs of poverty, recession and austerity policies on Britain's poorest children. *Children & Society*, 27, 406–417.
Roluto, G. and Palma, P. 2023. Understanding Covid-19 in children: immune determinants and post-infection conditions. *Pediatric Research*, 94, 434–442.
Schwiter, K. and Steiner, J. 2020. Geographies of care work: the commodification of care, digital care futures and alternative caring visions. *Geography Compass*, 14(12), e12546.
Shah, M., Rizzo, S., Percy-Smith, B., Monchuk, L., Lorusso, E., Tay, C. and Day, L. 2021. Growing up under Covid-19: young people's agency in family dynamics. *Frontiers in Sociology*, 6, 722380.
Spray, J. 2025. Children's care for public health and politically expedient care for children in Aotearoa New Zealand's COVID-19 pandemic. In *Care and Coronavirus: Perspectives on Childhood, Youth and Family (Emerald Studies in Child-Centred Practice)*, Eds T. Disney, L. Grimshaw, Bingley, Emerald.
Spyrou, S., Rosen, R. and Cook, D.T. 2019. Introduction: Remaining Childhood Studies: Connectivities... Relationalities... Linkages In *Reimagining Childhood Studies*, Eds S. Spyrou, R. Rosen, D.T. Cook, pp. 1-20, London, Bloomsbury Press.
Tatlow-Golden, M. and Montgomery, H. 2021. Childhood studies and child psychology: disciplines and dialogue? *Children & Society*, 35(1), 3–17.
Tronto, J. 1989. Women and caring: what can feminists learn about morality from caring? In *Key Concepts in Critical Theory: Gender*, Ed. C. Gould, pp. 282–289, Atlantic Highlands, NJ, Humanities Press.
Tronto, J. 2015. *Who cares? How to reshape a democratic politics*, Ithaca, NY, Cornell University Press.
Tyner, J. 2013. Population geography I: surplus populations. *Progress in Human Geography*, 37(5), 701–711.
UNESCO 2020a. *COVID-19 Educational Disruption and Response*. Available at: https://en.unesco.org/covid19/educationresponse. (Accessed 05 February 2024)
UNESCO 2020b. Addressing the Gender Dimensions of COVID-related School Closures. Available at: https://en.unesco.org/news/COVID-19-webinar-3-addressing-gender-dimensions-covid-related-school-closures. (Accessed 05/02/2024).
Walker, P. and Pidd, H. 2020. "Don't kill granny!" Message for preston youth aims to slow spread of covid-19. *The Guardian*. Available at: 'Don't kill granny' message for Preston youth aims to slow spread of Covid-19 | Coronavirus | The Guardian. (Accessed 19 May 2024).
Wells, K. 2017. *Childhood Studies – Making Young Subjects*. Polity Press, Cambridge.
WHO 2024. *The True Death Toll of Covid-19 – Estimating Global Mortality*. Available at: https://www.who.int/data/stories/the-true-death-toll-of-covid-19-estimating-global-excess-mortality. (Accessed 29 January 2024)
Wyness, M. 2012. *Childhood and Society*, 2nd ed., London, Palgrave MacMillan.

Section 1

Early Systems of Care

Chapter 2

Children's and Parents' Experiences of Care During the Pandemic: An International Review

Fabio Dovigo

Northumbria University, UK

Abstract

This chapter presents an international review of the experiences of children and parents regarding care during the COVID-19 pandemic. The pandemic profoundly impacted children and families, magnifying the influence of governmental policies, socio-economic disparities and cultural contexts on children's experiences and exacerbating global inequalities. Vulnerable families faced increased challenges affecting children's rights and well-being, while the transition to digital learning highlighted the critical need for equitable access to technology. Despite extensive documentation of these challenges, research focusing on the pandemic's impact on young children's development, well-being, socialization and learning opportunities, as well as the experiences of parents/carers, remains limited. This scarcity stems from the pandemic's constraints on research activities, requiring reliance on online methods and the increased burdens on parents/carers, making participation in research more challenging.

Employing the PRISMA 2020 method for a literature review, this chapter aggregates international research findings on the subject, examining the impacts of COVID-19 on health and well-being, knowledge of the pandemic, effects on learning, educational strategies, online activity engagement and collaboration with Early Childhood Education and Care (ECEC) services. It concludes with a synthesis of insights and recommendations drawn from the reviewed literature.

The chapter contributes to a comprehensive framework for understanding the pandemic's impact on young children and their families, emphasising the importance of targeted interventions, equitable resource distribution and ongoing support for the ECEC sector to address the challenges and opportunities presented by the COVID-19 pandemic and future crises.

Keywords: Children's well-being; COVID-19 pandemic; digital learning; Early Childhood Education and Care (ECEC); educational inequalities; parental involvement

Introduction

The COVID-19 pandemic has presented unprecedented challenges to the ECEC sector. The effects of the pandemic on the organisation of services for early childhood, teacher activities and the role of leadership have been extensively documented by research, both at the international and national levels. However, research concerning the pandemic's impact on young children, their development, well-being and opportunities for socialisation and learning has been limited. Similarly, there is a dearth of research on parents/carers, the challenges they have faced and the strategies they have employed to support the care and education of their children. This scarcity is not due to a lack of interest but rather the challenging conditions imposed by the pandemic on research activities. During COVID-19, research strategies have generally had to rely on online investigation methods that do not require direct contact with participants (Howlett, 2022; Lupton, 2020; Vindrola-Padros et al., 2020). Moreover, parents/carers, burdened by the additional stress and caregiving workload resulting from the lockdown, generally had less time and energy to respond to researchers' inquiries. Regarding young children, implementing appropriate inquiry strategies is a delicate and challenging task, involving numerous methodological and ethical issues (Greig et al., 2012). The pandemic has further complicated research efforts, as the isolation situation drastically limited the possibilities of directly gathering children's views through conventional approaches such as questions or spontaneous conversations.

One consequence of this limitation is the current lack of a comprehensive framework for understanding the experience of young children and their parents/carers during the pandemic. This chapter provides a broad overview of this experience through a review of the literature currently available internationally. Following a brief introduction on the impact of COVID-19 on the early childhood services sector, the review examines how children and their parents/carers have navigated the pandemic in key areas such as health and well-being, knowledge of the phenomenon, effects on learning, adopted educational strategies, engagement in online activities and collaboration with ECEC services. The chapter concludes with a synthesis of the main insights and recommendations arising from the research review.

Methods

To address the objectives of the study, a literature review following the PRISMA 2020 method was used (Page et al., 2021) to ensure that all relevant information regarding search strategy, selection criteria, data extraction and analysis was captured. The review included a systematic search of articles published between 2020 and 2023 in Scopus, Web of Science (WoS) and ERIC. These three databases encompass international peer-reviewed scientific literature on education with validated impact indices. The search strategy was performed through the Boolean operators (AND, OR) applied to core concepts related to the topic investigated (early childhood *, education *, care *, parents *, family *, children *, COVID-19 *, pandemic *). A search string was then generated, using the following inclusion/exclusion criteria, to select peer-reviewed articles (Table 2.1):

Following with PRISMA guidelines (Fig. 2.1), the review was conducted in five phases:

(1) Initial search of the literature included in Scopus ($n = 109$), WoS ($n = 261$) and ERIC ($n = 422$) electronic databases. A total of 432 studies were excluded because of the type of paper (IC1, EX1).
(2) 97 duplicated studies listed in another database were excluded (IC2, EX2).
(3) 112 studies were excluded, as not complying with the peer-review and language criteria (IC3-4, EX3-4).
(4) 21 studies not available in full text were excluded (IC5, EX5).
(5) 62 studies not focused on the topics investigated were excluded (IC6, EX6).

The described process is summarised in a PRISMA flow diagram (Fig. 2.1).

Table 2.1. Inclusion/Exclusion Criteria.

Inclusion Criteria	Exclusion Criteria
IC1: Journal article, book chapter or scientific report	EX1: Proceedings of congresses, conference papers and other nonpeer-reviewed publications.
IC2: The study is not listed in another database.	EX2: The study is listed in another database.
IC3: The study is peer-reviewed.	EX3: The study is not peer-reviewed.
IC4: The study is written in English.	EX4: The study is not written in English.
IC5: The full text of the study is available.	EX5: The full text of the study is not available.
IC6: The study focuses on ECEC, parents, children, and the COVID-19 pandemic.	EX6: The study does not focus on ECEC, parents, children, and the COVID-19 pandemic.

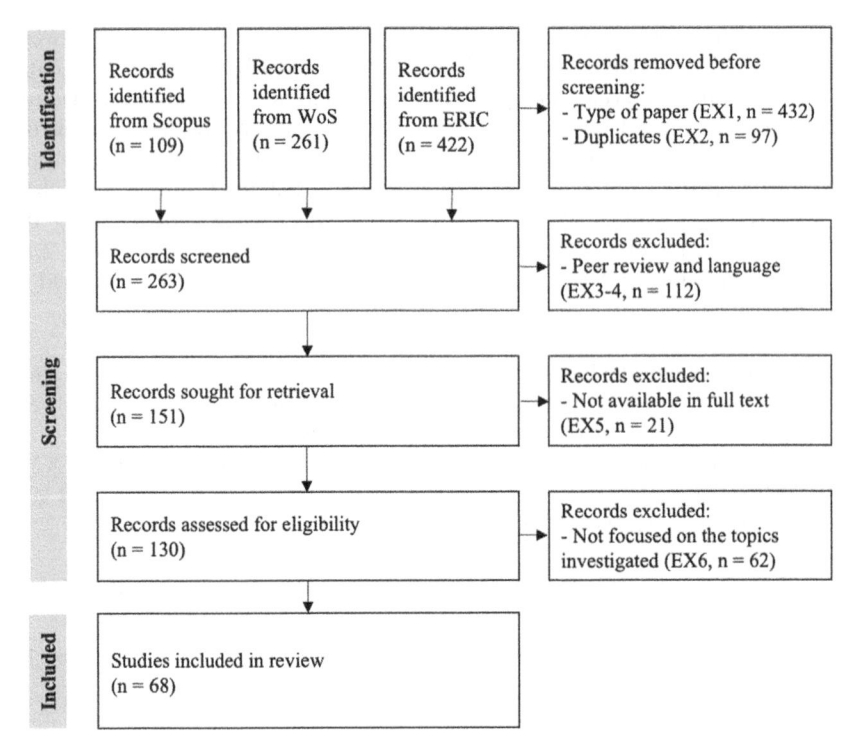

Fig. 2.1. Prisma 2020 Flow Diagram.

The Impact of the Pandemic on the ECEC Landscape

Acknowledged as a global crisis by the World Health Organization in March 2020, the COVID-19 pandemic had far-reaching consequences on young children and their families worldwide. Aiming to curb the virus's spread, governments globally imposed significant restrictions, such as social distancing and working from home. These measures varied across countries, influenced by factors including government responses, cultural contexts and socio-economic considerations. Notably, the ECEC sector faced diverse impacts, with variations in closure durations and provisions for essential worker access. Government responses and policies played a crucial role in shaping children's day-to-day experiences, either at home or in early childhood settings (Egan and Pope, 2022; European Commission, 2021a; Park et al., 2021; Rothe et al., 2022). The initial perception of children as potential disease carriers led to measures like social isolation, affecting their interactions, particularly with extended family (Yoshikawa et al., 2020).

Research indicates that vulnerable families bore a disproportionate burden, experiencing increased domestic violence, child poverty and violations of children's rights (Proulx et al., 2022). The disruption of nurturing care, exacerbated by strained parent–child relationships, increased screen time and limited outdoor play, underscored pre-existing global inequalities. Reports emphasised the fragility of the ECEC sector, already in crisis pre-pandemic, revealing inequalities and stressors for both children and caregivers (Speight et al., 2021). Gender disparities widened as well, as the burden of care disproportionately fell on women. Furthermore, the pandemic accentuated the limited readiness of governments to handle emergencies, highlighting challenges in interpreting and implementing guidelines (Henderson et al., 2022).

The consequences of COVID-19 exposed existing global disparities in families accessing ECEC services. Investigation from diverse regions indicated cultural, economic, safety, and psychological issues as key factors affecting the care and education of young children and their families during the pandemic. In this regard, UNICEF emphasised that the closure of services and imposed restrictions made it challenging for working parents with younger children to balance family and work life. 25% of quarantined parents exhibited symptoms of mental ill-health, a higher proportion compared to the 5% observed among those non-quarantined (Gromada et al., 2020). Examining the pandemic's effects on prekindergarten and kindergarten enrolment in the US, Weiland and Morris (2022), identified heightened potential negative effects on minority children concerning the reproduction of education inequalities. These findings were in line with the Study of Early Education and Development (SEED study), which scrutinised disparities in ECEC attendance and remote education across different lockdown phases in the UK, confirming that children from disadvantaged backgrounds and those with special educational needs encountered increased difficulties in accessing resources and achieving educational goals (Speight et al., 2021).

Another relevant consequence of the pandemic was the rapid shift to digital learning. In this respect, a comparison of policies and practices among ECEC services in Croatia, Hungary, Spain and Turkey highlighted that limited access to technology and socio-economic disparities significantly reduced the educational opportunities of disadvantaged groups when ECEC moved to distance learning (Visnjic-Jevtic et al., 2021). A study conducted in Ontario, Canada, in the spring of 2020, provided an overview of virtual kindergarten classes during the initial ECEC services shutdown. ECEC services faced multiple hurdles, from dealing with technology to supporting parental involvement and adapting the play-based curriculum to suit remote learning (Spadafora et al., 2022).

Finally, during the pandemic, the ECEC sector had to face various significant ethical dilemmas in ensuring care and education for all in an equitable way. Teachers were struggling to find a balance between staying healthy while simultaneously providing educational support to children and families. Choices related to the loss of in-person contact, coupled with the need to rely heavily on parents to preserve everyday educational activities, were another difficult quandary that had an impact on the quality of life of children, especially those with special needs, and their families (Samuelsson et al., 2020).

Young Children During the Pandemic

Health and Well-being

International research on the health and socio-emotional well-being of young children underscores the diverse impacts the COVID-19 pandemic had on their lives in terms of developmental challenges, socio-emotional responses and coping strategies. Studies from Denmark, Spain, Greece, Ireland, Germany and France revealed that young children experienced developmental regression, socialisation problems, increased screen time and heightened anxiety (European Commission, 2021a). Egan et al. (2021) conducted a comprehensive investigation emphasising the profound impact of disrupted routines on children's socio-emotional development, leading to anxiety, clinginess, isolation and low mood. Individual factors, such as age and gender, played a crucial role, highlighting the need for additional support. Children with disabilities faced especially heightened challenges, as closures of ECEC centres affected their emotional distress and loneliness (Underwood et al., 2021).

Other studies presented more mixed findings. In Brazil, Costa et al. (2022) identified both risk and protective factors influencing early childhood development, with family participation in cash transfer programs emerging as a significant protective factor, while families led by women were considered vulnerable. Living with grandparents, however, was protective, emphasising their essential role in early childhood care. Research on the associations between ECEC and socioeconomic status in the UK revealed non-uniform benefits across outcomes, with lower-SES children in ECEC showing enhanced language development during the pandemic (Davies et al., 2021). Focusing on US home learning environments, Sonnenschein et al. (2021a, 2021b) highlighted the positive relationship between children's digital usage and home literacy activities. Research from Slovenia found that children mostly enjoyed participating in home activities during the lockdown and had mixed feelings about missing preschool (Zorec and Peček, 2022).

Young Children's Experience During the Pandemic

Investigation of children's experiences during the pandemic shows that they created a complex interplay of vulnerability and systemic resilience built on dynamic shifts and play adaptations. Findings from a study conducted in three countries (New Zealand, Scotland and the UK) underscored that, despite disruptions, children exhibited remarkable adaptability upon returning to the ECEC centres, with practitioners playing a crucial role in managing transitions through building positive relationships with parents and children (Pascal and Bertram, 2021). However, the reduction in nursery hours posed additional challenges. Notably, the study reported that alterations in children's play became especially evident. Play deepened, intensified and extended, occurring in smaller groups, while the reduced number of children facilitated more elaborate and intricate play, encompassing both COVID-19-related and unrelated themes, such as mask-wearing and loss.

Mantovani et al.'s study (2021) provides additional insights on the topic, focusing on systemic resilience in families during the COVID-19 lockdown in the

Lombardy Region of Italy. According to the authors, several areas of vulnerability emerged, including changes in eating patterns, sleep disturbances, increased screen time and fears about going out. Depending on their age and maturity, children exhibited differing responses, highlighting the need for targeted interventions. Increased irritability and unreasonable behaviour were observed, alongside changes in sleep patterns reported by a significant number of families. Disruptions to social and play relationships with peers were acknowledged, causing distress among children unable to socialise. However, this study also highlights that the majority of parents perceived a sense of "systemic resilience," with high acceptance of restrictions among young children. More precisely, family systems demonstrated resilience through both internal dynamics and networking with other parents. Positive outcomes included improved parent–child relationships, enhanced sibling relationships and gains in linguistic development.

What Did Children Know About COVID-19?

Research on narratives developed by young children during the COVID-19 pandemic shed light on the way their perceptions, emotional expressions and well-being were shaped by their knowledge and understanding of the virus. Oral accounts gathered in Brazil from children aged 3–6 revealed their worries about the disease, awareness of hygiene measures and the manifestation of emotions such as sadness, irritation and frustration (Malta Campos and Vieira, 2021). The children expressed their perspectives through statements such as the need to 'stay at home all the time' as the medicine for the virus, the desire for a vaccine and longing for ECEC and friends.

A similar study was conducted in Slovenia, exploring preschoolers' perceptions of the COVID-19 epidemic (Zorec and Peček, 2022). The research investigated how children, especially those not attending preschool, spent the lockdown period. Children's preferences regarding staying at home or attending preschool varied, with some enjoying family togetherness and favourite activities at home, while others missed the social aspects of preschool life.

Interviews with young children in Chile, Venezuela and other countries in Latin America helped highlight children's dissatisfaction with online education during the pandemic (Fermín González, 2022). Children expressed a notable concern about the limitation of play during home-based activities, emphasising their preference for attending in-person ECEC centres, where they can interact with friends. The absence of physical contact, such as hugging and playing in the park, was explicitly mentioned as a disliked aspect of the lockdown period, underscoring the importance of social interactions for children's well-being.

Finally, Nikiforidou & Doni's research (2022) explored children's meanings and feelings of the COVID-19 pandemic through narrated drawings. Children aged 4–6 expressed their perceptions through drawings, demonstrating a comprehensive understanding of the virus's appearance and impact on health and daily life. The drawings, coupled with narrations, reflected children's access to age-appropriate information, allowing them to articulate their views and emotions about the pandemic. The study highlighted the significance of transparent and age-appropriate information-sharing in mitigating potential negative influences on children's well-being during the pandemic.

Young Children's Use of Technology During COVID-19 Pandemic

The COVID-19 pandemic has brought about significant changes in technology-based learning for young children, particularly those aged 3–6, a domain that was relatively unexplored before. Despite pre-pandemic recommendations discouraging technology exposure for this age group, children extensively embraced technology during the pandemic. A study from India delved into the repercussions of prolonged screen time on the cognitive, social and behavioural development of young children (Genimon et al., 2022). The research revealed that the average daily screen time significantly exceeded recommended limits, leading to immediate outcomes such as mobile dependency and health issues. Statistically significant impacts of screen time on mobile dependency, cognition, socialisation and behaviour were identified. Although cognitive domains were not significantly affected, excessive screen time exhibited a negative correlation with children's behaviour, emphasising the importance of control to prevent undesirable psychological consequences and screen dependency disorders.

A survey conducted in the Lombardy region of Italy further underscored concerns about potential addiction to digital technologies during distance learning (Mantovani et al., 2021). The study acknowledged positive responses to remote educational connections but highlighted worries about children's future experiences, including uncertainties about post-lockdown education scenarios and concerns about developmental delays, discipline issues, dietary behaviours and digital technology use.

Similarly, an Israeli study emphasised the increase in child screen time during lockdowns and its continued rise post-lockdown, possibly due to disrupted routines altering viewing habits, highlighting the dynamic nature of parental media use during pandemic routines (Gueron-Sela et al., 2023). Additionally, Koran et al.'s (2022) research on mobile technology usage in early childhood in North Cyprus revealed that children were introduced to mobile devices before 36 months, often surpassing recommended guidelines. The comparison between pre-pandemic and lockdown periods indicated an increase in mobile device usage, particularly for educational purposes. Parents predominantly regulated their children's mobile device usage through time restrictions, family protection, and age restrictions, underscoring the need for mindful use of technology in early childhood.

Young Children's Reading Experience

The impact of the COVID-19 pandemic on the reading experiences of young children was a subject of significant concern among ECEC stakeholders, considering the crucial role of early reading habits in shaping a child's academic future and overall development. A survey administered to 500 families with children aged two to four in the US shed light on the alterations in both the quantity and nature of shared reading experiences within families during the pandemic (Wheeler and Hill, 2021). Despite limitations in response rates, the data obtained underscored the heightened awareness among parents of the value of reading to their children during the COVID-19 period. The findings revealed an increase in the frequency of reading activities compared to the pre-pandemic era, signifying a positive shift in parental reading practices.

Another US study focused on the broader family media ecology during lockdowns, offering insights into children's media use patterns (Read et al., 2022). The research indicated an increase in child screen time during lockdowns, which continued to rise post-lockdown, potentially influenced by disrupted routines. Household background television exposure initially surged during the first lockdown due to the need for pandemic updates but subsequently decreased. Maternal use of media to regulate child distress witnessed a decline across lockdowns, suggesting an adaptive response to pandemic-related stress. The study highlighted the dynamic nature of parental media use during pandemic routines, emphasising the need for a nuanced understanding of the changing dynamics of young children's reading experiences in the context of COVID-19.

An Outdoor Activity of Young Children During COVID-19

A few studies focused on identifying changes that occurred in outdoor activities for young children in ECEC settings amid the COVID-19 pandemic. Liu et al. (2023) explored how the outdoor activities of young children in Australian ECEC settings underwent substantial modifications. While health advice promoted outdoor activities to minimise virus transmission, a significant number of educators maintained the same amount of outdoor time and access to outdoor spaces for children. However, a noteworthy discovery was that a majority of educators imposed restrictions on children's outdoor play compared to pre-pandemic conditions, potentially impacting the quality of outdoor experiences. Nevertheless, this finding contrasts with some studies in a systematic review reporting increased outdoor time for children in ECEC settings during the pandemic (Delisle Nyström et al., 2020; Liu et al., 2022). Pascal and Bertram (2021) further emphasised children's growing preference for outdoor pursuits during the pandemic, possibly in response to lockdown restrictions. Their study especially highlighted a resurfacing "Romantic" belief in nature's healing properties among practitioners and parents. The belief was supported by the assumption that nature-oriented activities, like berry picking, bring recovery and joy to both children and adults.

Parents/Carers During the Pandemic

The Impact of COVID-19 Pandemic on Parents/Carers

The COVID-19 pandemic had a profound impact on parents/carers of young children, intensifying existing disadvantages and increasing poverty, particularly for families with children from vulnerable groups. Lockdown periods presented specific challenges, including the difficulty of balancing professional and private lives while teleworking with young children at home, the reduction or loss of income and jobs, limited family support for childcare and decreased access to services for children with special needs.

The European Commission's (2021b) report identified diverse effects on parents/carers, emphasising the challenges of balancing paid work, childcare and health and financial concerns. During lockdowns, vulnerable families, and particularly mothers, bore an increased childcare burden, disrupting established childcare and work arrangements (European Commission, 2021a). Changes in family interactions were also emphasised, with mothers struggling to balance household, professional and parenting duties (Gelir and Duzen, 2021). This prompted governments worldwide to implement supporting measures such as financial assistance, childcare fee reductions and special provisions for parents unable to work due to childcare responsibilities. Other studies echoed these findings, emphasising gaps in health services, disruptions in early childhood education and changes in social interactions affecting parents' day-to-day lives (Sanders et al., 2022). Investigations outlined the social, psychological and physical effects on parents/carers, with changes in daily routines and communication limitations. However, growing stressors and disruptions in daily life also led to an increase in parental involvement and family sharing (Lee et al., 2021; Yazici and Yüksel, 2022).

Regarding education, Garbe et al. (2020) highlighted challenges faced by parents/carers during ECEC services closures, including juggling responsibilities, learner motivation issues and concerns about learning outcomes. Formosinho (2021) emphasised an emerging schoolification trend, requiring parental involvement in remote education. Moreover, studies from Ethiopia (Kim et al., 2021), Hong Kong (Lau et al., 2020), and Victoria (Levickis et al., 2022) revealed multiple challenges faced by parents/carers in supporting children's learning at home in terms of limited access to resources and disruptions in family engagement with ECEC. Yildiz et al. (2023) pinpointed inefficiencies in the educational process due to technological challenges and increased parenting responsibilities.

During the pandemic, families with children experiencing developmental delays were confronted with service disruptions and increased responsibilities (Kunze et al., 2023). In this regard, parents/carers of young children with special needs expressed strong concerns regarding the inadequacy of services (Fettig et al., 2023) Sonnenschein et al. (2022a, 2022b) highlighted that families with children with disabilities were often side-lined, as a result of the adoption of the virtual learning format.

The Coping Strategies of Parents/Carers During the Pandemic

During the COVID-19 pandemic, parents/carers worldwide adopted various coping strategies to navigate the challenges imposed by lockdowns and disruptions in the provision of ECEC. A qualitative study in the UK revealed the anxieties and uncertainties parents faced during the pandemic in supporting their children (Shum et al., 2023). Despite challenges, some parents reported positive outcomes, such as strengthened family bonds and hopeful perspectives. However, the study noted that parents, embodying characteristics of authoritative parenting, prioritised their children's needs at the cost of their well-being, experiencing low self-efficacy and heightened stress. Challenges included difficulties in controlling children's screen time, especially during lockdowns. McIsaac et al. (2022) explored the impact of changes in employment demands and income on family environments and childhood development in Canada. Families adapted to new routines and responded to challenges with the resources available in their homes and communities, emphasising the positive appraisal and reorganisation efforts of families in navigating challenges. However, the study also highlighted gender imbalances in parental responsibilities and concerns about increased screen time and sedentary behaviours among children.

A cross-cultural study conducted across Europe, the Middle East and the US revealed that loving behaviours were consistently reported as the most prominent parenting practice during lockdowns, emphasising its significance. However, challenges in spousal collaboration, particularly in partnership behaviours, were noted across cultures, indicating potential difficulties in collaborative parenting. Larger families and older parents faced increased difficulties coping with the circumstances, leading parents to promote independence in older children (Aram et al., 2022).

A Canadian study explored the relationships between children's activities, parental concerns and child care utilization during the pandemic (Zhang et al., 2023). The study identified three distinct profiles of children's activities: Screenies, Analog and Balanced. Parental concerns varied across activity profiles, with Screenies causing the highest worry. Pandemic-related changes in childcare arrangements were linked to children's activity patterns, emphasising the need for targeted post-pandemic planning. Demographic factors, such as caregiver age, education and family employment status, played a role in shaping activity profiles and parental intentions to use childcare services.

Finally, Dereli and Kurtça (2022) focused on parent engagement in young children's education during lockdowns, highlighting the role of parents as teachers. The study emphasised the parent's involvement in various activities and communication methods, despite challenges such as parents lacking technology skills and facing difficulties with computer use and internet connectivity at home. Positive outcomes included parents recognising the importance of spending quality time together with their children while focusing on education.

Collaboration Between Families and ECEC Services

During the COVID-19 pandemic, the collaborative efforts between families and ECEC services became pivotal for the education and care of young children. An online survey conducted in Northern Ireland emphasised that effective remote learning during ECEC service closures necessitated various factors, including appropriate assignments, strong service-home communication, home support and access to devices and the Internet (Bates et al., 2023). Disparities in support revealed the need for a consistent approach to ensure equity, suggesting interventions at higher levels, such as government or educational bodies, to establish a template for all

ECEC services. Challenges related to access to technology, the emotional needs of children and the impact on children with special educational needs underscored the importance of addressing inequities and providing support for future closures.

A study conducted in the US assessed parent–teacher relationships during the pandemic, revealing lower-quality relationships across various subscales (Keengwe and Onchwari, 2022). The study identified variations in collaborative practices during COVID-19, with positive aspects but challenges in areas like communicating about activities. Parental education levels, income and the age of children played roles in relationship scores, emphasising the need for tailored support tools and quality programs in rural areas. The study also highlighted the potential benefits of distance learning for connecting with programmes during the pandemic. A similar study conducted in Italy analysed the collaborative relationship between early childcare services and families during the pandemic as an educational alliance (Bosoni, 2022). Despite disruptions, the study recognised positive changes initiated by both teachers and families, emphasising the irreplaceable role of educational services in children's growth. The need for ECEC services to engage in dialogue with families and treat them as collaborators was stressed, especially for ongoing monitoring and support as challenges persist.

The Brazilian families' perspective on the relationship with ECEC services during the lockdowns was explored through research conducted by Pereira de Lima et al. (2022). Widespread use of remote activities faced difficulties, especially related to children's engagement and family reconfigurations, highlighting socio-economic disparities. The study called for a more inclusive and collaborative approach between institutions and families, emphasising the necessity of efficient communication, assistance in understanding proposals and providing training for meaningful experiences supporting child development. A study carried out in Wuhan, China, revealed a positive correlation between the frequency of parental participation in online parent–teacher meetings during ECEC centres closures and children's approaches to learning (Tan et al., 2021). The research outcomes underscored the valuable role of family-centred connections, particularly through parents' active engagement in online meetings to support pre-schoolers' development during the pandemic. The study underlined the importance of creating flexible and accessible opportunities for families and preschools to establish systematic connections.

Lastly, an investigation developed by McIntyre et al. (2022) shared insights and lessons learned from providing telehealth-delivered group parenting interventions for families of preschool-aged children with developmental delays and disabilities. The research project aimed to assess the efficacy of remote versus in-person group interventions, recognising the potential of telehealth interventions in meeting the needs of families and children, especially during challenging situations and times of crisis. Preliminary findings from the study showed that the transition to remote interventions, though initially challenging, revealed numerous advantages, emphasising the importance of having a variety of intervention options in early childhood education and family support.

Online Learning

The surge in digital and online learning during the COVID-19 pandemic, often lauded for its flexibility, wider access and cost-effectiveness, encountered challenges, particularly in the context of young children's education, as observed in Chinese families (Dong et al., 2020). Despite recognised advantages, Chinese parents expressed negative beliefs and attitudes toward online learning, preferring traditional methods in early childhood education. The unpreparedness of parents, exacerbated by pandemic-related hardships, resulted in resistance to online learning at home, citing concerns about children's inadequate self-regulation and parents lacking time and professional knowledge to support online learning. Carrell Moore's study (2022) further emphasised the substantial assistance required by young children during online activities, leading to increased parental responsibilities compared to traditional classrooms. Parents faced challenges related to younger children's difficulties in completing work independently and effectively using technology, emphasising the need for interactive, hands-on activities to enhance children's independence.

A study conducted in Indonesia highlighted the transformation of learning with parental assistance during the pandemic, revealing the multiple challenges involved in ensuring an effective parental assistance model in online learning (Juliana Pramono et al., 2020). Challenges included maintaining children's enthusiasm, time constraints, children's moods and distractions from toys, emphasising consistent parental assistance to enhance children's enthusiasm and guidance from ECEC services on using learning support applications. Along the same lines, Mota et al.'s investigation (2021) addressed concerns about access to distance education during the pandemic, revealing variations based on factors such as the number of children, age group, employment status and whether parents worked during the lockdown. The authors recommended future support measures for parents working from home, emphasising the importance of investing in digital competencies for both children and parents.

Further critical questions were identified by research on US parents' experiences with distance learning, which emphasised the importance of considering the implications of home-based learning activities on parents' stress levels (Sonnenschein et al., 2021b). The study highlighted the need for educators and policymakers to tailor distance learning demands to prevent potential negative consequences. Additionally, research carried out by Shaw et al. (2021) on parents' experiences supporting children with special needs and disabilities during the pandemic underscored a global trend of deficient remote learning for such children.

However, a few studies have shed a more positive light on the role of remote learning in the early years during the pandemic. An investigation in Italy detailed early intervention strategies implemented during ECEC services closure, emphasising successful engagement of families, particularly in activities tailored for younger children, highlighting the importance of supporting ongoing collaboration between educational services and families (Nossa et al., 2021). A study from Spain highlighted innovative ways in which parents and children established a virtual support network to mitigate the effects of social isolation (Cano-Hila and Argemí-Baldich, 2021). Through platforms like WhatsApp and YouTube, families formed a dynamic support system, fostering social connections and mutual assistance. This virtual network positively impacted participants' subjective well-being by providing emotional, material and informational assistance. The study emphasised the importance of such support in enhancing well-being, self-esteem and a sense of belonging, highlighting the role of parents' digital skills and educational capital in shaping children's educability.

Conclusion and Recommendations

The review provided in this chapter highlights how COVID-19 has significantly impacted the education and care of young children, prompting the need for comprehensive strategies to address the multiple challenges posed by the pandemic. The closure of ECEC facilities during lockdowns has highlighted its pivotal role as a support net for families and raised concerns about the deepening of inequities, particularly affecting vulnerable groups, including those with special educational needs.

During ECEC services closures, disparities in access to technology and parental support became apparent, affecting children's educational experiences. The widespread use of remote learning has brought attention to the risks of overexposure to screens for young children. This underscores the importance of raising awareness about screen time and implementing measures to identify potential learning loss, language developmental delays and social-emotional difficulties. However, the positive role of collaborative efforts between teachers and parents emerged as a critical factor in supporting children's developmental needs. Family-centred practices, such as embedding learning opportunities in children's daily routines, proved effective.

To address these challenges, it is recommended that interventions and mechanisms be established to provide equitable opportunities for children to catch up on missed learning and socialisation. The examined literature highlights that the impact of COVID-19 on the education and care of young children requires a multifaceted approach. Scaffolding and support for parents during school closures are essential tools to promote children's well-being and educational achievements, with a focus on improving access to dedicated information and resources for the early years. Maintaining and enhancing the focus on family-centred practices by increasing collaboration with parents is crucial for positive child and family outcomes. In addition, governments should ensure that other vital components of the ECEC system will receive continuous support in crisis times concerning facilities, financial assistance for families, awareness of screen time risks, and targeted interventions for learning loss.

Finally, there is a pressing need for research into the long-term impact of the pandemic on children's well-being and cognitive development and the role of their parents in sustaining these pivotal dimensions. Understanding the multifaceted effects of the crisis on the ECEC system is crucial for guiding current and future investments to better respond to the evolving needs of children and families. Research into the long-term effects of the pandemic will further inform evidence-based strategies for future crises, ensuring the well-being and development of young children and their families.

References

Aram, D., Asaf, M., Karabanov, G.M., Ziv, M., Sonnenschein, S., Stites, M., Shtereva, K. and López Escribano, C. 2022. Beneficial parenting according to the "parenting pentagon model": a cross-cultural study during a pandemic. In *The Impact of COVID-19 on Early Childhood Education and Care*, Eds J. Pattnaik, M. Renck Jalongo, vol. 18, pp. 215–236, Springer International Publishing. https://doi.org/10.1007/978-3-030-96977-6_11

Bates, J., Finlay, J. and O'Connor Bones, U. 2023. "Education cannot cease": the experiences of parents of primary age children (age 4-11) in Northern Ireland during school closures due to COVID-19. *Educational Review*, 75(4), 657–679. https://doi.org/10.1080/00131911.2021.1974821

Bosoni, M.L. 2022. Children's services and the COVID-19 pandemic in Italy: a study with educators and parents. *Children & Society*. https://doi.org/10.1111/chso.12676, chso.12676

Cano-Hila, A.B. and Argemí-Baldich, R. 2021. Early childhood and lockdown: the challenge of building a virtual mutual support network between children, families and school for sustainable education and increasing their well-being. *Sustainability*, 13(7), 3654. https://doi.org/10.3390/su13073654

Carrell Moore, H. 2022. "The whole experience is still very high touch for parents": parent moves to support young children's remote learning during the COVID-19 pandemic. *Journal of Early Childhood Research*, 1476718X2210986. https://doi.org/10.1177/1476718x221098671

Costa, P., Forni, E., Amato, I. and Sassaki, R.L. 2022. Risk and protective factors to early childhood development during the COVID-19 pandemic. *Revista da Escola de Enfermagem da USP*, 56, e20220196. https://doi.org/10.1590/1980-220x-reeusp-2022-0196en

Davies, C., Hendry, A., Gibson, S.P., Gliga, T., McGillion, M. and and Gonzalez-Gomez, N. 2021. Early childhood education and care (ECEC) during COVID-19 boosts growth in language and executive function. *Infant and Child Development 30* (4), e2241. https://doi.org/10.1002/icd.2241

Delisle Nyström, C., Alexandrou, C., Henström, M., Nilsson, E., Okely, A.D., Wehbe El Masri, S. and Löf, M. 2020. International study of movement behaviors in the early years (Sunrise): results from sunrise Sweden's pilot and COVID-19 study. *International Journal of Environmental Research and Public Health*, 17(22), 8491.

Dereli, F. and Türk-Kurtça, T. 2022. Parent engagement in early childhood education: pandemic period. *Southeast Asia Early Childhood Journal*, 11(1), 35–48.

Dong, C., Cao, S. and Li, H. 2020. Young children's online learning during COVID-19 pandemic: Chinese parents' beliefs and attitudes. *Children and Youth Services Review*, 118, 105440. https://doi.org/10.1016/j.childyouth.2020.105440

Egan, S.M. and Pope, J. 2022. *A Bioecological Systems Approach to Understanding the Impact of the COVID-19 Pandemic: Implications for the Education and Care of*

Young Children, pp. 15–31, Springer International Publishing eBooks. https://doi.org/10.1007/978-3-030-96977-6_2

Egan, S.M., Pope, J., Moloney, M., Hoyne, C. and Beatty, C. 2021. Missing early education and care during the pandemic: the socio-emotional impact of the COVID-19 crisis on young children. *Early Childhood Education Journal*, 49(5), 925–934. https://doi.org/10.1007/s10643-021-01193-2

European Commission. Directorate General for Education, Youth, Sport and Culture 2021b. *Governing Quality Early Childhood Education and Care in a Global Crisis: First Lessons Learned from the COVID-19 Pandemic: Analytical Report*. Publications Office. Retrieved from: https://data.europa.eu/doi/10.2766/642131

European Commission. Directorate General for Education, Youth, Sport and Culture 2021a. *Early Childhood Education and Care and the COVID-19 Pandemic: Understanding and Managing the Impact of the Crisis on the Sector*. Publications Office. Retrieved from: https://data.europa.eu/doi/10.2766/60724

Fermín González, M. 2022. Early childhood education in times of pandemic: the lived experience of children in Latin America. *Proceedings of the 2022 AERA Annual Meeting*. https://doi.org/10.3102/1897252

Fettig, A., Zulauf-McCurdy, C., Choi, G. and McManus, M. 2023. Qualitative investigation of educator and parent experiences of education services during COVID-19. *Journal of Early Intervention*, 45(4), 430–451. https://doi.org/10.1177/10538151221140322

Formosinho, J. 2021. From schoolification of children to schoolification of parents? – Educational policies in COVID times. *European Early Childhood Education Research Journal*, 29(1), 141–152. https://doi.org/10.1080/1350293x.2021.1872677

Garbe, A., Uzeyir, O., Ogurlu, Ü., Uzeyir, O., Logan, N. and Cook, P. 2020. COVID-19 and remote learning: experiences of parents with children during the pandemic. *American Journal of Qualitative Research*, 4(3), 45–65. https://doi.org/10.29333/ajqr/8471

Gelir, I. and Duzen, N. 2021. Children's changing behaviours and routines, challenges and opportunities for parents during the COVID-19 pandemic. *Education, 3–13*, 1–11. https://doi.org/10.1080/03004279.2021.1921822

Genimon, V.J., Agnes, T.M., Sneha, E., Stephiya, V. and Jebin, T. 2022. The impact of screen time and mobile dependency on cognition, socialization and behaviour among early childhood students during the covid pandemic- perception of the parents. *Digital Education Review*, 41, 114–123. https://doi.org/10.1344/der.2022.41.114-123

Greig, A.D., Taylor, J. and MacKay, T. 2012. *Doing Research with Children: A Practical Guide*, Sage.

Gromada, A., Richardson, D. and Rees, G. 2020. *Childcare in a Global Crisis: The Impact of COVID-19 on Work and Family Life*, vol. 2020/18, UNICEF Innocenti Research Briefs. https://doi.org/10.18356/16d757a1-en

Gueron-Sela, N., Shalev, I., Gordon-Hacker, A., Egotubov, A. and Barr, R. 2023. Screen media exposure and behavioral adjustment in early childhood during and after COVID-19 home lockdown periods. *Computers in Human Behavior*, 140, 107572. https://doi.org/10.1016/j.chb.2022.107572

Henderson, L., Bussey, K., Ebrahim, H.B. Eds 2022. *Early Childhood Education and Care in a Global Pandemic: How the Sector Responded, Spoke Back and Generated Knowledge*, Routledge.

Howlett, M. 2022. Looking at the 'field' through a Zoom lens: methodological reflections on conducting online research during a global pandemic. *Qualitative Research*, *22*(3), 387–402.

Juliana Pramono, R., Parani, R. and Djakasaputra, A. 2020. Transformation of learning for early childhood education through parent assistance in the pandemic COVID-19. *European Journal of Molecular & Clinical Medicine*, *7*(10), 2192–2206. Retrieved from: https://ejmcm.com/article_6939.html

Keengwe, G. and Onchwari, A.J. 2022. Assessment of parent–teacher relationships in early childhood education programs during the COVID-19 pandemic. *Early Childhood Education Journal*, *1*(22). https://doi.org/10.1007/s10643-022-01431-1

Kim, J.H., Araya, M., Hailu, B.H., Rose, P.M. and Woldehanna, T. 2021. The implications of COVID-19 for early childhood education in Ethiopia: perspectives from parents and caregivers. *Early Childhood Education Journal*, *49*(5), 855–867. https://doi.org/10.1007/s10643-021-01214-0

Koran, N., Berkmen, B. and Adalıer, A. 2022. Mobile technology usage in early childhood: pre-COVID-19 and the national lockdown period in North Cyprus. *Education and Information Technologies*, *27*(1), 321–346. https://doi.org/10.1007/s10639-021-10658-1

Kunze, M., Gomez, D., Glenn, E.C., Todis, B., Riddle, I., Karns, C., Glang, A. and McIntyre, L.L. 2023. Parenting young children with developmental disabilities: experiences during the COVID-19 pandemic in the US. *Journal of Childhood, Education and Society*. https://doi.org/10.37291/2717638x.202342264

Lau, E.Y.H., Lee, K. and Lee, K. 2020. Parents' views on young children's distance learning and screen time during COVID-19 class suspension in Hong Kong. *Early Education & Development*, *32*(6), 863–880. https://doi.org/10.1080/10409289.2020.1843925

Lee, S.J., Ward, K.P., Chang, O.D. and Downing, K.M. 2021. Parenting activities and the transition to home-based education during the COVID-19 pandemic. *Children and Youth Services Review*, *122*, 105585. https://doi.org/10.1016/j.childyouth.2020.105585

Levickis, P., Murray, L., Lee-Pang, L., Eadie, P., Page, J., Yi Lee, W. and Hill, G. 2022. Parents' perspectives of family engagement with early childhood education and care during the COVID-19 pandemic. *Early Childhood Education Journal*. https://doi.org/10.1007/s10643-022-01376-5

Liu, J., Wyver, S. and Chutiyami, M. 2022. Impacts of COVID-19 restrictions on young children's outdoor activity: a systematic review. *Children*, *9* (10), 1564.

Liu, J., Wyver, S., Chutiyami, M. and Little, H. 2023. Outdoor time, space, and restrictions imposed on children's play in Australian early childhood education and care settings during the COVID pandemic: a cross-sectional survey from educators' perspective. *International Journal of Environmental Research and Public Health*, *20*(18), 6779. https://doi.org/10.3390/ijerph20186779

Lupton, D. 2020. *Doing Fieldwork in a Pandemic*. ResearchGate. [crowdsourced document]. https://docs.google.com/document/d/1clGjGABB2h2qbduTgfqribHmog9B6P0NvMgVuiHZCl8/edit?ts=5e88ae0a

Malta Campos, M. and Vieira, L.F. 2021. COVID-19 and early childhood in Brazil: impacts on children's well-being, education and care. *European Early Childhood Education Research Journal*, *29*(1), 125–140. https://doi.org/10.1080/1350293X.2021.1872671

Mantovani, S., Bove, C., Ferri, P., Manzoni, P., Cesa Bianchi, A. and Picca, M. 2021. Children 'under lockdown': voices, experiences, and resources during and after the COVID-19 emergency. Insights from a survey with children and families in the Lombardy region of Italy. *European Early Childhood Education Research Journal*, *29*(1), 35–50. https://doi.org/10.1080/1350293X.2021.1872673

McIntyre, L.L., Gab, M., Hoskins, J., Tienson, J. and Neece, C. L. 2022. Lessons learned supporting families of young children with disabilities via telehealth during the COVID-19 pandemic. In *The Impact of COVID-19 on Early Childhood Education and Care*, Ed J. Pattnaik, M. Renck Jalongo, vol. 18, pp. 275–291, Springer International Publishing. https://doi.org/10.1007/978-3-030-96977-6_14

McIsaac, J.D., Lamptey, D., Harley, J., MacQuarrie, M., Cummings, R., Rossiter, M.D., Janus, M. and Turner, J. 2022. Early pandemic impacts on family environments that shape childhood development and health: a Canadian study. *Child: Care, Health and Development*, *48*(6), 1122–1133. https://doi.org/10.1111/cch.13046

Mota, S., Seabra, F., Teixeira, A. and Aires, L. 2021. Learning in troubled times: parents' perspectives on emergency remote teaching and learning. *Sustainability*, *14*(1), 301. https://doi.org/10.3390/su14010301

Nikiforidou, Z. and Eleni, D. 2022. 'Go away from this galaxy coronavirus': children's meanings and feelings of the COVID-19 pandemic through narrated drawings. *European Early Childhood Education Research Journal*, 1–13. https://doi.org/10.1080/1350293x.2022.2098993

Nossa, R., Biffi, E., Colnago, G., De Gregorio, G., Saudelli, L., Reni, G. and Caruso, C. 2021. Engagement of families attending early childhood services during 5-month school closure due to COVID-19: an Italian experience. *Frontiers in Psychology*, *12*. https://doi.org/10.3389/fpsyg.2021.722834

Page, M.J., McKenzie, J.E., Bossuyt, P.M., Boutron, I., Hoffmann, T.C., Mulrow, C.D., Shamseer, L., Tetzlaff, J.M., Akl, E.A., Brennan, S.E., Chou, R., Glanville, J., Grimshaw, J.M., Hróbjartsson, A., Lalu, M.M., Li, T., Loder, E.W., Mayo-Wilson, E., McDonald, S., McGuinness, L.A. and Moher, D. 2021. The PRISMA 2020 statement: an updated guideline for reporting systematic reviews. *International Journal of Surgery*, *88*, 105906. https://doi.org/10.1016/j.ijsu.2021.105906

Park, E., Logan, H., Zhang, L., Kamigaichi, N. and Kulapichitr, U. 2021. Responses to coronavirus pandemic in early childhood services across five countries in the Asia-Pacific region: OMEP policy forum. *International Journal of Early Childhood*, *52*(3), 1–18. https://doi.org/10.1007/s13158-020-00278-0

Pascal, C. and Bertram, T. 2021. What do young children have to say? Recognising their voices, wisdom, agency and need for companionship during the COVID pandemic. *European Early Childhood Education Research Journal*, *29*(1), 21–34. https://doi.org/10.1080/1350293x.2021.1872676

Pereira de Lima, L., Sbroion de Carvalho, R. and da Silva, A.P.S. 2022. The perspective of families towards remote activities for early childhood education in times of COVID-19. *Zero-a-Seis*, *24*(45), 265–285. https://doi.org/10.5007/1518-2924.2022.e84086

Proulx, K., Lenzi-Weisbecker, R., Hatch, R., Hackett, K., Omoeva, C., Cavallera, V., Daelmans, B. and Dua, T. 2022. Nurturing care during COVID-19: a rapid review of early evidence. *BMJ Open*, *12*(6). e050417. https://doi.org/10.1136/bmjopen-2021-050417

Read, K., Gaffney, G., Chen, A. and Imran, A. 2022. The impact of COVID-19 on families' home literacy practices with young children. *Early Childhood Education Journal*, 50(8), 1429–1438. https://doi.org/10.1007/s10643-021-01270-6

Rothe, A., Moloney, M., Sims, M., Calder, P., Blyth, D., Boyd, W., Doan, L., Dovigo, F., Girlich, S., Georgiadou, S., Kakana, D., Mellon, C., Opazo, M.J., O'Síoráin, C.A., Quinn, M., Rogers, M., Silberfeld, C. and Tadeu, B. 2022. Lessons from the COVID-19 pandemic: a qualitative study of government policies relating to the early childhood sector across ten countries. In *The Impact of COVID-19 on Early Childhood Education and Care: International Perspectives, Challenges, and Responses*, pp. 67–88, Springer International Publishing.

Samuelsson, I.P., Wagner, J.T. and Ødegaard, E.E. 2020. The coronavirus pandemic and lessons learned in preschools in Norway, Sweden and the United States: OMEP policy forum. *International Journal of Early Childhood*, 52(2), 1–16. https://doi.org/10.1007/s13158-020-00267-3

Sanders, C., Frank, T.J., Amyot, T., Cornish, K., Koopmans, E., Usipuik, M., Irving, L. and Pelletier, C.A. 2022. Day-to-day life during the COVID-19 pandemic: a longitudinal qualitative study with Canadian parents of young children. *Contemporary Issues in Early Childhood*, 146394912211154. https://doi.org/10.1177/14639491221115475

Shaw, P.A., Shaw, A. and Shaw, A. 2021. COVID-19 and remote learning: experiences of parents supporting children with special needs and disability during the pandemic. *Education, 3–13*, 1–15. https://doi.org/10.1080/03004279.2021.1960579

Shum, A., Klampe, M.-L., Pearcey, S., Cattel, C., Burgess, L., Lawrence, P.J., Waite, P. 2023. Parenting in a pandemic: a qualitative exploration of parents' experiences of supporting their children during the COVID-19 pandemic. *Journal of Family Studies*, 29(5), 2335–2355. https://doi.org/10.1080/13229400.2023.2168561

Sonnenschein, S., Stites, M.L., Grossman, J.A., Galczyk, S.H. 2022a. "This will likely affect his entire life": parents' views of special education services during COVID-19. *International Journal of Educational Research*, 112, 101941. https://doi.org/10.1016/j.ijer.2022.101941

Sonnenschein, S., Grossman, E.R. and Grossman, J.A. 2021a. U.S. Parents' reports of assisting their children with distance learning during COVID-19. *Education Sciences*, 11(9), 501. https://doi.org/10.3390/educsci11090501

Sonnenschein, S., Stites, M.L., Grossman, J.A. and Galczyk, S.H. 2022b. *"It Just Does Not Work": Parents' Views About Distance Learning for Young Children with Special Needs*, pp. 253–273, Springer International Publishing eBooks. https://doi.org/10.1007/978-3-030-96977-6_13

Sonnenschein, S., Stites, M. and Ross, A. 2021b. Home learning environments for young children in the US during COVID-19. *Early Education & Development*, 32(6), 794–811.

Spadafora, N., Reid-Westoby, C., Pottruff, M., Wang, J. and Janus, M. 2022. From full day learning to 30 minutes a day: a descriptive study of early learning during the first COVID-19 pandemic school shutdown in Ontario. *Early Childhood Education Journal*. https://doi.org/10.1007/s10643-021-01304-z

Speight, S., Taylor, I. and Taylor, B. 2021. *Study of early education and development (SEED): findings from the coronavirus (COVID-19) follow-up*, vol. 1168. Research report. National Centre for Social Research

Tan, F., Gong, X., Gong, X., Zhang, X. and Zhang, R. 2021. Preschoolers' approaches to learning and family-school connections during COVID-19: an empirical study based on a Wuhan sample. *Early Childhood Education Journal*, 49(5), 1–11. https://doi.org/10.1007/s10643-021-01217-x

Underwood, K., van Rhijn, T., Balter, A.S., Feltham, L., Douglas, P., Parekh, G. and Lawrence, B. 2021. Pandemic effects: ableism, exclusion, and procedural bias. *Journal of Childhood Studies*, 16–29.

Vindrola-Padros, C., Chisnall, G., Cooper, S., Dowrick, A., Djellouli, N., Symmons, S.M., Martin, S., Singleton, G., Vanderslott, S., Vera, N. and Johnson, G.A. 2020. Carrying out rapid qualitative research during a pandemic: emerging lessons from COVID-19. *Qualitative Health Research*, 30(14), 2192–2204.

Visnjic-Jevtic, A., Varga Nagy, A., Ozturk, G., Şahin-Sak, İ.T., Paz-Albo, J., Toran, M. and Sánchez-Pérez, N. 2021. Policies and practices of early childhood education and care during the COVID-19 pandemic: perspectives from five countries. *Journal of Childhood, Education & Society*, 2(2), 200–216. https://doi.org/10.37291/2717638X.202122114

Weiland, C. and Morris, P. 2022. The risks and opportunities of the COVID-19 crisis for building longitudinal evidence on today's early childhood education programs. *Child Development Perspectives*, 16(2), 76–81. https://doi.org/10.1111/cdep.12445

Wheeler, D.L. and Hill, J.C. 2021. The impact of COVID-19 on early childhood reading practices. *Journal of Early Childhood Literacy*, 1–20. https://doi.org/10.1177/14687984211044187

Yazici, D. and Yüksel, N. 2022. Investigation of the reflections of the pandemic process on early childhood education by taking the opinions of teachers and parents. *International Journal of Psychology and Educational Studies*, 9, 908–921. https://doi.org/10.52380/ijpes.2022.9.4.850

Yildiz, S., Kilic, G.N. and Acar, I.H. 2023. Early childhood education during the COVID-19 outbreak: the perceived changing roles of preschool administrators, teachers, and parents. *Early Childhood Education Journal*, 51(4), 743–753. https://doi.org/10.1007/s10643-022-01339-w

Yoshikawa, H., Wuermli, A.J., Britto, P.R., Dreyer, B.P., Leckman, J.F., Lye, S.J., Ponguta, L.A., Richter, L. and Stein, A. 2020. Effects of the global coronavirus disease-2019 pandemic on early childhood development: short- and long-term risks and mitigating program and policy actions. *The Journal of Pediatrics*, 223, 188–193. https://doi.org/10.1016/j.jpeds.2020.05.020

Zhang, J., Smith, J. and Browne, D. 2023. Children's activities, parental concerns, and child care service utilization in the early stages of the COVID-19 pandemic. *Frontiers in Public Health*, 11, 1047234. https://doi.org/10.3389/fpubh.2023.1047234

Zorec, M.B. and Peček, M. 2022. Preschoolers' perceptions of the COVID-19 epidemic: an interview study with children in Slovenia. In *The Impact of COVID-19 on Early Childhood Education and Care*, Eds J. Pattnaik, M. Renck Jalongo, vol. 18, pp. 105–125, Springer International Publishing. https://doi.org/10.1007/978-3-030-96977-6_6

Chapter 3

Childcare, Responses to Poverty in Preschool and a 'New Normal' After COVID-19 Pandemic?

Donald Simpson[a] *and Sandra Lyndon*[b]

[a]Teesside University, UK
[b]University of Chichester, UK

Abstract

This chapter discusses research exploring preschool practitioners' beliefs about child poverty and their responses to it before and during the COVID-19 pandemic. Previously, in 2014, the authors' research found notable levels of poverty insensitivity amongst preschool practitioners within prescribed formal pedagogical contexts emphasising early education over care. With COVID-19 pandemic, some commentators speculated care's place in public consciousness would be raised allowing it to go viral across society. Exploring this, the authors replicated the earlier study in 2021. Drawing upon these recent data from England, the authors consider preschool practitioners' views about the extent to which COVID-19 posed challenges for children in poverty and how much they agreed poverty was something they needed to be sensitive to during the pandemic. The authors then examine preschool practitioners' pedagogical adaptions and their prioritising of care alongside early education during the pandemic. The chapter ends by questioning conjecture about a 'new normal' emerging in preschool, allowing pedagogical space for an energised focus upon care.

Keywords: Care; COVID-19; early education; new normal; poverty; preschool

Introduction

Globally, there has been widespread consensus that preschool settings will continue to be key in providing early childhood education and care (ECEC) to children and families in poverty as recovery from COVID-19 is implemented. Pre-COVID-19, during the early decades of the new millennium, policymakers in many countries positioned preschool as having a key socially progressive function, claiming it can remediate poverty's negative grip on children's holistic development through the provision of integrated ECEC. Preschool is also expected to fill an informal 'care deficit' as record numbers of women enter labour markets across several countries (Hayes, 2017). To perform this role, the preschool system in England has expanded greatly since 2000 and is a 'mixed economy of care', a childcare market consisting of a patchwork of private and public preschool providers/settings with differing organisational arrangements and resources.

Preschool in England is expensive although some 'free early educational places' are subsidised by the state for all 3–4 year olds. Since 2010, these free places have been for 15 hours a week for 38 weeks a year for all families. Some working families can also be eligible for 30 free hours per week, raising concerns about inequality and disproportionate benefits for higher income families (Campbell et al., 2019). Poorer families are less able to afford additional hours. Before COVID-19, the hours preschool settings were open could vary, and during the pandemic, some settings remained open throughout while some did not. This highlighted how across England children have no guaranteed right to childcare. It is estimated around 50% of preschool settings stayed open during the first COVID-19 lockdown from 23rd March 2020 across England (Staffordshire County Council, 2021: 6).

We begin this chapter by highlighting how in this preschool context a long standing early care and education divide has been evident in England. Indeed, the introduction of the Early Years Foundation Stage (EYFS) Statutory Framework in 2008 was underpinned by a desire to integrate early care and education more closely across preschool in England. We then briefly consider our research completed in 2014 exploring preschool practitioners' views on poverty and their responses to it which found them operating within prescribed formal pedagogical contexts and prioritising early education over care of impoverished children. Drawing upon research we completed in 2021 replicating our earlier study, we then explore if practitioners felt COVID-19 presented challenges and would impact upon children in poverty and whether they felt poverty was something they needed to be sensitive to during their interactions with children. We consider adaptions to practice, with care concerns being foregrounded when working with children during the pandemic, and contemplate the balancing of care and educational concerns by our practitioners during the pandemic. Some speculate a greater focus upon care may endure in the post-COVID-19 'new normal,' but we critically consider this possibility in preschool within England.

Preschool and a Long Standing Care and Education Divide

The concept of childcare is generally used to indicate the maintenance or promotion of well-being of a child or children. Cousins and Knight (2016: 22) define childcare as being 'about the actions associated with attending to someone's physical and emotional needs'. They indicate how childcare is 'necessarily enacted within relationships' through which 'early years practitioners may need to call on their inner-selves to perform their duties of care'. In some countries, historically there has been a long-standing separation between early education and care for young children, with recent attempts to move away from these 'split systems' to integrate early care with early education (Kaga et al., 2010). This divide has been evident in England (Bennett, 2003) and is regarded as damaging (Braumer et al., 2004) since the evidence base outlining the benefits of integrating care and education is significant, especially for children in poverty who are more likely to present additional needs (Penn et al., 2004; Kaga et al., 2010). As noted earlier, the introduction of the EYFS in 2008, in theory, was meant to more fully integrate care and education.

This attempt to integrate early care and education more closely through preschool has been fully situated within England's socio-political and cultural contexts. The pre-COVID-19 context in England was one in which early years policies and language prioritised 'school readiness', and this has dominated preschool policy and practice. Framed by a focus upon readying children educationally for learning, successive governments have attempted to 'remotely control' and strongly influence preschool's work with children across England. They have moved to shape what is delivered in early years, how it is delivered and the timing and pace at which it is delivered. There has also been an attempt to cement deeper notions about what knowledge is valuable in this process and why. Despite the talk of aligning care with education, the heavier emphasis in policy – including the EYFS statutory framework – has been upon 'schoolification' in the early years and the delivery of early education (Moss, 2008). It has been suggested preschool can 'do it alone' addressing poverty by promoting school-readiness and reducing the educational attainment gap between impoverished children and their peers.

Poverty and Preschool: Findings From Our 2014 Research

Indeed, in our research with preschool practitioners in England and the USA in 2014 about their work with poverty we found a heavy emphasis on this schoolification agenda (Simpson et al., 2017). Education, not care, was the central language, and we found in pursuing this agenda preschool practitioners downplayed the influence of socio-economic factors in children's immediate lives. Practitioners revealed children in poverty were 'seen but not heard' as poverty was organised out of their work via prescriptive curricula which stymied pedagogical pace and space (Simpson et al., 2017). A minority of practitioners we consulted at that time expressed confliction about this situation. But many did not question the emphasis upon school-readiness and reducing the attainment gap, its influence upon issue prioritisation or its obscuring of the everyday realities in impoverished children's lives which make raising their attainment extremely difficult. Many identified how children in poverty have additional needs, but they simultaneously indicated a preference for working with children in poverty in an identical way to other children.

We also found evidence of deficit-based discourse, othering and some practitioners disassociating and socially distancing themselves from parents in poverty. This was a threat to the important parent–child–practitioner triangle in the early years. At that time, the majority of practitioners participating in our study felt negative outcomes of disadvantaged children are a problem located within their families, with their parents being singled out for particular critique. They talked of parent pedagogy with the poor being about 'doing to' rather than 'doing with' and emphasised the importance of addressing alleged parental deficiencies and of their struggles to engage impoverished parents. Practitioners reported that reciprocal and co-constructed relations with parents in poverty were rare despite these being considered important to supporting impoverished families. Many practitioners blamed parental beliefs and practices for this disconnect.

COVID-19 and a Window of Opportunity for Care in Preschool

As such, previously we found care being downplayed and education dominating practice in preschool. We note elsewhere, though, how since 2014, austerity and a cost of living crisis placed pressures upon preschool to work in a more flexible and inclusive way with children and families in poverty, with care becoming more prioritised even prior to COVID-19 pandemic (Simpson et al., 2023). The pandemic certainly has emphasised preschool's important caring role. Childcare's place in the public conscience became much more obvious during the ongoing pandemic (Fine and Tronto, 2020: 302). Care of children was a notable discourse during societal lockdowns (Tregenza and Campbell-Barr, 2023). Our 2021 research aimed to explore if experience of the pandemic resulted in a realignment in preschool practitioners' beliefs about poverty and their practice and the potential for a realignment between early education and care enduring in a post-lockdown 'new normal' context.

Methodology

In general, data collection for this research was a direct replication of our previous 2012–2014 research. This research involved both a quantitative survey strand and a qualitative interview strand undertaken in both England and the USA. Below, we report the analysis of data from England. Data collection occurred in 2021 which meant we added additional questions to reflect the context of the COVID-19 pandemic. Ethical approval for the research was gained from the appropriate ethics bodies in each of the collaborators' institutions.

The survey was administered to preschool practitioners in England online via Qualtrics. After cleaning up the data, a final sample size of 119 was achieved in England. Survey participants from England were drawn from local authorities from the South East, the East Midlands and the North East. Participants were reached via emails to individual settings, general social media network postings and through personal networks of educators. We achieved our intention of a reasonably diverse sample of a sufficient size to explore issues around responses to poverty in preschool. Semi-structured interviews considered in-depth the views of a sub-set of practitioners who had completed the questionnaire. Thirty preschool practitioners were interviewed in the three locations across England (10 in the North East, East Midlands and the South East, respectively). The COVID-19 pandemic was a dominant societal phenomenon during the entire data collection period with all the interviewing completed online.

The survey data were analysed using descriptive and inferential statistical procedures including t-tests. The questionnaire included seven blocks considering the following themes: (1) Beliefs about the causes of poverty; (2) Poverty (in)sensitivity; (3) Child development; (4) Attitudes to challenges connected to children in poverty; (5) Practitioners' perceptions of parents; (6) COVID-19 (in)sensitivity and (7) Keep children home during COVID-19. Each of the seven themes contained several items (statements), and respondents were asked to indicate the extent to which they disagreed or agreed with these statements on scales from 1 to 10. For purposes of the analysis, the statements under each theme were then combined and averaged into a composite measure. The reliability coefficient (α) indicated a good level of inter-item consistency across statements under each of the seven themes. Qualitative interview data were considered using thematic analysis with the assistance of NVivo software.

Our 2021 Findings

We begin the discussion of data from England with a focus upon survey results and practitioners' beliefs in the context of COVID-19. As the pandemic took hold, preschool practitioners became change agents, charged with working differently. Theories of human agency suggest it is collective, as 'agentic power lies in humans' capacity to reflect on and evaluate social contexts, creatively envisaging alternatives and collaborating with others to bring about their transformation' (Pantić, 2015: 763). Any realignment of education and care was to be carried out collectively by practitioners 'who do, think and feel and who draw on their personal subjectivities' (Cousins and Knight, 2016: 22). What they were thinking was, therefore, interesting to explore.

COVID-19 and (In)sensitivity to Care Needs of the Poor

Our five-item COVID-19 (In)Sensitivity Scale assessed (in)sensitivity to the impacts that COVID-19 presented for children living in poverty (e.g. 'Children living in poverty have experienced more negative impacts due to the COVID-19 pandemic'; 'I worry that children living in poverty will be especially at risk if they are not able to physically attend pre-school'). Participants responded to these items on a 10-point scale. The items were scored appropriately and then averaged into a composite score with higher composite scores closer to 10 indicating greater sensitivity to the impacts of COVID-19 on children living in poverty. Table 3.1 reveals the composite mean score of 7.11 (SD = 1.61), showing a level of

Table 3.1. Means Across All Composite Measures (England Only).

Scale	M (SD)
COVID (In)sensitivity	7.57 (1.46)
Attendance During COVID	2.51 (2.08)
Poverty (In)sensitivity	4.89 (1.52)
Poverty Beliefs	7.76 (1.50)

Notes. English cell means range between 108 and 116.

sensitivity for the challenges COVID-19 would present to children living in poverty. Practitioners' preferences for either children attending preschool settings or staying at home during the COVID-19 pandemic were also assessed. Participants responded to two items on a 10-point scale. These two items were combined into a composite, with higher scores indicating a desire to keep children at home during the pandemic. A lower composite mean score of 2.51 showed agreement amongst our English survey respondents that children in poverty should continue to attend preschool during the pandemic.

While practitioners responding to the survey tended to agree COVID-19 would present challenges for children in poverty and they tended to agree children in poverty should attend preschool during COVID-19, this did not mean they collectively showed strong agreement that poverty was something they needed to be especially sensitive to taking actions around. Our Poverty (In)sensitivity Scale included eight items assessing sensitivity to childhood poverty in terms of perceptions of the need for actions on the part of the practitioner to meet the needs of impoverished children. Items either related to sensitivity (e.g. 'I provide extra support to children living in poverty') or insensitivity (e.g. 'I try to treat children living in poverty identically to other children'). We considered not accommodating children who have higher needs a form of harmful insensitivity. Participants responded to these items on a 10-point scale. The items were scored appropriately and then averaged into a composite such that higher composite values closer to 10 indicated higher levels of poverty insensitivity. For our English sample, the mean score on this scale was 4.89 (SD 1.52), close to the mid-point and indicating some indifference to the necessity of taking actions associated with poverty.

Indeed, when completing t-tests we found a limited interconnection between scores upon the COVID-19 (In)sensitivity and Poverty (In)sensitivity scales across the English respondents ($r = -0.15$). Table 3.2 shows that slightly stronger relationships were found between our Poverty Belief Scale and other composite variables, and these were all statistically significant meaning they had not happened by chance. This indicated poverty belief is certainly amongst the factors influencing these other variables. Our Poverty Belief Scale used nine items that attributed poverty to individual factors or situational factors, participants responded to these on a 10-point scale. A composite was produced such that higher composite score closer to 10 indicated the belief that poverty is more due to

Table 3.2. Intercorrelations Between Poverty Beliefs and Other Study Measures (English Data).

Scale	Poverty Beliefs
COVID (In)sensitivity	0.37**
Attendance During COVID	–0.21*
Poverty (In)sensitivity	–0.22*

Notes. Degrees of freedom ranged between 100 and 118. * = $p < 0.05$. **$p < 0.01$.

situational than individual factors. Table 3.1 shows the composite mean score of 7.76 (SD = 1.50), indicating support amongst practitioners for situational, rather than individual, factors. Table 3.2 reveals the stronger a belief poverty is situational in nature meant practitioners were more likely to (1) hold a stronger sensitivity to the particular challenges posed by COVID-19for children in poverty; (2) preferred that children in poverty kept going to preschool during the pandemic and (3) exhibited greater poverty sensitivity – i.e. agreed more that the needs of the poor require a particular response.

Care Needs of the Poor and Adaptions to Practice During COVID-19

As care provision is about relationships, physical distancing requirements attached to COVID-19 raised a serious threat to such provision. As indicated, about 50% of preschool settings in England remained open during the first COVID-19 lockdown. During the initial lockdown (23rd March 2020) only those children of key workers and those identified as vulnerable were allowed to attend preschool settings remaining open, and some of these children were living in poverty. For those children continuing to attend, they found themselves in preschool environments adapted to prevent the spread of the virus with a focus upon children's health and safety. Practitioners we interviewed in England seldom mentioned poverty as a central organising factor in making these adaptions. Rather they talked of general adaptions made to benefit all children, including impoverished children. For example, for those children who were attending, 'bubbles' were created, where children could only interact with those children in their key person group. These attempted to prevent the spread of COVID-19 but were also beneficial to children's socio-emotional needs. Carol noted how children were scared during Covid and creating these bubbles helped them to feel more relaxed. Socialising and having fun with bubbles reduced stress:

> The children needed it, I think especially at this time, they just needed to be with their friends and have fun, and do things that – not necessarily that they've been stopped doing - but, you know, socialising[...] I would say the children that have stayed with us throughout the lockdown and have attended settings seemed a lot

> happier when they came back altogether than the children who didn't. (Carol – Wrap-around Care Lead, Primary School)

Jean revealed how expecting very young children to socially distance in bubbles was unrealistic and, therefore, persuading parents about the safety aspects of provision was essential to their children attending. More widely it is recognised how during the height of lockdown, some settings struggled in maintaining social distancing for young children and 'eventually policy shifted to accommodate the fact that social distancing is not appropriate for younger children' (Holt and Murray, 2022: 490). This reminds us of the adaptions children were making in the COVID-19 context:

> I know there's always stories in the press about how are they going to socially distance? Obviously under 5, they can't, they're not going to. But the parents are aware of all our risk assessments in place. (Jean – Nursery Manager)

While evidence suggests a social divide in the negative impacts of COVID-19 upon children (Hobbs and Bernard, 2021), and several of our practitioners mentioned negative impacts; it was also stated there were positives of creating bubbles for children attending settings due to increased opportunity to relate much more closely with practitioners within bubbles. Erica felt this had been a really good thing. She indicated below how those children in poverty continuing to attend at her setting were 'thriving':

> [...] any vulnerable children, which would be the children in child poverty, they've still been able to come into school if they want to. So that's one of the positives about, for them, Covid[...] Well, those children that are in school are absolutely thriving with class sizes being so much smaller. for them, it's been a really, really positive thing. So they've been doing really, really well. (Erica – Outreach Lead in Primary School)

As others consulting the preschool workforce in England during the pandemic have found (Baker and Bakopoulou, 2023), our interviewees revealed extra workload was attached to making pedagogical adaptions. Hygiene procedures, always a concern in preschool, became even stricter and further embedded for children attending and use of resources was carefully regulated with implications for play, etc. All this took place in the dangerous context of a deadly pandemic involving constant daily stress for our interviewees:

> [...] like the workload has like ramped up since Covid like astronomically because we were doing toy rotation and cleaning [...] And also you don't know if kids have got it until we get in their test results and everyone is like waiting with their fingers crossed for three days to see if that child you've been with for ages has got it or not. (Angela – Early Years Teacher, Nursery)

Physical distancing meant contact with parents of children attending was severely restricted by COVID-19, for instance, with adaptions to drop-off and pick up arrangements. This meant potentially less interaction, and some of our interviewees felt it created a disconnect compromising the important parent–child–practitioner triangle in preschool. Dialogue with parents about children's development and the bigger picture around what was going on in their lives was lost:

> [...] like the families can't come into nursery. And we've noticed a big difference with that, because when we would normally have them come in and they would tell us what was going on, now we just don't find out what's happening at home and that's sad. (Andrea – Nursery Manager).

Quite unexpectedly, some felt parents' lack of access to their setting and practitioners was a good thing and it is an adaption they will be keeping post-COVID-19:

> [...] our parents don't come in anymore, they don't come in. Where children are dropped at the door and they say goodbye and it actually works so much better for everybody[...] So we've just decided to keep it. (Annis - Manager – Not-for-profit Preschool)

For settings which closed during the first COVID-19 lockdown 'child care and early learning communities ended abruptly and children's relationships with teachers and friends were no longer accessible' (Swadener et al., 2020: 314). The likely negative consequences were clear as we know the effects of poverty means impoverished children are more likely to have care needs relating to stress, mental illness, food, health, etc. Many children in poverty did not attend preschool, for a lengthy period from March 2020 onwards, continuing to remain away even as lockdowns eased. Why families stayed away is not fully understood, but Linda whose nursery setting remained open throughout COVID-19, believed parent concerns around safety was the chief reason many children continued to remain at home:

> [...] the school has been open the whole time... we've changed a few things. We're not mixing in school. We keep very separate. We're not going into the hall for lunches, we're keeping in our room. But we had – from sort of the November there were quite a few parents who said actually I'm working from home or I'm not working, I'm keeping them [their child] at home because they're safer. (Linda – Nursery Manager)

Obviously, indirectly addressing the care needs of children not attending was extremely challenging. Practitioners mentioned adapting by increasing telephone or online contact with parents of children, with some emphasis on checking the well-being of children. Erica questioned the effectiveness of telephoning parents compared with face-to-face meetings:

> [...] this is the thing – you lose that contact with them, and I think most people are better face- to-face rather than telephone call. It's easier on the telephone to say, "Yeah, I'm fine", whereas if you can get people in and you can just have a conversation, I think that's a better way of doing things and you find out more. (Erica Outreach Lead, Primary School)

Cath indicated how in her setting a staff member's role was adapted and they took on an obligation to liaise with families in need and to pay socially distanced visits to homes. This involved the staff member providing basic care needs. Cath noted how through the pandemic her setting 'had got involved in home life much, much more' despite only being able to communicate in doorways and over garden gates with parents:

> Some of the home visits we've been doing have been around helping them set up broadband, just keeping a pastoral eye, actually doing the shopping for them[...] So, we have got involved in homelife much, much more[...] There's no point in doing any kind of home learning if everything else is falling apart first. (Cath, Early Years Lead, Primary School)

Other examples of responding to care needs of children in poverty not attending included the provision of food packs.

There were examples of care needs of children not being met even when they wanted to attend. Sian's setting had struggled to meet the care needs of some children in poverty with significant needs, and their attendance was described as 'sporadic' throughout the initial and later COVID-19 lockdowns. Indeed, during the first lockdown from March 2020, a small number of families had accessed grandparents and other sources of one-to-one support for their children, with arrangements around support for some children in poverty with additional needs not being in place initially at the setting:

> In the first lockdown it [the attendance of children eligible for EYPP[1]] was sporadic because what we were doing, as a setting, we weren't able to meet the needs that they had[...] So, the additional needs needed extra support as well, so it was kind of putting that all in place for them. (Sian – Teacher, Maintained Nursery)

---

[1] Early Years Pupil Premium. This is additional funding available to early years providers to improve education for qualifying children.

COVID-19 Lockdowns and the Early Care and Education Balance

The above adaptions to practice made within the pandemic demonstrate how care's place in preschool practitioners' conscience was unsurprisingly raised by COVID-19 across England. But was care the dominant language and practice concern within preschool during the pandemic? While caring aspects of early childhood provision were clearly deemed essential during COVID-19, our interviewees' narratives indicate educational aspects of preschool continued to be emphasised, increasingly after the initial lockdown. There remained a heavy focus upon continuing provision supporting children's 'readiness for school' and the educational development that prepares children to meet school requirements, typically embracing specific cognitive, linguistic and numeracy skills.

This raised challenges connected to management of children in settings during the pandemic. Sara noted how in her setting they moved to a larger group of children with a wider range of ages. She indicated how this presented difficulties when attempting to ready older children (four year olds) for school as they started to mimic the younger children in the merged group by not doing things like fastening coats:

> [...] everything is sort of being mushed together, and it's not always necessarily the best for the children whereas we could be challenging some of our older children and getting them a bit more ready for school, trying to pull a two year old along to do those same things is really kind of tricky at times. you're then helping the two year old out and then the four year old sees that and all of a sudden can't do their buttons anymore, because they want that same help you're giving the two year. (Sara – Early Years Teacher, Nursery)

For those children staying at home, there was a keen focus upon ensuring the home learning environment and educational work by parents/families. The 'learning pack' became ubiquitous:

> The council provided a list of vulnerable children that had to come to nursery, but a lot of the vulnerable children that were on that list just didn't come[...] we were putting things together like home packs for children to like have colouring in and things like that, and maths and things going home. (Andrea, Nursery Manager)

Hilda revealed how there was some thought connected to financial costs for families using the learning packs – implying poverty proofing:

> [...] we were sending out sort of learning packs and things for the children that were staying at home, to kind of support their families at home. Lots of resources and things[...] we try and think of activities that didn't involve a lot of cost and stuff like that as well. (Hilda - Practitioners, Maintained Nursery School)

Online interaction was attempted – although several interviewees alluded to the digital divide structuring an unequal participation of poorer families relative to their peers in this regard:

> [...] we've been doing a lot of home learning and videos, because we have a closed parent Facebook group as well so we have been contacting all the families weekly anyway that haven't been coming in, and been giving them tips and strategies. (Jean Manager, Nursery)

> there has been an emphasis with this online work[...] I do worry that whenever they do return to school it will be like starting again from scratch, and that's a shame. It's my personal view that those parents won't be doing things at home. (Kate Teaching Assistant – Primary School)

Cath noted during the initial part of the COVID-19 pandemic care had been emphasised, but a movement back to the predominance of an educational focus re-emerged as the COVID-19 lockdowns in England rolled out:

> We were much more focused in the last lockdown [5th January 2021 in England] on home learning, the first time [23rd March 2020] it was about keeping body and soul together because we were worried about what was going to happen. (Cath – Early Years Lead, Primary School)

The emphasis across settings, though, could differ. Joanne mentioned how care needs were not initially prioritised in support to parents, but the pandemic had brought into light the difficult situations families were struggling to cope with in all sorts of ways. While support for parents had been steered towards helping them help their children's learning, it soon became about care requirements:

> [...] they [parents] needed help. But we actually – we weren't thinking of it in terms of helping parents financially, or helping parents mentally; we were actually thinking of it in terms of purely helping them with the education of the children, but it evolved into something different[...] It became about supporting the families. I mean, it was quite tough for some of them. (Joanne – Head of Maintained Nursery).

Conclusion – Care in Preschool and a 'New Normal'?

Data above collected in the English context show how during the height of the COVID-19 crisis preschool practitioners provided essential care, supported responses to the pandemic by opening their setting doors to children of key workers and the vulnerable, dealt with anxieties of children and parents – including those in poverty – and supplied food in local neighbourhoods to families in need. While our survey found practitioners agreed that the COVID-19 had presented challenges to children in poverty, it also revealed some indifference to the idea poverty was an issue which should be a central concern in thinking about and organising access to care during the pandemic. From the first lockdown in England, preschool settings and practitioners were required to adapt practice around a general focus upon care, but poverty concerns were only occasionally mentioned as a specific factor shaping responses. Practitioners talked in very general terms about needing to ensure all children's health and socio-emotional well-being were protected. In providing this care they risked their lives, so much so that there has been debate about whether these low paid practitioners were considered essential but expendable in providing it (Simonton, 2020). Our practitioners' accounts reveal something of the difficulties attached to their brave efforts within unprecedented, stressful and difficult circumstances.

While the emphasis in settings became more focused upon care, certainly initially during the first English lockdown, education and home learning remained a priority. Indeed, a priority remained trying to prevent children in poverty falling further behind in early educational attainment and with many not attending settings a heavy emphasis was placed upon home learning. Something some of our interviewees felt, and wider evidence from England suggests (Holt and Murray, 2022), has been in vain.

Speculation about a 'new normal,' where alongside the stress, suffering and dislocation of COVID-19, 'a huge window of opportunity has opened to leverage the best of the present into a future that works for all' – with a particular 'centre around care' (Howard, 2020: 21) – seems wide of the mark across preschool in England. Our research found the ethics and actions that demonstrate caring as part of responses to poverty were less evident before COVID-19 in 2014 than during the pandemic in 2021, and they will continue to be present across preschool in the future. But as we move on from COVID-19 it will likely be 'in small places' locally (Swadener et al., 2020: 324). For care to become more integrated with education in preschool this transformation would need to take place within pre-existing structures (e.g. a preschool market and inequality of access to preschool) and cultures (e.g. central government policy discourse and messages around care and education as part of COVID-19 recovery) and would require leadership, action at all levels and strategy (Kaga et al., 2010).

The strategic focus of national COVID-19 recovery plans in the post-lockdown context made clear such a transformation is remote. Recovery plans in England prioritise preschool's contribution to the constant drive towards school readiness and educational priorities, while downplaying the holistic caring and socioemotional needs of children in poverty (Cooper, 2022). Furthermore, recovery is to be attempted in a preschool sector described in England as 'shamelessly' and 'knowingly underfunded' (Nursery World, 2021) and 'at breaking point' (EYA, 2021). While in March 2023 the UK government announced further funding attached to childcare expansion plans for England, they have been heavily critiqued. Claims have been made that the £4 billion funding is insufficient to cover the expansion and ensure quality care and education, with concern reduced ratios will compromise existing caring arrangements (Nursery World, 2023). The expansion has also been called a missed opportunity with a claim that the new investment risks entrenching rather than changing the unequal preschool childcare system, which will continue to disproportionately benefit families with higher incomes (Jarvie et al., 2023).

References

Baker, W. and Bakopoulou, I. 2023. Children's centres, parenting, and education in a post-pandemic world. *Education*, 3–13. 10.1080/03004279.2023.2186967

Bennett, J. 2003. The persistent division between care and education. *Journal of Early Childhood Research*, 1(1), 21–48.

Braumer, J., Gordic, B. and Zigler, E. 2004. Putting the child back into childcare: combining care and education for children aged 3-5. In *Social Policy Report, XVIII*, Washington DC, National Association for the Education of Young Children.

Campbell, T., Gambaro, L. and Stewart, K. 2019. *Inequalities in the Experience of Early Education in England: Access, Peer Groups and Transition*. London School of Economics: Centre for Analysis of Social Exclusion. Retrieved from: https://sticerd.lse.ac.uk/dps/case/cp/casepaper214.pdf

Cooper, K. 2022. Early years catch-up must go further. *TES Magazine*. (Accessed 26 April 2022). Retrieved from: https://www.tes.com/magazine/analysis/early-years/early-years-catch-must-go-further

Cousins, S. and Knight, P., 2016. Quality experience for babies and very young children. In E. Slaughter, *Quality in the Early Years*, pp. 16–29, London, Open University Press.

Early Years Alliance [EYA] 2021. *Breaking Point – The Impact of Recruitment and Retention Challenges on the Early Years Sector in England*. Accessed on 26 April 2022. https://www.eyalliance.org.uk/breaking-point-impact-recruitment-and-retention-challenges-early-years-sector-england

Fine, M. and Tronto, J. 2020. Care goes viral: care theory and research confront the global COVID-19 pandemic. *International Journal of Care and Caring*, 4(3), 301–309.

Hayes, L. 2017. *Stories of Care: A Labour of Law. Gender and Class at Work*, London, Palgrave.

Hobbs, A., and Bernard, R. 2021. *Rapid response: impact of COVID-19 on early childhood education & care*. Available at: https://post.parliament.uk/impact-of-covid-19-on-early-childhood-education-care/. (Accessed 13 April 2022).

Holt, L. and Murray, L. 2022. Children and COVID 19 in the UK. *Children's Geographies*, 20(4), 487–494.

Howard, N. 2020. A world of care. In *Life After Covid-19: The Other Side of Crisis*, Ed M. Parker, pp. 21–30, Bristol, Bristol University Press.

Jarvie, M., Ollerearnshaw, R. and Goddard, E. 2023. *Tackling disadvantage through childcare*. Coram Family and Childcare and Joseph Rowntree Foundation.

Kaga, Y., Bennett, J. and Moss, P. 2010. *Caring and Learning Together: A Cross-National Study on the Integration of Early Childhood Care and Education Within Education*, UNESCO, Paris.

Moss, P. 2008. What future for the relationship between early childhood education and care and compulsory schooling? *Research in Comparative and International Education*, 3(3), 224–234.

Nursery World 2021. *Government 'knowingly underfunded' the early years sector.* (Accessed 18 May 2022). Retrieved from: https://www.nurseryworld.co.uk/news/article/government-knowingly-underfunded-the-early-years-sector#:~:text=The%20Government%20stands%20accused%20of,funded%20childcare%20places%20for%20three%2D

Nursery World 2023. *Budget 2023: Nurseries Warn They 'Need to See the Sums' as Government Plans Major Expansion in Childcare for One- and Two-Year-Olds.* (Accessed 07:08:23). https://www.nurseryworld.co.uk/news/article/budget-2023-nurseries-warn-they-need-to-see-the-sums-as-government-plans-major-expansion-in-childcare-for-one-and-two-year-olds

Pantić, N. 2015 A model for study of teacher agency for social justice, *Teachers and Teaching*, 21(6), 759-778

Penn, H., Barreau, S., Butterworth, L., Lloyd, E., Moyles, J., Potter, S. and Sayeed, R. 2004. *What is the Impact of Out-of-Home Integrated Care and Education Settings on Children Aged 0-6 and Their Parents?*, Social Science Research Unit, Institute of Education.

Simonton, S. 2020. *Essential, Not Expendable'—Child Care Workers on the Frontlines of COVID-19*. (Accessed 03:08:23). https://scalawagmagazine.org/2020/05/childcare-workers-coronavirus/

Simpson, D., Loughran, S., Lumsden, E., Mazzocco, P., McDowall Clark, R., and Winterbottom, C. 2017. 'Seen but not heard'. Practitioners work with poverty and the organising out of disadvantaged children's voices and participation in the early years. *European Early Childhood Education Research Journal*, 25(2), 177–188.

Simpson, D., Mazzocco, P., Loughran, S., Lumsden, E., Lyndon, S., and Winterbottom, C. 2023. 'New normal' or continued 'social distancing'? Preschool practitioners' responses to poverty across post-lockdown England and the USA. *Journal of Early Childhood Research.* https://journals.sagepub.com/doi/full/10.1177/1476718X231175459

Staffordshire County Council 2021. *Annual childcare sufficiency report 2020 – 2021.* Available at: https://www.staffordshire.gov.uk/Children-and-early-years/Childcare/Documents/Annual-Sufficiency-Report-v3.pdf. accessed April 26, 2022

Swadener, B. B., Peters, L., Frantz Bentley, D., Diaz, X. and Bloch, M. 2020. Child care and COVID: precarious communities in distanced times. *Global Studies of Childhood*, 10(4), 313–326.

Tregenza, S. and Campbell-Barr, V. 2023. Quality early childhood education and care in a time of COVID-19, *Journal of Early Childhood Research*, 21(2), 198–211.

Chapter 4

COVID-19 Anxiety and Early Childhood Development: Reflections From Practitioners in Early Years Settings

Charmaine Agius Ferrante and Elaine Chaplin

Northumbria University, UK

Abstract

The COVID-19 pandemic had a profound impact upon early childhood practice. This chapter presents reflections from discussions with practitioners based on their experiences through and coming out the COVID-19 pandemic. Whilst acknowledging the extreme circumstances for the practitioners, children, families and the settings, the authors sought to value and share these contributions in a way that highlight developmentally appropriate practice speech around language delay, delays in physical development, relationship and self-regulation problems, mental health and well-being issues and children's safeguarding. The authors place a strong focus on young children's developmental outcomes, which should be a priority for early years research. The narratives presented should also be of interest to policymakers to aid them in developing strategies to ensure young children's holistic development.

Keywords: COVID-19; developmentally appropriate practice; early childhood development; early years settings; practitioners

Introduction

The COVID-19 pandemic has disrupted almost all facets of young children's daily lives, and the impact has been seen in developmental terms in children within several early years' settings. This chapter is a short reflection documenting the experiences, challenges and more importantly the strategies and practices that they have implemented to try to mitigate the adverse consequences of the

---

Care and Coronavirus, 55–61
Copyright © 2025 Charmaine Agius Ferrante and Elaine Chaplin
Published under exclusive licence by Emerald Publishing Limited
doi:10.1108/978-1-83797-310-120241004

pandemic on the holistic development of young children. We present narratives of practitioners working in seven different settings which comprised conversations with early years practitioners, with the intention to highlight their voices.

A developmental perspective, namely bioecological theory (Bronfenbrenner and Morris, 2006), has been used as a lens to help our understanding of the pandemic's impact on the children's development. Bioecological theory (Bronfenbrenner and Morris, 2006) asserts that development is driven by individual characteristics, the proximal to distal systems in which the child is embedded and the historical time in which development and associated interactions occur. Reflecting this perspective the practitioners present some of the potential adverse effects of the COVID-19 pandemic by identifying processes and mechanisms that have buffered the pandemic experience. However, it is important to note that young children continue to grow and develop whilst COVID-19 is still an emerging and evolving phenomenon. Facilitating young children's good development and well-being should be an important focus for all stakeholders.

Setting 1

A local authority nursery in an area of deprivation who currently only take two-year old, funded children. The setting has several children with Special Educational Needs and Disabilities (SEND) and Children in Need. SEND may impact upon a child's ability to learn, and a child in need is a child who is considered unlikely to achieve, or their development is likely to be impaired without the support from children's services. The setting has a strong focus on parent partnerships to ensure positive outcomes. The setting has recently been judged as outstanding by Ofsted. Ofsted is the regulatory body in England who set key standards by which all early years providers must adhere to.

Rachael in the setting noted particular concerns around gross motor skills:

> We have seen a decrease in children's gross motor skills development following lockdown. More children are arriving at the setting in buggies rather than walking. These children are unaware of risk in the outdoors, and we have seen an increase in trips and falls.

To address the gap the setting organised attendance at mini mover sessions at the local leisure centre, arranged outings to the local park and held sessions with the parents to address the use of buggies and to reinforce its importance for their child's development to walk them to nursery. The setting has a large outdoor environment which was not being fully utilised, and they refreshed this to promote gross motor skill and risky play development.

Staff continue to expand on gross motor skill and risky play development with the introduction of activities such as climbing, jumping, obstacle courses and walks in the local community. Recently, they held a family walk and parents shared with practitioners they had not realised how far their child could walk and how enjoyable it was to be out with them exploring the local area.

Setting 2

A private day nursery in an area which covers all demographics with a wide mix of funded and fee-paying children. The provision operates for children aged 0–11 years, operating 0–5 years term time with breakfast and out of school club and 0–11 years during school holidays. It is part of a small chain of nurseries and has developed over the last 20 years. It is a purpose-built nursery with various outdoor areas.

Debdon from this setting provides the following observation about heightened anxiety of the children in their care:

> We have a few children who live in flats and during lockdown they have never stepped foot outside of the [home]. These children are very anxious and are struggling to adjust to being back within the settings.

Following the COVID-19 lockdowns, the setting identified various development gaps and introduced a range of targeted interventions to support the children. To offset the physical developmental gap, practitioners planned various activities to enable children to express their feelings through play. For example, they used the colour monster story and developed potion mixing activity. The children were keen to share how they were feeling by being animated and fully engaged in the activity. In the 'two-year-old room' the practitioners created a cosy sensory room where children had the opportunity to go either alone or with an adult and have one-to-one time. They were able to use emotion cushions to demonstrate feelings, and practitioners promoted the use of appropriate language to facilitate this.

This initiative is augmented by ongoing staff training in mental health and wellbeing. This training has supported not only the children but also the practitioners working with them.

Setting 3

A private day nursery in an area of high deprivation with a mix of funded and fee-paying children, aged between 0–5 educated across six rooms. There are a high number of children with SEND and Child in Need. In addition, one in four children has had either an early help assessment (EHA) or a Child Protection Plan put in place.[1] An EHA is used to identify a family's strengths and weaknesses and the support plans required for them at an early stage.

---

[1]Section 47 of the Children Act (1989) states that a local authority must investigate to safeguard a child's wellbeing if it has "reasonable cause to suspect that a child who lives, or is found, in its area is suffering, or is likely to suffer, significant harm"; or is informed that a child in its area is the subject of an emergency protection order or is in police protection.

Daisy from this setting highlights concerns around children's self-regulation:

> We have seen an increase in children struggling with self-regulation. They are unable to resolve conflicts between peers and through discussions with parents, it is evident they have not mixed with any other children of their own age due to closures of soft plays and toddler groups.

To support the children to develop self-regulation, many small group activities were made available where a practitioner would work with two children in interactive turn taking games. This allowed the children to understand the need to accept others' views and opinions as well as working together. For some of the youngest children, it was about adjusting the environment and resources to offer opportunities for children to have space to self-regulate.

Setting 4

A private day nursery within a residential area where most of their children are fee paying. They have a small number of two-year-old funded children. The provision is a converted residential care home and consists of four rooms. One room requires some additional work as it is not working as an educational space and was identified in a recent Ofsted inspection. The facility was judged as requiring improvement by this Ofsted inspection. Staff were supported via a focused improvement plan and noticeably the Department for Education (DfE) Expert and Mentor Programme and on reinspection they were graded 'Good.'

Dani from this setting notes concerns around speech and language development:

> We have identified an increase in speech and language delays with many of our two-year-olds. They do not have the correct phonetical sounds and appear to be struggling with identification of everyday environmental sounds.

To address these speech and language delays, practitioners needed to refer several of the children to speech and language therapy services. For some children simply being back into the provision and exposed to high-quality interactions was enough to improve language development. Practitioners ensured they modelled correct phonological sounds whilst narrating the children's play. 'Environmental sound walks' in the local area were completed as well as 'sound lotto games' to support identification of everyday environmental sounds.

A communication and language audit was carried out with the manager and practitioners to identify areas which are working well and those that required additional support to continue to maintain improved outcomes.

Setting 5

A private day nursery in another residential provision where the majority of the children are fee paying. There are however a small number of two-year-old funded children. The provision is a converted house which has been adapted to become a nursery. The setting takes children aged 0–5 years.

Parental anxieties were noted in settings, as Nikki from this setting states

> We are finding babies are taking longer to settle when starting our provision. Parents are very anxious about leaving their little ones as they have not been left with family's members due to the restrictions. We are finding we must give greater support to the parents and children are needing longer settling in periods.

Staff reintroduced their 'parent and baby sessions,' for new parents which allowed them to be accustomed to the setting and the staff. Parents were offered shorter and more settling in sessions to support with their anxieties and allow them to build relationships with the children's key person. Parents had the opportunity to meet their child's key person before their child started the setting, and during this meeting, the key person gathered as much information about the child and asked the parents to identify their concerns to try and alleviate them. As Nikki from the setting states,

> Many children did not return when the setting reopened initially and gaps in their knowledge could be identified on their return. The setting needed to adapt their curriculum for these children to try and close gaps.

When the children returned to the setting practitioners undertook baseline assessments to identify the developmental stage of the children and this identified the gaps in their knowledge. From these assessments, the practitioners were able to modify their curriculum to ensure the activities planned were developmentally appropriate and challenging for the children. They provided small group interventions for some children who required greater levels of support.

Setting 6

A private day nursery in the centre of the city was previously a children's centre and purpose built for nursery provision. The setting takes children from 0 to 5 years. It has a high number of children with SEND and Child in Need referrals as well as a mix of fee paying and funded children. It is in an area of high deprivation.

Behavioural issues were noted by practitioners, as Karter from this setting explains

> An increase in children with additional needs has been noted. Children are returning with behavioural challenges. These include inability to partake in group activities, unable to follow simple instructions and inability to self-regulate.

Staff adapted the curriculum and activities to meet the individual needs of the children. They ensured that small group activities were available to support children's behaviour. A review of the settings Behaviour Policy was undertaken to ensure it reflected the settings expectations.

Play plans were implemented for children who were identified as needing additional support to begin monitoring processes. These play plans support the child's health, care and education needs. As Karter states,

> We have identified an increase in mental health and wellbeing needs of some of our children and their families. We are finding this difficult to source additional support for this. Children who have attended the setting during the lockdown are feeling more anxiety than those who were absent. They ask a lot of questions such as "is it safe for us now?", "why can we not be with our friends?" and "can I still be with my sister/brother?"

Staff attended mental health and wellbeing training to gain new knowledge to support the children. The objective of this was to ensure that the children who had been attending and feeling anxious, had the opportunity to remain in their existing bubbles at the start, to enable them to feel safe and secure. Staff discussed with the children the changes which were occurring and their feelings regarding being able to mix with others and that it was now safe to do so.

Karter also highlighted concerns around language acquisition:

> A big focus for us since returning is early language acquisition. We have identified a lot of our children who are nor pronouncing words correctly or have very broken English.

The practitioners undertook 'the speech and language toolkit,' a language acquisition intervention, with some of the children they had identified as having gaps. This enabled them to gain a greater understanding of the level of support required. If it was felt the gaps were greater than could be supported within the setting the children were referred to speech and language therapy. Modelling and narrating children's language and play was key to improving outcomes.

Despite this staff ensure activities are used to support children's emotional development and offer opportunities for a safe space for children to share how they are feeling. Labelling the emotions children are feeling and having a listening ear are regarded as significant.

Setting 7

A pack away playgroup in a village hall with funded children aged two to four years of age. Most of the children leave the setting at three to go to school nursery. Support has been provided to this setting through the DfE experts and mentors programme to support and challenge practitioners. Again, the theme of developmental delay is evidenced, as Shelly from the setting explains

> On reopening we have had an increase in children with dummies. These children have delayed speech, and they are beginning to show signs of issues with their teeth as an impact of the dummy use. These children struggle to settle without their dummies, and this is impacting on their ability to learn. Since the return of all children, we have referred ten children to speech and language for support. This is a big jump from two in the year prior to lockdown. We have had an increase in applications for early years inclusion fund from 1 pre lockdown to 8 post lockdowns.

Practitioners have shared information relating to the use of dummies with parents highlighting the impact this can have on children's language and their teeth. The setting has promoted accessing a dentist and importance of good oral hygiene. Practitioners have supported the children to find an alternative comforter with the support of parents to ensure children have something they are emotionally attached to settle.

To address language delay staff are using 'the language toolkit' as well as the additional services of the speech and language therapist when needed.

Concluding Reflection

The emerging evidence presented based on the COVID-19 pandemic presents a global scenario of a gamut of social problems for early years children returning from lockdown. These include speech and language delay, delays in physical development, relationship and self-regulation problems, mental health and well-being issues and children's safeguarding. This is compounded by the mental health and well-being issues experienced by the staff. A significant gap in the narratives was the practitioners' lack of self-reflection of the impact of the pandemic on their own mental health and well-being. This together with a focus on the influence of the pandemic on young children's developmental outcomes should be a priority for early years research. These narratives should also be of interest to policymakers to aid them in developing strategies to ensure young children's holistic development.

References

Bronfenbrenner, U. and Morris, P. 2006. The bioecological model of human development. In *Handbook of Child Psychology: Vol. 1. Theoretical Models of Human Development*, Series Eds W. Damon, R.M. Lerner and Vol. Ed R.M. Lerner, 6th ed., pp. 793-828, New York, John Wiley.

Children Act 1989. *c. 41*. Available at: https://www.legislation.gov.uk/ukpga/1989/41/contents. (Accessed 13 May 2024).

Section 2

Children and Young People's Health and Wellbeing

Volume 2

Children and Young People, Travel and Adventure

Chapter 5

Experiences of Vulnerable Girls From an Informal Settlement in South Africa During COVID-19 Lockdowns

Lucy Currie[a], Sibusisiwe Tendai Sibanda[b] and Athenkosi Mtumtum[b]

[a]Northumbria University, UK
[b]Sizakala Wellness Counsellors, South Africa

Abstract

This chapter reports on a study that examined the impact of COVID-19 within a context of poverty and existing emotional vulnerabilities amongst girls in an informal settlement in South Africa. Findings highlight the young people's resilience, hope and determination to stand together and draw upon each other's strengths through extremely difficult experiences. Data were collected through a survey with 19 girls aged between 12 and 17 years and analysed using Maslow's theory of human motivation (1943) and Brammer's crisis theory (1985). Living conditions and socio-economic status influenced the girls' experiences of the COVID-19 lockdowns. Social distancing, in particular, was found to be a challenge in their living conditions. Despite this, the study found the girls to be sophisticated caring agents; they were resourceful, supportive of each other and resolute in their plans for the future, despite the impact of the pandemic. Recommendations are made for further research with female adolescents to inform future strategies and interventions in South Africa's informal settlements.

Keywords: COVID-19; educational inequalities; gender inequalities; informal settlements; poverty; vulnerable girls

Introduction

In this chapter, we present a case study that lends a voice to young Black girls who, by virtue of being female are often socialised to be seen and not heard. This is a collaborative chapter between practitioners working in youth counselling and academia. In addition to cultural inequalities, the girls in this study experience social exclusion due to South Africa's socio-economic inequalities and a system that has relegated young black females to the bottom. Their precarious situation puts them at risk of poorer outcomes in later life such as substance misuse, economic and sexual exploitation. Family and home are often considered a safe haven for children, but for the girls in the study, homes and local communities could be harmful and risky spaces at a time when their health, well-being and safety should have been a priority to those they looked up to. Compounding this situation was a patriarchal culture that effectively silences victims of abuse by questioning the morals and credibility of a child that reports abuse to an adult or the authorities (World Health Organisation, 2009). Nonetheless, our findings show that despite being abandoned by the state, their community and families, the girls cared for each other and those around them, including those who had seemingly turned their backs on them at the most critical time of their lives. Our chapter highlights the need for all concerned to be accountable for the safety, health and well-being of children and young people at a local, national and global level.

Poverty and Informal Settlements

The United Nations (2020: 2) predicted that the pandemic would be the most damaging for children in 'the poorest countries, and in the poorest neighbourhoods, and for those in already disadvantaged or vulnerable situations'. Although South Africa is by no means a poor country, it has some neighbourhoods with very high levels of poverty, which are home to some of the most marginalised groups within the population. Prior to the pandemic, some progress had been made in reducing poverty amongst Blacks in South Africa since the end of apartheid in 1994. However, poverty rates remained high for an upper middle-income country. An estimated half of all South Africans live in poverty, economic growth is stagnant, and inflation remains high. Meanwhile the unemployment rate has climbed towards 30% (World Bank, 2018; Francis and Webster, 2019). According to the OECD Economic Survey (2017), low growth and high unemployment means that income inequalities remain wide and social progress is poor.

This disparity has been manifested in South Africa's failure to provide appropriate accommodation for 13.9% of its population, leading to a high incidence of informal settlements (OECD, 2017). Informal settlements are defined in South Africa's National Housing Code (DoHS, 2009) as illegal, inappropriately located dwellings, with restricted public and private sector investment. Despite a progressive legal and policy framework governing the right to housing (DoHS, 2009), informal housing is a major contributor to social inequalities in South Africa. The Socio-Economic Institute of South Africa (SERI) (2018) reports that implementation of the housing policy framework is plagued by poor planning, a lack of coordination, insufficient capacity, inadequate monitoring, as well as a lack of political will. An estimate in 2011 suggested that between 2.9 and 3.6 million people were living in informal settlements in South Africa (SERI, 2018). Life in informal settlements is often characterised by poverty, vulnerability and social stress, especially for girls and young women. This was particularly acute during the COVID-19 pandemic.

The COVID-19 pandemic induced fear and led to heavy losses of life globally, triggering world-wide national lockdowns to contain it. One major concern with these precautions was the impact on the mental health and well-being of diverse groups of people, including children. South Africa went into national lockdown on March 16th, 2020, but, according to Fisher et al. (2020), the government's official response made little or no provision for the impact on mental health. There was no provision for the necessary health care such as psycho-social support. In many senses, the children within these settlements represented neglected and abandoned groups whose well-being was negatively impacted by state inaction (Davies et al., 2017). Yet, in our study, the young girls in Stjwetla informal settlement were able to document caring agency in the face of such neglect. Instigated by two organisations (anonymised for the purposes of this research): NGO Counsellors and a Charitable Foundation, the aim of the research was to find innovative ways of continuing the girls' support during and post COVID-19.

The Lockdown, School Closures and Home

In relation to education, it should be acknowledged that South Africa invests a large budget into education (OECD, 2019). However, there are still massive educational inequalities within informal settlements, which make it much harder for residents to succeed in life. These inequalities were exacerbated by COVID-19, negatively affecting already disadvantaged children and their families. For example, Reddy et al. (2020) predicted that learning loss amongst children in non-fee-paying schools would be higher than in fee-paying schools. Lack of access to basic needs had a significant impact on children's educational attainment.

The lockdown and closure of schools cut access to education for children living in settlements where resources were already scarce. As a result, families had to rely on government supplied food parcels which most families did not receive. This meant that low paid, poor parents with no savings could not afford data bundles to access online learning mandated by the Department of Education. Some children had no access to a smart device to enable online learning (Reddy et al., 2020).

Additionally, for children, the lockdown could be stressful, with the potential for conflict where family relationships were already strained. This was particularly the case in volatile home environments due to an already overstretched system lacking in resources. For girls in particular, such family environments can be dangerous, risky places, according to Kheswa (2020). Kheswa (2020) examines the challenges faced by women and adolescent girls living in informal settlements in South Africa and highlights the impact of the difficult living conditions on women and adolescents who are often victims of physical and sexual abuse. Poor infrastructure and inadequate facilities such as electricity and toilets put the girls at even higher risk of sexual assault while walking some distance from their homes in the dark to dispose of sanitary towels in the few shared toilets. Kheswa (2020) argues that in settlements, girls are vulnerable to abuse from older men and teenage gangs. Girls can also be forced to engage in transactional inter-generational sex. Girls orphaned at a young age can also be compelled to have sex with older men to earn money to support their siblings. This environment means that sexually transmitted diseases, unwanted pregnancies, substance abuse and high rates of psychological distress are prevalent amongst teenage girls (Kheswa, 2020). Some girls engage in substance abuse as a way of coping, resulting in more severe emotional, physical and mental ill health (Otwombe et al., 2015). Kheswa (2020) argues that in certain cultures, women and girls are socialised to be submissive, as well as respectful and fearful of men and elders. This means that girls often live in silence when abused, especially where family members are the perpetrators. Fear of repercussions makes it difficult for them to report to the police (Otwombe et al., 2015). With schools closed, and families locked down in small living spaces with no income, the girls were more vulnerable than they had ever been before.

Research Methodology

Aims of the Research

The purpose of this research was to examine the impact of COVID-19 and the ensuing lockdown on a specific group of marginalised girls in Stjwetla settlement and how their living conditions and pre-existing emotional vulnerabilities contributed to their experiences of the lockdown.

Alexandra Township and Stjwetla Informal Settlement

Sjtwetla is an informal settlement with a population of 5131 as of the 2011 census. It is located in the township of Alexandra which was established in 1912 close to the centre of Johannesburg. Sitting on an area of over 800 hectares, its infrastructure was designed for a population of about 70,000, but over the years, the population has ballooned to an estimated 350,000 within a geographic area of 1.6 km^2 (Mere, 2011; The World Bank, 2000). The original housing stock was characterised by sizeable houses (500–600 square metres) of reasonable standard. These have been extended over time with 3–6 additional separate rooms built in the original gardens, each usually housing an additional family who rent from the main householder who enjoys a significant income. There are an estimated 20,000 such shacks in the settlement, with approximately 7000 in backyards (Mere, 2011; The World Bank, 2000). Amenities are overstretched with 3 in 10 households having to use bucket toilets and the rest sharing portable chemical toilets. The prospect of keeping these clean in the face of COVID-19 was a significant challenge.

Experiences of Vulnerable Girls **69**

The Participants

Aged between 12 and 17, the girls in the study had suffered trauma from various experiences ranging from sexual abuse, sexual exploitation to domestic violence. In a culture that often silences children, when girls report such experiences, they are either not believed or forbidden from reporting to the police as the perpetrators are sometimes family members. Bottled up emotions can escalate to crisis levels, occasionally with tragic consequences. In some cases, before the pandemic, the emotions had presented as observable behaviours in school, impacting on learning but also prompting interventions from various volunteer professionals, groups and charities that had recognised the need to do something about the fate of girls in such complex situations.

The girls in Stjwetla informal settlement had previously accessed services from counsellors in an NGO, in partnership with a Charitable Foundation, a non-profit organisation that had set up an after-school project to offer practical support. COVID-19 and the lockdown presented new challenges to the project team who could no longer meet regularly with the girls to continue weekly therapy sessions. The team were concerned about the impact to the progress made thus far with the girls' therapy and feared that potential infection and forced confinement in volatile family situations would impact heavily on the girls in the sudden absence of their safety nets and support networks. However, the team were able to maintain contact with the girls through telephone calls to their offices and on mobile phones, highlighting the important role technology can play in facilitating care (see Brown Chapter 13 and Burg Chapter 14 in this volume). Access was limited, however, as not all the girls had access to a phone. The Charitable Foundation was able to provide a few devices for some of the girls and to facilitate some visits to the after-school club with social distancing measures in place.

Data Collection

Questionnaires were sent to 26 girls, in May 2020 who were receiving counselling and therapy from the NGO Counsellors and the Charitable Foundation. The girls were informed that participation was voluntary, confidential and anonymous, with pseudonyms used in any reporting of responses. They were also told that they would not be impacted in any way if they chose not to participate. It was explained that if they did participate and later changed their minds, they could withdraw from the study and their responses would not be included. Nineteen girls responded, ranging in age from 12 to 17. The participants were asked 10 questions relating to their understanding of COVID-19, social distancing, how they had been impacted and how they were copying with the situation. With limited contact with the girls, the after-school club was used to distribute the questionnaires and the rest were sent electronically to those who had access to mobile devices. Questions included:

(1) What is your understanding of COVID-19/Coronavirus?
(2) How has it affected you?

(3) How has it affected the family? (How has it changed your family lifestyle/home environment?)
(4) How has it affected your community?
(5) What challenges have you encountered (come across) since the national lockdown?
(6) How has the national lockdown upset your lifestyle/way of living?
(7) How are you coping, given the circumstances?
(8) What is your understanding of social distancing/physical distancing?
(9) How are you practicing physical distancing?
(10) How are you keeping your friendships/relationships going?

Theoretical Framework

The girls' responses were analysed using two theoretical frameworks, Maslow's theory of human motivation (1943) and Brammer's crisis theory (1985).

Brammer's Crisis Theory

The sudden and severe disruptions of routines, separation from families, wage losses and social isolation were undoubtedly what made COVID-19 a worldwide situational crisis. According to Brammer's theory (1985), a situational crisis arises when an individual is confronted by unexpected events that are seemingly out of their control. The situation is usually sudden, shocking, intense and accidental. Parad and Caplan (1960) developed a framework with five essential features for a stressful event to be classified as a crisis:

(1) The event must pose a problem which is perceived as unsolvable in the immediate future.
(2) The problem taxes the resources of the individual or family, since they cannot apply traditional problem-solving approaches to it.
(3) The situation is seen as a threat to the life goals of the individual or family.
(4) The situation induces a generalised physical tension that is symptomatic of anxiety.
(5) The situation awakens unresolved key problems from the near and distant past.

Maslow's Hierarchy of Needs Model

According to Maslow (1943), we have five categories of needs: physiological, safety, love, esteem and self-actualisation. Physiological, security, social and esteem needs are deficiency needs, which arise due to deprivation. Satisfying these lower-level needs is important to avoid unpleasant feelings or consequences (Taormina and Gao, 2013). These categories are intertwined with the giving and receiving of care, particularly in the role of therapists' day-to-day professional work but also central to this research.

Knowledge About the Virus

In many contexts across the globe, there was a desire to protect young people from the virus, often emerging from an assumption that children and young people did not fully understand what was happening. Such approaches have tended to sideline young people's perspectives and experiences (see Spray, 2022). The girls in our study were aware that the virus had travelled far and wide and was still spreading. They were aware that it continued to evolve and that there was no immediate solution to it so there was a need to try to minimise its spread. In the analysis of the responses to the first question, there was a general understanding of what the virus was and its origins from China in 2019; that it was deadly, had spread worldwide and killed indiscriminately through attacking the lungs. The girls also mentioned the cross-over from animals to human and that it was essential that the disease was contained. This understanding was crucial to the girls' perception of the pandemic and how they managed their own safety and well-being and that of others. This was also a key factor in how they rationalised and coped with this experience. The girls' description of the virus fell within the first of Parad and Caplan's 5 characteristics of a crisis event (Parad and Caplan, 1960).

This concern of transmission was indicative of a general desire to care:

Sophie: 'Coronavirus is a pandemic that affects everyone ...it has no specific race ...gender ...it is spread through the mouth where the droplets from the mouth come out'.

Karabo: 'A monstrous and deadly virus that attacks physically, which infects one in various ways such as: by sneezing, coughing, hugging, touching of hands and so forth'.

Thuli: 'Coronavirus is a disease, and my understanding is that the virus, it continues to evolve. It was first detected in China and has now been detected in over 100 countries, including the United States. The virus is believed to have originally occurred from animal to person contact and spread person to person'.

Sisa: '... [It] is a deadly virus that we must try and minimize its spread to save lives'.

Within Maslow's (1943) hierarchy, this represents a threat to safety and life, and what is clear is that these young girls had a sophisticated understanding of the virus and the risks it posed.

Concerns for the Future

In relation to their own well-being, the girls were most concerned with the shut-down of schools and loss of learning time. School was seen as a route to a better life, apart from the immediate benefit of spending time with friends. The mandatory move to online learning brought challenges such as poor network in the area, limited access to electronic devices, lack of money to buy data to access the resources since the parents had stopped working and difficulties to understand the content without the support of the teacher.

The loss of learning time was indicative of Parad and Caplan's (1960) third point of crisis criteria; a threat to life goals of the individual or family, as the girls explain:

> Novuyo: 'This year I was ready to do well in my studies and pass Grade 10 and pass to another grade and finish school early to change the situation at home, and now it will take time'.
> Sophie: '... I can't access the online learning because our community has network issues ... learning through TV is difficult because if I don't understand I can't ask questions'.
> Thuli: '... Schools have been shut down in the nation lockdown and it's putting me at risk of losing out learning time'.
> Langa: 'It's affecting me so bad... it's hard to study ... some work needs teachers to explain'.
> Bongie: 'I am behind with schoolwork'.

These worries expressed by the girls come in the wake of concerns over the quality of the South African education system. In The World Economic Forum (2016–17) Global Competitiveness Report, the South African education system was ranked 126 out of 138 countries (Schwab, 2017). The South African Education system is allegedly inefficient, and its learners cannot read or count at an appropriate level (Govender, 2012).

On the other hand, the girls' concerns indicated a desire to succeed and reach their full potential. This would equate to esteem and self-actualisation, the highest levels in Maslow's hierarchy. Onah (2015) perceives self-actualisation as self-fulfilment, the need to develop one's full potential. This encourages people to be innovative in their various social settings in an endeavour to improve their living conditions in the society (Aruma and Hanachor, 2017). Also featuring significantly in this question was social isolation and the subsequent emotional impact. High on the participants' concerns were the inability to have physical contact or play with friends, not being able to share the 'burning issues' with them.

> Lizzie: '...I can't go and play with my friend or share ... burning issues'.
> Sandile: 'It affect me a lot because every day I get scared because I think that am affected without knowing'.
> Karabo: '... I'm not able to communicate with my friends physically and this sometimes makes me feel depressed and bored'.

Despite these fears, the girls also articulated elements of care and concern for themselves and others, which we now turn to.

Caring About Community

Maslow's theory examines the need for individuals to be part of a group such as family, friendships, church and other social groups. These meet the need for love and belonging (Anyanwu et al., 1985) which in turn gives them the confidence to contribute to the development of their communities.

The impact of poverty on the girls' experiences of the pandemic and lockdown is most evident in their accounts of how the community has been affected. The abject living conditions were seen to precipitate the situation. The difficulties of social distancing in the overcrowded settlement and confined home spaces come to the forefront in responses, as do the risks presented by limited communal amenities such as water taps and toilets. The girls also mentioned the impact that parents working or not being able to work had in their family and communities. This reflects feature four of the crisis criteria, with the event inducing a generalised physical tension that is symptomatic of anxiety (Parad and Caplan, 1960). While the community may have developed a way of normalising their life circumstances and living conditions, the sudden appearance of COVID-19 and the lockdown taxed the resources of the community; not working meant not meeting their family's needs or if they did go out to work this increased the risk of infection. In essence, they could not apply traditional problem-solving approaches to the situation (Parad and Caplan, 1960):

> Novuyo: 'As we are using one toilet and a tap it is very difficult for us to use those things because we don't know if the person who used the toilet or the tap last has Coronavirus'.
> Sandile: 'The community is very affected because we share a toilet, for example six families to one toilet'.
> Sindi: 'My community is more affected, and it has high risks of being infected by Coronavirus because people get out and hustle so that they can bring food to the table for their families and when it comes to social distancing people can't maintain it because we are overpopulated'.
> Buhle: 'People are scared of dying and also, they have to support their families with the little businesses they have'.
> Bongie: 'People are not working so there have been a lot of house break-ins because of no income'.

In their accounts of the challenges encountered since the national lockdown, the girls reiterated the dismal living conditions. There were concerns about the spread of the virus due to lack of knowledge about it and unhygienic conditions, posing a problem which is perceived as unsolvable in the immediate future, in line with characteristic one of Parad and Caplan's framework (Parad and Caplan, 1960), posing a threat to safety and security (Maslow, 1943):

> Thembie: 'People in my community don't take this pandemic seriously because they aren't educated enough about Corona. Hygiene is lacking when it

comes to our community, and you can't prevent corona in this kind of environment'.

Sandile: '...when I want to go to the toilet I feel guilty and scared because I think that the soldiers will beat me'.

Ntombi: '... at home we are too many and we don't give each other space'.

Sophie: 'Staying in the house has been difficult ... having no one to talk to you about how you really feel ... it's been a real challenge'.

The girls' descriptions of how the lockdown has disrupted their lifestyle highlights the bottom three of Maslow's hierarchy of needs; physiological needs like food, water, shelter and sleep; safety and security needs like health, family, social stability; love and belonging, including friendships, family intimacy. It also, however, underscores the importance of social networks and the importance of sharing experiences, feelings and support from friends. Within these responses was a strong theme of caring about their community, wanting it to be protected.

Family Tensions

The major issue in how the family was affected, was lack of income and therefore inability to obtain basic needs like food and rent, putting the parents under a lot of pressure, and leading to arguments. There were also expressions of feeling trapped in the house with the family, causing unwanted tension and conflicts; typical of feature five of the crisis-inducing events, where the event induces a generalised physical tension that is symptomatic of anxiety:

Thembi: 'It affected my family by spending a lot of time together, caused more conflict and unwanted tension between us'.

Sophie: 'Both my parents aren't working so ... there is no income coming in ... which causes arguments between my parents because they are under a lot of pressure. I can't visit my friends anymore and I hate being trapped in the house'.

This is also reflective of the most basic level of Maslow's hierarchy where the families are struggling for basic needs like food and rent:

Sandra: 'It affects the family because parents no longer go to work and at home there is no food, and they don't have money to pay rent'.

Naledi: 'It has affected my family very badly because my mother is not working, and she has to buy me data so that I can learn online and buy food ... she needs to buy warm clothes ... very bad'.

The experiences of lockdown transformed the sense of home for many of the girls; regarding safety and security needs such as health, family and social stability. Home was no longer seen as a safe haven, with economic and emotional concerns at the forefront.

Despite this, as in other sections of the questionnaire, love and belonging needs (friendship, family and intimacy) were strongly represented. For many, the focus was on how the virus impeded forms of intimacy:

> Sophie: 'I never hug my friends or hold hands and we have to be one meter apart always and I liked going out with my friends and now everything has stopped'.
> Thuli: 'In the battle against the high infection Covid 19 social distancing is extremely important to help curb the spread'.
> Thembi: 'This is very hard to avoid because we live in a community, where we are close.... Social distancing means we must stay away from each other at least 1m away ... we shouldn't get in contact like hugging and kissing and touching'.

This last response is also indicative of a feature of one of the crisis criteria where the individual cannot apply their usual ways of coping. The preoccupation with hugging indicates the girls' desire for human contact, a demonstration of level three of Maslow's framework; love, friendship and intimacy. Research has associated hugging and other forms of contact with health and mental well-being; Keating (1995 cited in Forsell and Åström, 2012: 4) observed the importance of touch for facilitating well-being. Despite the desire for physical contact, the girls' avoidance of physical contact is demonstrative of their own caring agency in protecting themselves and their family from catching the virus.

Coping and Self-Care

These girls clearly had a sophisticated understanding of the need for social distancing, and while taking measures to protect themselves, they still sought out safe contact with friends as a means of caring for their own well-being:

> Sophie: 'We communicate through social media, and we meet sometimes at [the Charitable Foundation]'.
> Sandra: 'By chatting on the phone....sometimes I get a chance to see them in the afternoon and have a chat and ask each other how we are feeling and stuff'.
> Sandile: 'When I feel like I miss my friends I talk with them on Facebook or when I go to fetch water I see them so we get an opportunity to talk'.

The main message on how they practiced social/physical distancing was that the girls were doing their best but crowding in the settlement made it difficult. They were adhering to the recommended precautions and using social media to keep in touch with their friends on the mobile phones provided by the Charitable Foundation:

> Sindi: 'by trying to communicate with my friends and the group over WhatsApp, Facebook and over a phone call since [the Charitable Foundation] collected some donations to buy us cell phones'.

In reflections about how they were coping in the circumstances, the two supporting organisations were mentioned, where social distancing measures were applied, as important for facilitating meetings where the girls could discuss, read books and complete some homework. The Charitable Foundation also gave the girls food and mobile phones. It was hard for some of the girls, but their responses indicate that they found ways of coping (alongside the communication with friends) through forms of self-care:

> Sophie: 'My coping mechanism is writing about how I feel and sometimes meeting up with my group helps me a lot'.
> Sandile: 'Every day in the morning when I am done with home chores I take my grade 9 reader and read, after reading I do Maths'.
> Sindi: 'I cope by sharing my burning issues with the girls in [the Charitable Foundation]. Doing all the homework that [the Charitable Foundation] gives us'.
> Linda: 'Putting my faith in God'.

Discussion

Maslow's hierarchy of needs highlights the challenges imposed by poor incomes and living conditions already experienced by the girls before the pandemic, putting them on a back footing in terms of their reactions to and management of the new and unexpected challenges. The girls' crowded living conditions were already a barrier to attaining the higher levels in the hierarchy. COVID-19 posed an additional threat to their security and safety needs, the next level in the hierarchy. Muvunyi (2020) states that the majority of South Africans, at least 54% of households, have no access to clean water, while at least 14% live in crowded informal settlements. These unmet physiological needs make it difficult for individuals to transcend to the next level in the hierarchy, which is safety. This level focuses on the people's need for security and protection (Aruma and Hanachor, 2017). COVID-19 has not only exposed the social inequalities but has also amplified poor living conditions in informal settlements. As mentioned in their responses, the national lockdown rendered the girls' caregivers jobless, creating financial instability and insecurity.

A further theme indicates that a sense of belonging in the form of intimate relationships was threatened by the social distancing measures imposed by the need to contain the virus through lockdown and closure of schools. Aruma and Hanachor (2017: 20) note the human need for security, protection and survival from chaotic situations, social disorder, social disturbance and physical dangers in their environment. COVID-19 was a threat to the status quo in the community, particularly so for the girls who were already emotionally vulnerable and undergoing therapy in the face of a situation they had no control over, with no prior experiences to draw upon (Brammer, 1985). The unexpected emergence of COVID-19 and the unprecedented measures taken by governments globally represented a potential crisis event to the girls. The COVID-19 pandemic undeniably thrust the world into a situation unparalleled by any other since the Spanish flu of 1918. From events globally, it can be argued that all five features in Brammer's (1985) framework are applicable to this pandemic, from individual, family, community to national levels. For the girls in the informal settlement, the impact was made more complex by their prevailing situation and living conditions. Yet, what our findings show is that the girls demonstrated sophisticated knowledge of the risks associated with the virus and deployed nuanced forms of caring; for themselves, for their community and their families. These are important to reflect upon; they should not excuse a form of state inaction in relation to care (Davies et al., 2017), but emphasise the needs and importance of care to this population who have in many respects been abandoned by the South African government.

Conclusion

The girls at Sjtwetla informal settlement may have found themselves in a situation that had the potential to overwhelm them, but the findings of this small study indicated that they were aware of the threat and were finding ways of caring and coping at that early stage of the pandemic. This study brought to light the challenges that poverty and crowding can bring to girls and young women living in less-than-ideal environments, in a culture where the odds are stacked against them. The extracts from the girls' responses tell their story in their own words which indicate a good level of understanding of the situation and an appreciation of the care they give and receive from each other and the organisations supporting them. It is noted that although these challenges are likely to be common to most informal settlement residents, these findings are not readily generalizable due to the very small sample and the specific context of the study. However, the implications of the living conditions revealed here highlight the need for further research focusing on informal settlements and the need to address the inequalities in the South African education and social systems. Furthermore, with COVID-19 cases rising in South Africa at the time of research, it was recommended another study should be conducted after the pandemic to inform therapy and other potential interventions to secure the girls wellbeing going forward. Cultures are not easy to change. However, community education programs should be prioritised to create an awareness of the impact of cultural gender biases.

References

Anyanwu, C.N., Omolewa, M.A., Adeyeri, C.L.K., Okanlawon, A.B. and Siddiqui, A.A. 1985. *Adult Education and Community Development*. Heinemann Educational Books (Nig.) Ltd., Ibadan.

Aruma, E.O. and Hanachor, M.E. 2017. Abraham Maslow's hierarchy of needs and assessment of needs in community development. *International Journal of Development and Economic Sustainability*, 5(7), 15–27.

Brammer, L.M. 1985. *The Helping Relationship: Process and Skills*, New Jersey, Prentice-Hall.

Davies, T., Isakjee, A. and Dhesi, S. 2017. Violent inaction: the necropolitical experience of refugees in Europe. *Antipode*, 49(5), 1263–1284.

Department of Human Settlements (DoHS) 2009. National Housing Code. Available at: https://www.dhs.gov.za/content/national-housing-code-2009. (Accessed 11 10 2023).

Fisher, J., Languilaire, J.C., Lawthom, R., Nieuwenhuis, R., Petts, R.J., Runswick-Cole, K. and Yerkes, M.A. 2020. Community, work, and family in times of COVID-19. *Community, Work & Family*, 23(3), 247–252. https://doi.org/10.1080/13668803.2020.1756568

Forsell, L.M. and Åström, J.A. 2012. Meanings of hugging: From greeting behavior to touching implications. *Comprehensive Psychology*, 1(13).

Francis, D. and Webster, E. 2019. Poverty and inequality in South Africa: Critical reflections. *Development Southern Africa*, 36(6), 788–802. https://doi.org/10.1080/0376835X.2019.1666703

Govender, P. 2012. Expulsion on the cards for school heads who fail. Sunday Times, 9. Available at: http://www.cluteinstitute.com/. (Accessed 02 11 2024).

International Bank for Reconstruction and Development/World Bank March 2018. Overcoming Poverty and Inequality in South Africa. An Assessment of Drivers, Constraints and Opportunities. Available at: https://documents1.worldbank.org/curated/en/530481521735906534/pdf/Overcoming%20Poverty-and-Inequality-in-South-Africa-An-Assessment-of-Drivers-Constraints-and-Opportunities.pdf (Accessed 11/02/2024).

Kheswa, J. 2020. Conditions and challenges associated with women's risk sexual behaviour in informal settlements across South Africa. *Journal of Human Ecology*, 70(1–3), 124–131.

Maslow, A.H. 1943. A theory of human motivation. *Psychological Review*, 50, 370–396.

Mere, O.M. 2011. Geographical Patterns and Disaster Management: Case study of Alexander Township (Masters Mini-dissertation), North-west University. Available at: https://pdfs.semanticscholar.org/7456/587b00a020ca02ded780727443c9ffcbf23c.pdf. (Accessed 11/02/2024).

Muvunyi, F. 2020. COVID-19: South Africa's social divide and economic woes exposed. Available at: https://www.dw.com/en/coronavirus-south-africas-social-divide-and-economic-woes-exposed/a-53739914 (Accessed 11/02/2024).

OECD. 2017. *OECD economic surveys: South Africa 2017*. OECD Publishing, Paris. https://doi.org/10.1787/eco_surveys-zaf-2017-en

OECD. 2019. "South Africa", in education at a glance 2019: OECD indicators. OECD Publishing, Paris. https://doi.org/10.1787/c5c8fd33-en

Onah, F.O. 2015. *Human Resource Management*, fourth ed. John Jacob's Classic Publishers, Enugu.

Otwombe, K.N., Dietrich, J., Sikkema, K.J., Coetzee, J., Hopkins, K.L., Laher, F. and Gray, G.E. 2015. Exposure to and experiences of violence among adolescents in lower socio-economic groups in Johannesburg, South Africa. *BMC Public Health*, 15(1), 450.

Parad, H.J. and Caplan, G. 1960. A framework for studying families in crisis. *Social Work*, 5(3), 3–15.

Reddy, V., Soudien, C. and Winnaar, L.D. 2020. Impact of school closures on education outcomes in South Africa. Available at: https://theconversation.com/impact-of-school-closures-on-education-outcomes-in-south-africa-136889. (Accessed 10 November 2023).

Schwab, K. 2017. The Global Competitiveness Report. World Economic Forum, pp. 2016–2017. Available at: https://www3.weforum.org/docs/GCR2018/05Full Report/TheGlobalCompetitivenessReport2018.pdf. (Accessed 02 11 2024).

Socio-Economic Institute of South Africa 2018. Informal Settlements and Human Rights in South Africa. Available at: https://www.ohchr.org/Documents/Issues/Housing/InformalSettlements/SERI.pdf. (Accessed 02 11 2024).

Spray, J. 2022. *Children's Inclusion and Participation in COVID-19 Health Promotion in Aotearoa New Zealand - Report for Participants, Parents, and Stakeholders*, Auckland, University of Auckland.

Taormina, R.J. and Gao, J.H. 2013. Maslow and the motivation hierarchy: measuring the satisfaction of the needs. *American Journal of Psychology*, 126(2), 155–177.

United Nations 2020. Policy Brief: The Impact of COVID-19 on Children. Available at: https://unsdg.un.org/resources/policy-brief-impact-COVID-19-children. (Accessed 02 11 2024).

World Bank Group 2000. Project spotlight: Alexandra township, Johannesburg, South Africa. Available at: http://web.mit.edu/urbanupgrading/upgrading/case-examples/overview-africa/alexandra-township.html. (Accessed 11/02/2024).

World Health Organization 2009. *Changing Cultural and Social Norms Supportive of Violent Behaviour*, Geneva, WHO Press.

Chapter 6

Children's Care for Public Health and Politically Expedient Care for Children in Aotearoa New Zealand's COVID-19 Pandemic

Julie Spray

Children's Studies, University of Galway, Ireland

Abstract

Managing public 'affect' was a critical component of Aotearoa New Zealand's COVID-19 policy approach, which was predicated on collective emotional feelings of calmness, compassion and trust. A long history of health promotion efforts have involved co-opting children as tools to manipulate (adult) public affect towards motivating behavioural change or accepting health interventions. Little research has yet considered the consequences of objectifying children for affect management in the name of public health. The Pandemic Generation study compared the perspectives of Auckland children aged 7–11, generated through co-drawing comics about their pandemic experience, with a critical discourse analysis of children's representation in New Zealand COVID-19 public health messaging. In this chapter, I argue that by leveraging performative care for children to manipulate an adult public affect, the New Zealand government erased children's subjectivities, their care-giving roles and contributions, further disenfranchising children as members of the 'public' in public health.

Keywords: Affect management; COVID-19; child-centred research; child participation; New Zealand; public health

Introduction

On April 6th 2020, New Zealand Prime Minister Jacinda Ardern stepped onto a stage in front of the nation's media representatives.[1] Flanked by national flags and banners branded with now familiar yellow and white stripes and the 'Unite against COVID-19' slogan, Ardern stood behind a podium imprinted with the national coat of arms. This was the Prime Minister's press conference, already an established daily event since the global COVID-19 outbreak had prompted the government to lock down the country 12 days earlier. Intended primarily for briefing the press, these conferences were broadcast over television and radio and livestreamed online, routine viewing for the New Zealand public who gathered to hear the day's case numbers and policy updates.

During this day's conference, Ardern frowned earnestly as she announced the details of a business subsidy. Then, her tone softening, she voiced concern for the population's mental well-being: 'I know there are some people who are feeling distressed, anxious, or worried at this time, and that is completely understandable'. Gently explaining the forthcoming release of resources to support with stress, she then pivoted to briskly describe the surveillance testing her government was using to determine that all regions would remain under level four, the most severe lockdown, for at least four weeks. These announcements were, as usual, followed by questions from the press. Emphatically parrying media challenges, Ardern maintained her characteristic upbeat poise, frowning to convey seriousness and concern as she clarified the role of the military in enforced quarantines. Then in the final minutes of the conference, a media representative put forward a question 'on a slightly different note… from some younger viewers who are quite concerned this weekend—'

'—the Easter Bunny?' Ardern's face broke into a glowing smile. 'Yes, you'll be pleased to know that we do consider both the tooth fairy and the Easter bunny to be essential workers', she informed the nation's children. Acknowledging that the Easter bunny would also be quite busy with their own family, Ardern suggested families might help by drawing an Easter egg for the front windows to create neighbourhood egg hunts as they had earlier with teddy bears (Fig. 6.1). This announcement apparently charmed the global press, who picked up the message in news articles published in major outlets around the world, from *NPR* to *the BBC* to *the New York Times*.

New Zealand, and Ardern in particular, received global acclaim for the country's 'zero tolerance elimination' approach to COVID-19 policy. After a strict lockdown in March 2020 eliminated the virus from the country, extensive public health measures prevented its re-emergence, including a four-tier alert level system, lockdowns, contact tracing, border closures and hotel quarantines for returning citizens and essential immigrants (full details available at Ministry of Health, 2021). These policies, implemented between March 2020 and December 2021, successfully minimised morbidity and mortality during this period—by January 2022, New Zealand had

---

[1] Archived at https://web.archive.org/web/20200515093112mp_/https://covid19.govt.nz/latest-updates/daily-COVID-19-media-conferences-6-april/

Fig. 6.1. Screenshot From the Prime Minister's Press Conference; Ardern Encouraging Families to Display Easter Eggs.

reported a total of 52 deaths. Although the restrictions were among the most severe in the world, representing extraordinary impositions into public lives and the broadest enactment of state power in New Zealand history, the public overwhelmingly accepted these measures (Trnka, 2020). The protests and politicisation of public health efforts observed in many other countries were notably absent in the first one and a half years of New Zealand's pandemic, in part because of very intentional management of public 'affect' by Arden's government. As scholars have observed, Ardern counterbalanced announcements of heavy government intrusions with 'rhetorical softeners' that connected care and compassion for the vulnerable with a positive nationalism (Gilray, 2021; Trnka, 2020). Characterising the public as the 'team of 5 million', Ardern's communications strategy used rugby metaphors to connect grassroots communities with national pride, and termed locked-down household units as 'bubbles', evoking pretty, transparent fragility (Trnka and Davies, 2020). And images of children, innocent and vulnerable, stood in for communities and the nation, reminders of for whom adults were sacrificing their autonomy. Through the semiotics of bunnies and fairies, bubbles and games, the adult public's fear, anxiety, frustration or anger could be converted into care, concern and compassion for the dependent generation of future citizens.

A long history of health promotion efforts has involved co-opting children as tools to manipulate (adult) public affect towards motivating behavioural change or accepting policy interventions. By 'affect management' I refer to the way that collective emotions are produced and managed as part of governance. Affect is rarely explicitly considered in public health, which as Deborah Lupton (2013: 634) has noted, tends to represent itself, as a field, as 'dispassionately expert and rational'. In practice, however, public health frequently engages covert or overt affective strategies to, for example, incite fear, shame or disgust. Because public health operations involve disease prevention and health promotion at a collective, population level, policies and messaging are often enacted through government bodies and leverage common political tools such as affect management for increasing public acceptance of impingements on individual autonomy (e.g. safety regulations; seatbelts) or discouraging unhealthy behaviours (e.g. smoking; drink driving). In the case of the COVID-19 pandemic, affect management was particularly core to public health strategy because of the need to solicit public buy-in to what were dramatic intrusions into private life. New Zealand's successful zero-covid strategy was predicated on collective feelings of concern but not panic, compassion, trust, solidarity and calm.

There are consequences to using children in this way, however. As Ian Hacking (1986) has so compellingly theorised, representations do not reflect but constitute the subjectivities of those represented, prescribing the range of social roles available to them and influencing how the objectified see themselves. Commenting on the public health approach to the HIV/TB epidemic in Zambia, for example, Jean Hunleth (2017) showed how the orphan tropes pervaded public discourse also influenced how children navigated their dependency to the extent that even those who were already technically orphaned expressed fear of becoming an orphan. In my research with a New Zealand community targeted by a rheumatic fever campaign featuring sad-eyed children, I found many children could recite the campaign messages about death verbatim, while also expressing a fear and anxiety about rheumatic fever that drove them to over-use a school-based sore throat clinic (Spray, 2020). How Othered groups of people are represented also shapes how group members are seen and understood and treated, contributing to stereotyping, bias, discrimination, neglect or stigma. As childhood studies scholars have critiqued since the field's inception, representations of children as innocent, vulnerable and passive recipients of adult care have come to dominate social constructions of childhood in hegemonic Western cultures over the last few decades (James and Prout, 1990). These simplistic constructions of children that now pervade the public imaginary are accompanied by increasing segregation and surveillance of children's lives in the name of their 'protection' and 'development' (Lee, 2001; Spray, 2023; Valentine, 2004). Children's reduced autonomy and exclusion from public life engenders new forms of risk and silencing, impacting their social participation and value, care-giving, diversity of relationships, knowledge acquisition, independence and political voice (Bessant, 2021; Cohen, 2005; Zelizer, 1985). As children disappear from public view so do their subjective perspectives, leaving only one-dimensional, paper cut-out representations. As these representations influence conceptions of children in models of processes and practices like development, health and citizenship, they in turn reify those social constructions of children as incomplete and inchoate humans – public-in-waiting (Spray and Samaniego, 2023).

In this chapter I ask, how were children implicated in public affect in New Zealand's COVID-19 public health strategy? And what were these representations obscuring about how children actually contributed to public health through their own affective and agentive practices? I investigate this question through a study called the Pandemic Generation, which sought to assess and compare children's representation in COVID-19 political and media discourse with children's own perspectives of their contributions to public health care, generated through co-making comics of their stories. This comparison shows that while children were objectified as affective tools in political discourse, as subjects, children also enacted their own forms of affect management for 'public' health in the domains in which they had agency. Children's narrow representation as affective objects also obscured the array of health promoting practices which contributed to public health.

Participants and Methods

I initiated the Pandemic Generation study in response to my early observations, echoed by other scholars, of children's narrow representation in political and media discussions of COVID-19 policy and impacts (Alwan, 2021; Lomax et al., 2022; Spray and Hunleth, 2020). The study took a critical childhood studies approach, which examines how childhood is socio-historically constituted within dynamic, structural relations of power and oppression (Alanen, 2011). Part one of the study assessed children's representation across three forms of government and media COVID-19 public health policy and communications. Part two investigated children's perspectives through a novel method, co-making comics with 26 Auckland children aged 7–11 (further detailed in Spray, 2022).

This chapter focuses on data from press conferences and comics. A student researcher extracted 182 transcripts of government press conferences held during the period 1 January 2020 and 30 March 2022 from the government's COVID-19 website (sample includes all available). Within NVivo 12, we ran keyword search queries to identify transcripts and sections relating to children or related subject areas for coding. We developed a coding framework by applying a critical childhood lens to a subset of the sampled communications to identify initial themes, which we then iteratively refined throughout the coding process. We then coded the material to identify how children and their perspectives were represented (full details reported in Spray and Samaniego, 2023).

Part two of the study occurred between November 2021 and April 2022. I recruited participants through personal networks and advertisements posted to a selection of community Facebook groups representing diverse geographic areas of Auckland. Invited to select their preference, 16 families chose an in-person visit with health protection measures (masks, hand sanitisers, outdoors) and 10 families elected to participate online over Zoom. Introducing the study, I explained I was a researcher interested in children's views about the pandemic because adults making decisions for children sometimes made mistakes. If the child chose to participate, we would first make a mind-map of their experiences, and then they could choose the stories for their comic. Extending my research approach, *drawing together* (Spray, 2021), which attends to the researcher's mode of participation, I positioned myself as co-drawer to facilitate empathetic co-construction of stories. Children could choose to draw their own comic, or they could tell me what to draw, or we could draw it together. I also shared a comic of my own pandemic experience for a reciprocal exchange of stories. I audio recorded our interactions and analysed the data first by viewing all the comics on a wall and identifying themes with coloured sticky tags. Refining those initial themes into a set of codes, I then coded the recording transcripts in NVivo. During this process, I noted the frequency with which affective dimensions of children's care appeared in the data, which led me to this analysis of children and affect in public health.

Children in Affect Management

The New Zealand governments' manipulation of public affect can be usefully understood through Sara Ahmed's (2004) conception of how affect is produced. In Ahmed's conception, emotional valences are attached to objects circulating between people (e.g. in the form of images, words), each transmission ratcheting the emotions they convey – emotions that are then impressed upon and embodied by their recipients. Analysing white nationalist rhetoric, Ahmed identifies how hate groups use images of home, nation and family to invoke the love attached to those objects to secure their collective identity, creating and justifying hate for perceived threats (e.g. immigrants) to those beloved objects. Harnessing a dialectical force whereby threat to love produces hate and intensifies love, the circulation of objects shapes collective affect to consolidate in-group membership and out-group threat. In the case of New Zealand's pandemic response, circulated imagery included nationhood, community and family as objects of love to be protected from foreign coronavirus invaders through border closures and lockdowns.

As Ahmed theorises, some objects, due to their political salience, become particularly 'sticky' or saturated with affect, positive or negative. Children, at least in the contemporary West, are one such sticky object. As Erica Burman (1994) notes of humanitarian campaigns, children's iconography semiotically invokes and reinforces associations with helplessness, innocence and vulnerability to elicit adult sympathy and reassert adult control. Because it is difficult to argue that children should not be protected, perceived threats to children are powerful tools that have frequently been deployed in the form of moral panics over the latter 20th and early 21st century to stigmatise, exclude or silence groups who threaten the status quo, such as gay or Black men, trans women, single mothers, immigrants or youth (Bessant, 2021; Goode and Ben-Yehuda, 1994). Moreover, as children represent the reproduction of society, the 'improper' place, behaviour, activities and raising of children is politicised as potential threats to social order and indicators of social crisis. These ideologies also seep into public health policies and initiatives to discursively attach affective valences to the images of children and parents, for example, to justify surveillance of First Nations mothers and children on health grounds (Salmon, 2004).

The use of children as affective objects is of critical concern not only for the way they obscure and justify prejudice against marginalised groups but also for where they leave children. When children are used as objects, they are not recognised as subjects. Though Ardern spoke of being 'all in this together', analysis of children's representation suggests otherwise. While many children we spoke to described their families gathering around the television each day to hear the government's latest updates, across transcripts of these events children were rarely addressed and their perspectives rarely represented (Spray and Samaniego, 2023). Ardern's references to the Easter bunny on April 6th was one occasion when the child audience was acknowledged. During these early days, Ardern also held a press conference for children, capturing global headlines (again, referencing the tooth fairy) and inspiring several other national leaders to do the same. Unlike the daily media conferences, however, no video or transcript record of the children's conference is accessible, and the event was not repeated, even as children, ineligible for vaccination, were among the most vulnerable in the subsequent Delta and Omicron outbreaks.

Thus, children's representation in the early stages of the pandemic appears tokenistic, used to convert public alarm into a sense of collectivity and care. By crafting young children's images alongside the cute and fantastical – Easter bunnies, fairies, teddy bears – Ardern's government could channel public anxiety into compassion and affection for children. In turn, this reduced children's roles to drawing Easter eggs, framed as indulgences for children's entertainment and charming tired adult carers. Children's drawings, as I have argued elsewhere (Spray, 2023), are not insignificant contributions, as affective care and community-building are vital parts of a crisis response. But while children were used as affective objects, their own affective practices were not recognised as serious and substantial contributions to public health, while their other forms of public health care practices were erased. Moreover, children's feelings were largely excluded from acknowledgements of public sentiment. In one extended example, Education Minister Chris Hipkins fielded a number of media questions about teachers' and parents' worries about schools reopening with repeated assurances about safety (Press Conference, April 21st 2020). There was no mention that students may also have feelings about safety; in the only discussion of young people's perspectives Hipkins advised senior students worried about end-of-year exams to 'don't let themselves get totally strung out about it'.

As the immediate shock and uncertainty of crisis subsided with the end of the first lockdown, so too disappeared attempts to include children. Children were not directly addressed again after April 2020 except for the occasional request to students to be tested following a school outbreak. Meanwhile, reductive representations of children persisted. The second and final major national lockdown coincided with a mass campaign to achieve 90% vaccination rates across the eligible population (over age 16). Adults who declined vaccination were subject to social sanctions, including exclusion from public indoor spaces if they could not produce a 'vaccine pass'. While the government deliberately avoided the language of compulsion, critics pointed out that the restrictions effectively made the policy mandatory, and, as the lockdown dragged on, for the first time the country saw significant backlash and protests. During this time, images of children headlined government appeals for the adult public to get vaccinated. Here, children were silent and vulnerable, ineligible for vaccination and in need of adult protection. Often using the Māori words for children (tamariki), youth (rangatahi) and family (whānau) to target Māori communities who trailed in vaccination rates,[2] Ardern packaged her vaccine promotion in notions of moral duty to loved ones:

> I think actually the most impactful message is that if you're vaccinated, you keep your family safe. We've seen that, actually, time and time again, that has been one of the biggest motivating factors for people to get vaccinated. It's often not about them; it's about their whānau, and that's still the biggest message. Do it to protect your family, your rangatahi, your tamariki, and your babies. (Jacinda Ardern, Media Conference, September 23rd 2021).

These emotive pleas for adults to get vaccinated often highlighted the numbers of sick children, emphasising children's vulnerability to counter epidemiological evidence that children were less severely affected by infections than adults:

> There have been many devastating stories in this outbreak, including the case of a one-year-old child who fell ill with the virus. In fact, 121 of the New Zealanders who have tested positive in the last three weeks are under nine years old. These are children, who at this stage cannot be vaccinated, so they need us to be—all of us. (Jacinda Ardern, Media Conference, September 9th 2021)

Conversely, when parents became anxious about their children's safety, particularly around school reopenings, officials shifted to reassure the public by emphasising children's resilience. As Hipkins responded to a media question about the spread of Omicron through children:

> My advice to parents is to stay calm. [...] Younger people, and, you know, the evidence and the advice we're getting from our health professionals is that younger people do tend to be much more resilient against COVID-19. They tend to have milder symptoms, they tend to recover more, they are very under-represented. We're certainly seeing higher case numbers in our younger age cohorts now, but they're very under-represented at the other end, which is around hospitalisation and so on. (Media Conference, March 2nd 2022)

Although children's risk can both be low enough to justify open schools and high enough that they benefit from a vaccinated adult population, the rhetorical contradiction in shifting children's positioning from vulnerable to resilient suggests these images of children are being used to *do work* on behalf of the government. Indeed, when the paediatric vaccine was introduced in January 2022,

---

[2] Largely due to histories of systemic racism and inequitable health care.

children were again repositioned to promote public calming, this time through emphasising parental rights and choice:

> Look, I want to be absolutely clear about one thing—which you'll note I put in the statement—we will not be making it mandatory for young people to be vaccinated. This will ultimately be a choice for their parents. It's a choice that I strongly encourage parents to take. (Chris Hipkins, Media Conference, December 21st, 2021)

The paediatric vaccine's un-mandated status reflected an uneasy relationship between children and the State, where consecutive governments had reallocated responsibility for children's welfare to adult caregivers through a framework of parental rights (Angus, 2000). While public backlash to lockdowns and vaccination mandates was growing, culminating in a three-week occupation of Parliament grounds, the government attempted to placate unrest by firmly positioning children under the parental authority. Meanwhile, children's perspectives were notably absent. As social scientists of childhood have suggested, control of the young often stands in for maintenance of the social order, rendering the child's 'best interests' secondary to the rights of certain adults to decide (Bessant, 2021; Lee, 2001). Indeed, four months after the paediatric vaccine became available, only 25% of eligible 5–11 year olds had been fully vaccinated (Ternouth, 2022); consequently, the highest number of cases in New Zealand's first wave were in the 10–19 year old age group (Martin and Xia, 2022).

Visibilising Children's Perspectives

'How did you feel about lockdown?' asked nine-year-old Ananya in my Zoom screen. We had just finished her mind-map and she was waiting for me to clear the screen for her comic-making. She continued, 'How did you feel when you just came to New Zealand and like, imagine you just coming straight to New Zealand on a plane, and then when you, when you, when you go outside, you see people talking, you see some people coughing and you – how would you feel? Would you feel like worried? What would you feel?'

'I mean mostly I was afraid that the US wasn't taking it very seriously', I replied. I had opened our conversation by showing her my own comic, which featured my relocation between countries. Now, I described my fear in those days when I saw case numbers doubling. 'What was it like for you?'

'I wouldn't like to go to America if it doesn't take stuff seriously', Ananya responded.

It was unusual for children to ask me so directly about my experiences. I was a stranger to most, and they tended to maintain the polite boundaries that social custom demanded when an adult authority spoke with children. Ananya, however, made explicit what I observed in many other children's stories – a deep interest and attunement to the affective state of the others in their world. Indeed, the comic Ananya produced, drawn rapidly on the screen in front of me, told a story underpinned by emotive states (Fig. 6.2). In Ananya's world, it was not an

90   Julie Spray

Fig. 6.2.   Ananya's Comic.

adult mediator who broke the news of COVID-19 to children via highly managed government communications, but another child in her class. Not even the teacher had known, and in Ananya's telling: 'once [the boy] finished he looked at all of us, like, really he just stared at all of us, and then we all had a big gigantic gasp'. After drawing the boy's announcement, Ananya represented their collective shock and worry – 'my whole class's feelings merged together' – through an emoji.

Ananya's comic suggests children's affective experiences look very different from how they are represented in political – and public health – discourse. Children's ability to attune to others' affective states is often described in popular discourse as potentially harmful. Early in the pandemic, for example, an article by celebrity microbiologist Siouxsie Wiles (2020) advised parents, 'Don't talk to your kids if you are feeling anxious or fearful. They will pick up on your anxiety and that will make them anxious'. Such advice underestimates children's ability to discern when parents are concealing their emotions, an oversight which can, as anthropologists have documented, create relations of silence and mutual pretence (Bluebond-Langner, 1978; Hunleth, 2017). As Ananya demonstrated, children are humans with empathy, capable of inferring emotional state simply through imagining another's position – the worry one might feel emerging from a plane into a land where people coughed freely.

Moreover, the ability to discern the emotional states of the people around them is critically important to children's survival. As Jean Hunleth (2017) writes, children's structural vulnerability renders them highly dependent on adults for economic support, but children are not passive recipients in this exchange. Zambian children positioned themselves as important givers of affective and other forms of care, making themselves indispensable to the adults who protected them. New Zealand children,

Fig. 6.3.　Fifi's Comic.

too, often responded to the pandemic's upheaval by attuning to the emotional needs of the adults they depended upon. This was particularly noticeable among children of essential workers; nine-year-old Poprocks described how he observed his mother was stressed when she would stay only half the normal time at the gym. He cared for her by singing her a lullaby. Ten-year-old Fifi depicted herself hugging her mother when she arrived home, telling her 'I love you. Don't worry. It's going to be okay'. (Fig. 6.3). Children also described adjusting their own needs and behaviour to support the emotional distress of the adults in their lives. For example, 10-year-old Secret Sloth drew an image of herself alone at the table, refraining from asking her parents for help with her schoolwork because she detected their stress and frustration.

Like many other children's, Fifi and Ananya's comics also show other forms of children's public engagement and care beyond the affective.[3] Both depict engaging with health information (Ananya represents the news with the national flag, reflecting the iconography of Arden's podium). Both feature their participation in public health measures, including lockdowns (symbolically represented by Ananya as jail bars), and hand-washing, masking and vaccination (Fifi). Contrary to the government's representation of children as objects under parental authority, children often represented themselves engaging in these behaviours independently or even influencing or instructing adults. Nine-year-old McKenzy's comic narrative of her experience with vaccinations implicitly critiques the extended vulnerabilising of children created by the lengthy delays to the paediatric

---

[3] All children's comics can be viewed in an online gallery: https://juliespray.com/pandemic-generation/pandemic-generation-comic-gallery/

92   *Julie Spray*

Fig. 6.4.   McKenzy's Comic.

vaccine in the name of protection (Fig. 6.4). She provides support while her mother is vaccinated, watches jealously as her older brother receives his, until finally it is her turn. Subverting the narrative that children's vaccinations were entirely a matter of parental choice, it is she who convinces her mother. Whether or not these subversions are enhanced as narrative devices in a genre that makes protagonists into agentive heroes of their own destinies, children clearly could see themselves, at least sometimes, as active participants in public health. And, while children were not addressed as political subjects, they engaged in political commentary and action, hearing and responding to Ardern's plea for compassion and care, including her figure in their drawings of the news, and role-playing Ardern in imaginary media conferences.

Finally, children's comics suggest what reducing children to affective objects obscures about their emotional experiences. In a culture where children's feelings, often refracted through developmental models, are rendered inchoate and simple, children represented a complex array of emotional states and ambivalences, including guilt, worry, boredom, joy, disappointment, fun, anxiety and loneliness. In particular, many children like Fifi drew their sadness from the disruptions to their friendships. They drew their efforts to maintain friendship connections and care, including digital correspondences and dropping notes or gifts to friends' homes. This aspect of children's experience, the rupture to their carefully cultivated social support networks, was rarely mentioned in adult public discourse except for occasional references to children's 'social development' which positioned children's friendships as training grounds for the future adult rather than, as adult relationships are, critical to thriving in the present.

Conclusion

In fairness, Ardern and her government deployed children's images towards protecting public health, and children are served when their parents and communities are cared for. This is not always the case when adults invoke the need to 'protect' children. Yet even when children's objectification arguably serves a public good, it cannot be good for children to be erased as subjects. Already systematically excluded from political voice, children have few opportunities to supplement or challenge their objectification with multi-dimensional and nuanced representations of their perspectives. When they can represent themselves, children demonstrate they are not paper cut-outs passively waiting for care and instructions from parents, shielded from the adult world and feelings. Children know and use their capacities to infer and shift the affective states of others; they influence and enact health practices. But because their political representation was only as affective objects, not as citizen-subjects, their needs and priorities were not represented to those who had power to address them. Children's real emotional experiences were relegated to the private responsibility of parents, as politically expedient for a government that prioritises the interests of eligible, adult voters.

References

Ahmed, S. 2004. *The Cultural Politics of Emotion*, Edinburgh, University Press.
Alanen, L. 2011. Editorial: critical childhood studies?. *Childhood*, 18(2), 147–150. https://doi.org/10.1177/0907568211404511
Alwan, N.A., 2021. We must call out childism in COVID-19 policies. *BMJ* 375 (October), n2641. https://doi.org/10.1136/bmj.n2641
Angus, J. 2000. The code of social and family responsibility as a family policy initiative. In *Another New Zealand experiment: A code of social and family responsibility*, Eds J.A. Davey, N.Z. Wellington, Institute of Policy Studies.
Bessant, J. 2021. *Making Up People: Youth, Truth and Politics*, London, Routledge.
Bluebond-Langner, M. 1978. *The Private Worlds of Dying Children*, Princeton, NJ, Princeton University Press.
Burman, E. 1994. Innocents abroad: western fantasies of childhood and the iconography of emergencies. *Disasters*, 18(3), 238–253. https://doi.org/10.1111/j.1467-7717.1994.tb00310.x
Cohen, E.F. 2005. Neither seen nor heard: children's citizenship in contemporary democracies. *Citizenship Studies*, 9(2), 221–240. https://doi.org/10.1080/13621020500069687

Gilray, C. 2021. Performative control and rhetoric in Aotearoa New Zealand's response to COVID-19. *Frontiers in Political Science*, 86.

Goode, E. and Ben-Yehuda, N. 1994. *Moral Panics: The Social Construction of Deviance*, Oxford, UK, Blackwell.

Hacking, I. 1986. Making up people. In *Reconstructing Individualism: Autonomy, Individuality, and the Self in Western Thought*, Eds T. Heller, C. Wellbery, pp. 222–236, Stanford, Stanford University Press.

Hunleth, J. 2017. *Children as Caregivers: The Global Fight against Tuberculosis and HIV in Zambia*, New Brunswick, NJ, Rutgers University Press.

James, A. and Prout, A. 1990. *Constructing and Reconstructing Childhood: Contemporary Issues in the Sociological Study of Childhood*, London; New York, Falmer Press.

Lee, N. 2001. *Childhood and Society*, Buckingham, Open University Press.

Lomax, H., Smith, K., McEvoy, J., Brickwood, E., Jensen, K. and Walsh, B. 2022. Creating online participatory research spaces: insights from creative, digitally-mediated research with children during the COVID-19 pandemic. *Families, Relationships and Societies*, 11(1), 19–37. https://doi.org/10.1332/204674321X16274828934070

Lupton, D. 2013. Risk and emotion: towards an alternative theoretical perspective. *Health, Risk & Society*, 15(8), 634–647. https://doi.org/10.1080/13698575.2013.848847

Martin, H. and Xia, L. February 8, 2022. COVID-19: most of New Zealand's Omicron cases are in young people. *Stuff*. Retrieved from: https://www.stuff.co.nz/national/health/coronavirus/300512669/covid19-most-of-new-zealands-omicron-cases-are-in-young-people

Ministry of Health. 2021. History of the COVID-19 alert system. Unite against COVID-19. https://covid19.govt.nz/about-our-covid-19-response/history-of-the-covid-19-alert-system/

Press Conference April 21, 2020. Retrieved from: https://www.beehive.govt.nz/sites/default/files/2020-04/2104%20Joint%20Min%20of%20Ed%20and%20DG%20Daily%20Covid-19%20Press%20Conference%20.pdf

Salmon, A. 2004. "It takes a community": constructing aboriginal mothers and children with FAS/FAE as objects of moral panic in/through a FAS/FAE prevention. *Journal of the Motherhood Initiative for Research and Community Involvement*.

Spray, J. 2020. Towards a child-centred public health: lessons from rheumatic fever prevention in Aotearoa New Zealand. *Children & Society*, 34(6), 552–566. https://doi.org/10.1111/chso.12389

Spray, J. 2021. Drawing perspectives together: what happens when researchers draw with children? *Visual Anthropology Review*, 37(2), 356–379. https://doi.org/10.1111/var.12244

Spray, J. 2022. Disruption in bio-psycho-social context: children's perceptions of the COVID-19 pandemic in Aotearoa New Zealand. *Anthropological Forum*, 32(4), 325–350. https://doi.org/10.1080/00664677.2022.2113501

Spray, J. 2023. Re-childing the COVID-19 pandemic; and what we lose from the un-childed public. *Anthropology and Humanism*, 48(1), 88–100. https://doi.org/10.1111/anhu.12426

Spray, J. and Hunleth, J. 2020. Where have all the children gone? Against children's invisibility in the COVID-19 pandemic. *Anthropology Now*, 12(2), 39–52. https://doi.org/10.1080/19428200.2020.1824856

Spray, J. and Samaniego, S. 2023. The public-in-waiting: children's representation and inclusion in Aotearoa New Zealand's COVID-19 public health response. *Critical Public Health*. https://doi.org/10.1080/09581596.2023.2227334

Ternouth, L. May 6, 2022. Children eligible but less than a quarter fully vaccinated for covid. *RNZ*. Retrieved from: https://www.rnz.co.nz/national/programmes/checkpoint/audio/2018840916/children-eligible-but-less-than-a-quarter-fully-vaccinated-for-covid

Trnka, S. 2020. From lockdown to Rāhui and teddy bears in windows: initial responses to COVID-19 in Aotearoa/New Zealand. *Anthropology Today*, 36(5), 11–13. https://doi.org/10.1111/1467-8322.12603

Trnka, S. and Davies, S.G. 2020. COVID-19, New Zealand's bubble metaphor, and the limits of households as sites of responsibility and care. In *COVID-19: Volume I: Global Pandemic, Societal Responses, Ideological Solutions*, Ed J. Michael Ryan, pp. 167–183, Oxon; New York, Routledge.

Valentine, G. 2004. *Public space and the culture of childhood*, London, Routledge. https://doi.org/10.4324/9781315245638

Wiles, S. March 3, 2020. COVID-19 and kids: how to talk to children about the coronavirus. *The Spinoff*. Retrieved from: https://thespinoff.co.nz/society/03-03-2020/COVID-19-and-kids-how-to-talk-to-children-about-the-coronavirus

Zelizer, V. 1985. *Pricing the Priceless Child*, Princeton, NJ, Princeton University Press.

Chapter 7

We Were the Only Ones Still Seeing Families, We Just had to Be Creative About How! A Reflection on Health Visiting Practice During the COVID-19 Pandemic

Frances Gunn

University of Stirling, UK

Abstract

This practitioner chapter is a reflection on how health visitors (HVs) working in a health and social care partnership (HSCP) in Scotland worked safely and innovatively throughout the COVID-19 pandemic to build and sustain professional relationships with families and uphold children's rights, continuing to empower and support families despite the necessary restrictions. HVs shared their lived experiences of working through the pandemic in a variety of ways including contributing to data collection for the author's PhD research and through reflective discussion. All quotes within this reflection are anonymised.

Keywords: Family centred; health visiting; relationships; rights-based care; universal health visiting pathway

Introduction

In Scotland, our Childrens Services policy ethos is shifting tangibly towards emphases on relationships and rights. The aim of our 'Getting It Right For Every Child' (GIRFEC) (Scottish Government, 2015a, 2015b) framework for professionals is clearly noted in the name. GIRFEC is underpinned by the commitment and progress Scotland has made to incorporating the United Nations Convention on the Rights of the Child (UNCRC) (1989) into law, meaning that children's rights are embedded across policy and practice.

In Scotland, Health Visiting practice is underpinned by the Universal Health Visiting Pathway (UHVP) (Scottish Government, 2015a, 2015b), which outlines the enhanced role of the HV in Scotland. The UHVP comprises 11 home visits offered between 32 weeks gestation and the transition to school. This is the minimum care standard offered to families allocated a core health plan indicator i.e. no known health, developmental or social issues. For families where additional need, vulnerability or risk is identified, an additional health plan indicator is allocated and additional assessment and support by the HV and wider services is offered. As a universal service, HVs are 'uniquely positioned to improve outcomes for children and families' (Scottish Government, 2021, p. 3). The overarching aim of the UHVP is the development of a trusting HV–family relationship, which empowers families to engage with health promotion and education, improving outcomes and reducing inequalities. The investment in building meaningful professional relationships enables a robust platform for health promotion, assessment of need and supportive intervention when indicated.

Given the strongly embedded focus on relationship-based working throughout HV practice, the COVID-19 pandemic, and mandates to isolate were hugely challenging for HVs, with one HV reflecting that the changes in how we worked during the pandemic felt completely alien. The pandemic was intensely frightening and the announcement of the first lockdown led to much uncertainty and fear. This was partly because there was no tried and tested evidence base supporting actions to prevent the virus spreading and minimising potential harm. In later periods of restrictions however, while feelings of fear and uncertainty remained, there was a sense that the focus of these shifted, possibly due to a degree of cognitive dissonance noted by some HV's. We were very aware of the robust evidence base on the impact of social isolation and the emerging concerns around the impact of reduced visibility of children who were at risk of harm within their homes. This resulted in worry and fear focussing on both the unintended consequences of lockdown and restrictions, as well as the virus itself. We were aware of the need to keep people safe from increased risk of spread of the virus; however, we were also keenly aware of the risks to children and families from staying away. This resulted in an uncomfortable foundation for HV practice.

Despite the challenges and isolation associated with the pandemic, in Scotland policymakers and researchers responded quickly with guidance to keep the health and social care force connected despite the mandated distance. National clinical guidance for community nursing was published, underpinned by legislation via the Coronavirus (Scotland) Bill and Subsequently Act (Coronavirus (Scotland) Act, 2020), which made specific provisions for childcare, protection and justice. Child Protection Committees Scotland published weekly 'Keeping Connected' newsletters and research-based organisations including Institute of Research in Social Sciences (IRISS) published guidance to support social workers working through the pandemic (Dominelli, 2020) and the Centre for Excellence for Children's Care and Protection (CELCIS) quickly created a microsite collating developing research and practice updates on caring for vulnerable children during the pandemic. These resulted in a sense of attempting to make sense of the unknown which was helpful for practitioners including HVs.

Developing knowledge of the impact of the pandemic motivated HVs to work safely around the restrictions to provide care in innovative and creative ways which was a genuine privilege to witness. I worked with the HV teams at that start of the pandemic as their Child Protection Advisor and latterly as their Service Manager, so I had an oversight around how they were working to support families. Some examples of exemplary innovative HV practice during the pandemic will now be considered, with reflection on underpinning policy and research.

In March 2020 at the start of the pandemic, the emerging research and policy around violence against women and girls (VAWG) highlighted concerns around potential increase in domestic abuse. An unintended consequence of lockdown was that for those subject to abuse within their homes, there was a cumulative effect of both being isolated with the perpetrator and significantly reduced opportunity to benefit from external supports (VAWG Helpdesk, 2020) resulting in increased risk and trauma for victims. In response to this, the Scottish Government increased funding to local authorities to support the increasing levels of gender-based violence (Scotland Government, 2020). Within her HV practice, Alice became aware of Clara, a service user who was subject to domestic abuse within her home during lockdown. Clara's baby Cameron was also at risk of harm from exposure to the domestic abuse. While safely working within the sphere of the restrictions on home visiting, Alice sought opportunities to continue to build a professional relationship with Clara aiming to enable her to talk safely about her experiences, so that supports to reduce risk and mitigate trauma could be considered. Alice facilitated walks in a local park with Clara and Cameron so that HV care and support could be offered safely while adhering to social distancing requirements. This is a wonderful example of how HV's in North Ayrshire achieved the NMC standard of prioritising people (NMC, 2023) during the challenging circumstances of the pandemic.

Part of the HV role is signposting families to community services and initiatives to foster and build natural friendships and support systems. There is a clear understanding of the importance of the first 1001 days in establishing the foundations of healthy child physical, social and emotional development and the key role of establishing supportive networks (Parkes and Sweeting, 2018). During the pandemic, Scotland was subject to restrictions more stringent and longer in duration than other parts of the UK, meaning that these natural supports ceased to exist for prolonged periods of time. Suddenly, families with no pre-existing vulnerabilities became isolated and were navigating the transition to parenthood alone. The babies in lockdown study (Saunders and Hill, 2020) had 5474 participants from across the UK, and the findings highlighted the impact of reduced home visiting on families. 68% of participants reported their ability to cope with pregnancy or parenthood was affected by the pandemic, and 61% reported significant concerns around their mental health. Echoing these data, HVs across the service noted a rise in anxiety in new mothers related to the necessary isolation during periods of lockdown and restrictions and they felt that this increased the need for professional supports. The restrictions on home visiting allowed for home visits utilising safety measures when concerns around mental health or emotional well-being were noted.

HV Shona shared that families appreciated HVs visits, as their natural network of supports was significantly reduced leaving families feeling unable to access the reassurance and support that Young et al. (2019) suggest supports the transition to parenthood and builds confidence in parenting.

In an attempt to bridge the gaps, the restrictions necessitated, the virtual platform Near Me was implemented so that developmental assessments could be completed virtually. Shona reflected on what became a common practice during lockdowns. HVs carried out the developmental assessment or review virtually and then followed up by dropping off resources like vitamins or health promotion information or Bookbug bags (Scotland's national programme of free books to promote development of language, social skills and emotional well-being) or Childsmile (Scotland's national programme to improve oral health and reduce inequalities in dental health) products. This allowed them to safely have face to face contact with families outside while adhering to social distancing. This allowed HVs to continue to offer space for parents to share sensitive concerns that they may not have felt able to share virtually and supported holistic assessment of health, development and well-being. Home visits utilising personal protective equipment (PPE) continued to some families following an additional HPI and Shona reflected that: 'this felt right as prior to the pandemic we had worked really closely with some families and walked with them in times of crisis, so during the pandemic, some families really valued having us still visit to offer support and advice. Like a bit of a constant amidst all the uncertainty'.

Shona reflected on the HV role in being a point of contact with up-to-date information about community hubs and services which felt like a natural continuation of the named person function of HVs in Scotland which GIRFEC outlines as being a single point of contact and information for children and families (Scottish Government, 2022). For families navigating the changing goalposts around restrictions, the HV was a welcome point of contact. Shona received this feedback: 'It was actually really nice the way she said it. I don't know what to do, but I know who will know – the Health Visitor!'

Alice was aware of a family having infant feeding challenges and worrying about their baby's growth trajectory, but struggling to balance these concerns with the increased risk of transmission associated with a HV home visit. To compromise, Alice offered virtual support but obviously this could not facilitate physical review of the baby. Alice offered to visit and review the baby outside. She recalls: 'I actually had to weigh the newborn baby in a back garden and measure length on a changing mat outside, which was quite an experience!' She was pleased with the outcome which served to both reassure and empower the family. Alice further reflected on the increased stress associated with worry about increased possibility of transmission of the virus to her own family due to having more contact with others than most people had during the pandemic. This coupled with the challenges of trying to home educate and juggle working commitments resulted in increased stress and tension for HVs to manage alongside coping with the new challenges associated with attempts to work differently.

Conclusion

Health visiting was one of the few community health services that continues to operate unchanged during the pandemic, which resulted in a sense of increased pressure on staff who felt the pressure of increased expectation from families. This may have been driven by the HV role in searching for health needs (NMC, 2022), and during the pandemic, where need was identified, there were far fewer resources available to meet those needs and the concept of identifying need and leaving it was difficult for HVs. This further inspired and drove HV creativity in working with and for families during the pandemic.

HV Lucy concluded: 'Mums were still having babies, families were still becoming new families, and things like feeding challenges continued despite the pandemic.' HVs had a privileged position during periods of lockdown, due to the importance of our role, we were able to work to continue to support families during times of extreme challenge and crisis. These reflections suggest that our effort yielded positive results in improving outcomes for children. The effort and creativity shown by HVs resulted in increased trust in the HV service, and anecdotally, it is reported that some families are now more likely to be proactive in both contacting the HV and valuing the service. Alice reflected that the work of HVs during the pandemic cemented countless relationships. This is a meaningful legacy of the hard work and dedication demonstrated during the pandemic.

References

Centre for Excellence in Children's Care and Protection 2020. *COVID19 Knowledge Bank*. Available online: https://www.celcis.org/knowledge-bank/covid-19. (Accessed 1 September 2023)

Coronavirus (Scotland) Act 2020. asp 7. Available online: https://www.legislation.gov.uk/asp/2020/7/contents. (Accessed 28 August 2023)

Dominelli, L. 2020. *Guidance for Social Workers During the COVID Pandemic*. Available online: https://www.iriss.org.uk/news/features/2020/03/25/guidelines-social-workers-during-covid-19-pandemic. (Accessed 1 August 2023)

Nursing and Midwifery Council 2022. *Standards of Proficiency for Specialist Community Public Health Nurses*. Available online: https://www.nmc.org.uk/globalassets/sitedocuments/standards/post-reg-standards/nmc_standards_of_proficiency_for_specialist_community_public_health_nurses_scphn.pdf. (Accessed 1 September 2023)

Nursing and Midwifery Council 2023. *The Code: Professional Standards of Practice and Behaviour for Nurses, Midwives and Nursing Associates*. Available online: https://www.nmc.org.uk/standards/code. (Accessed 27 August 2023)

Parkes, A. and Sweeting, H., 2018. Direct, indirect, and buffering effects of support for mothers on children's socioemotional adjustment. *Journal of Family Psychology* 32 (7), 894.

Saunders, B. and Hill, S. 2020. *Babies in Lockdown: Listening to Parents to Build Back Better. Best Beginnings, Home-Start UK, and the Parent-Infant Foundation.* Available online: Babies-in-Lockdown-Main-Report-FINAL-VERSION.pdf. (Accessed 20 July 2023).

Scottish Government 2015a. *Getting It Right for Every Child (GIRFEC).* Available online: https://www.gov.scot/policies/girfec/. (Accessed 18 July 2023)

Scottish Government 2015b. *Universal Health Visiting Pathway in Scotland: Pre-birth to Pre-school.* Available online: https://www.gov.scot/publications/universal-health-visiting-pathway-scotland-pre-birth-pre-school/. (Accessed 18 July 2023)

Scottish Government 2020. *Support for Victims of Domestic Violence During the COVID-19 Outbreak.* Retrieved from: www.gov.scot. (Accessed 2 September 2023).

Scottish Government 2021. *Universal Health Visiting Pathway Evaluation - Phase 1: Main Report - Primary Research with Health Visitors and Parents and Case Note Review.* Available online: https://www.gov.scot/publications/evaluation-universal-health-visiting-pathway-scotland-phase-1-main-report-primary-research-health-visitors-parents-case-note-review/. (Accessed 1 August 2023)

Scottish Government 2022. *Getting it Right for Every Child (GIRFEC): Policy Statement.* Available online: https://www.gov.scot/publications/getting-right-child-girfec-policy-statement/pages/2/. (Accessed 1 September 2023)

UNICEF UK 1989. *The United Nations Convention on the Rights of the Child.* Available online: https://downloads.unicef.org.uk/wp-content/uploads/2010/05/UNCRC_PRESS200910web.pdf?_ga=2.78590034.795419542.1582474737-1972578648.1582474737. (Accessed 3 August 2023)

Violence Against Women and Children Helpdesk 2020. *Evidence on How the Covid-19 Pandemic Might Impact on Violence Against Women and Girls.* Available online: https://www.sddirect.org.uk/resource/query-284-impact-covid-19-pandemic-violence-against-women-and-girls. (Accessed 1 September 2023)

Young, C., Roberts, R. and Ward, L. 2019. Application of resilience theories in the transition to parenthood: a scoping review. *Journal of Reproductive and Infant Psychology*, 37(2), 139–160.

Section 3

Parents as Subjects and Recipients of Care

Chapter 8

A Simple Life? Parents' Early Narratives of Babies Raised During the COVID-19 Pandemic

Laura Bellussi and Siân Lucas

University of Stirling, Faculty of Social Sciences, Centre for Child Wellbeing and Protection, UK

Abstract

COVID-19 pandemic significantly impacted the nature of support available to new parents. Previously we conducted a study to explore parents' experiences of shifting to 'digitalised' caregiving specifically focussing on parents' access to online parenting groups. That study is re-examined in this chapter, presenting parents' narratives about their attempts to provide the best environment for their children while most of their face-to-face support networks were unavailable. The analysis aims to determine parents' constructions of the 'COVID baby', a term introduced by Brown (2021), although never defined in detail. Three themes were identified: 'Hopes and fears for the babies' future'; 'Peaceful and oblivious babies'; 'Babies as a perceived mirror of parents' abilities'. Parents in this study depicted a positive portrait in which babies thrived at home; however, they expressed worries about their children's future, as they lacked opportunities for development and socialisation usually offered by paid or unpaid group activities. To compensate, some parents engaged in extra labour at home in the face of home-made activities, inspired by previously attended group sessions. We argue that new parents, specifically mothers, are often pressured to display 'intensive mothering' to provide the best opportunities for development for their babies and fulfil gender and class expectations: such pressure leads to increased consumerism. Limitations of this approach have been emphasised by the simpler life that the lockdown forced on them, with apparent benefits to the babies' well-being. On the other hand, the need for new parents to be connected to nurturing networks of support remains essential.

Keywords: Caregiving; digital parenting; display work; feminism; new parents; postnatal support

Introduction

Ties between the individual and the social are particularly evident when we consider the concept of parenthood. The classic literature around gender, care and work offers us perspectives on how to understand why parenthood, and particularly motherhood, has been historically and still is an issue affected by inequality. Both John Stuart Mill and Karl Marx acknowledged the fundamental role of households in sustaining the daily and generational productivity of the labour force, even if it's debatable whether there was an adequate recognition of gender dynamics in Marx's theory, and, Elson (1998) contended that the absence of recognition for domestic structures in societal understanding consistently hindered the advancement of women's rights and gender equality (Brown, 2013). This invisibility of domestic life significantly restricted women's participation in economic and political spheres more than it did for men, thereby impacting their agency and opportunities. Women's unpaid work of childcare and household maintenance, defined as 'the second shift' by Hochschild (1989), is still a burden that stalls the revolution towards gender equality, due to the disempowering effect of macro-level policies, family and work institutions, and personal experiences of gender, intimacy and moral commitments (Blair-Loy et al., 2015; Hochschild and Machung, 2012).

Chodorow (1978) explored women's motherhood in her pivotal work, 'The Reproduction of Mothering', discussing how this role transcends generations within the sexual division of labour. She sought, akin to many feminists of the 1970s, to grasp the complexities behind the enduring nature of traditional heterosexual parenting and gendered subjectivity, her inquiry pondering why many women not only desired to have children but also aspired to exclusively take on the role of mothering (Heenan, 2002). Hochschild (2022) posited that women, historically socialised to be adept at managing emotions in private spheres, have commodified emotional labour more than men, comprehending its personal toll. She contends that individuals from lower and working classes typically engage more with tangible goods, while those from middle and upper classes tend to focus on interpersonal interactions; given this, a larger proportion of working women compared to men find themselves in roles involving human interaction, revealing distinct gender and class dynamics in the commercial utilisation of emotional capacities – although there has been a shift in modern times towards increased paternal input in childrearing (Hochschild, 2022).

At the juncture of class and gender, it could be argued that the enduring sentiment of heightened responsibility and consequent feelings of inadequacy as a mother persist across generations, shaping maternal behaviours, expectations and their public presentation. Traditionally, motherhood has been constructed as a concealed, private and domestic experience, confined to the home (Federici, 2012; Thompson and Walker, 1989; Yoshida, 2012). However, contemporary practices of mothering came to encompass both 'private' and 'public' dimensions, with a collective dimension manifesting in public spaces such as shopping centres, cafes and internet forums (Turner and Norwood, 2013; Säilävaara, 2016). These public displays often emphasise intensive care as a marker of 'good' motherhood (De Benedictis and Orgad, 2017). The reliance on digital technologies for parenting practices during the pandemic arguably brought further scrutiny to parents' display work, as this chapter will explore.

The erosion of collective support and elevated consumption expectations have intensified the burden of social reproduction, predominantly borne by women as mothers (Anderson and Moore, 2014; Rich, 2021). Examining the privileged perspective further exposes the normalisation of structural inequalities. Class dynamics are present in narratives concerning economic mobility and women's labour; some privileged women commodify their mothering practices into personal brands, presenting themselves as 'business models' of ideal motherhood, while others transfer privilege to their children through consumption choices aimed at fostering mobility (Demo et al., 2015).

Lockdown measures during the COVID-19 pandemic further influenced the landscape of caregiving and parenting, particularly the transition to parenthood – and particularly motherhood (Dib et al., 2020; Reid, 2020; Xue and McMunn, 2021). The impact of the COVID-19 pandemic extends beyond the experience of parenthood, significantly affecting perinatal care with potential consequences on babies' well-being: in the UK, data analysed by Brown in her comprehensive review of the literature called 'COVID Babies' (2021) reveals the substantial disruption to essential healthcare access – caused, according to Brown, by media scaremongering more than the actual risk posed by COVID-19. Lockdown impacted maternal moods and experiences, causing distress in many women and emphasising the need for more consistent in-person support, as highlighted in several studies (Dib et al., 2020; Dickerson et al., 2022; Vazquez-Vazquez et al., 2021). Many birth experiences became traumatic, marked by loneliness, partner separation, mask-wearing and discouragement or lack of support for breast-feeding, leading to a lack of bonding opportunities with the baby and potential health hazards (Brown, 2021; Costantini et al., 2021). Furthermore, the disruption of the continuum of care and healthcare consistency raised questions about the actual risk of COVID-19 infection versus the risks to parents' and babies' health and well-being when World Health Organisation guidelines were not adhered to, such as, the need to prioritise breastfeeding and mother-baby bonding (Brown, 2021).

During the pandemic and all over the world, access to community spaces, both formal and informal, was severely curtailed, dismantling fundamental support systems for new parents, with relevant negative impacts on their mental health (Dickerson et al., 2022; Fallon et al., 2021; Vazquez-Vazquez et al., 2021). The shift to 'digitalised' caregiving altered the caregiving landscape, prompting parents to adapt their home environments to this new reality. Online spaces played a pivotal role in the caregiving transformation, fostering reflections about technology and children's rights, as babies were constantly recorded while unable to provide their consent for it. According to Brown (2021), whereas many parents felt lonely and disoriented, babies arguably thrived by spending more time bonding with their parents, provided their basic needs were met; nevertheless, their behaviour was influenced by the atmosphere at home, which had a significant impact on their mood and receptiveness (Brown, 2021).

Amidst the pandemic, mothers faced increased pressure and an amplified sense of responsibility for their infants, as they lost access to usual networks of support and education and health professionals (Gray and Barnett, 2022; Emmott et al., 2023). However, further research revealed that many mothers endeavoured to reshape conversations about gender norms and the intense demands of parenting: their efforts challenged conventional notions of 'good mothering' and promoted more compassionate discussions in online fora, where most peer support happened during the lockdown (Bailey, 2022; Handley, 2023). While gender disparities in caregiving persisted during the lockdown, studies indicate that wherever there was a more equitable distribution of household responsibilities, that was linked to improved mental health outcomes for mothers (Dib et al., 2020; Reid, 2020; Xue and McMunn, 2021).

Methodology

In this chapter, we explore how parents adapted to the digital transition during the pandemic and how it changed their conceptualisation of themselves and their babies, as they discuss their experiences of managing anxieties, social expectations and caring responsibilities. In 2020, our study sought to explore the shift from community caregiving to digitalised community caregiving by examining narratives from new parents accessing online support groups (Lucas and Bellussi, 2023). We re-examined data from this study to shed light on parents' concerns and hopes as they navigated an unprecedented period, while striving to create the best environment for their children.

We gained ethical approval from the University of Stirling's Ethics Committee in April 2020 and recruited participants by posting adverts on social media, between May and June 2020; at this point, it was the first lockdown in the United Kingdom with 'stay-at-home' instructions given by the government. Out of 20 initial responses, 13 mothers and one father were interviewed remotely, after providing consent. Interviews lasted around 1 hour and were carried out by both authors. We transcribed and analysed interviews thematically using NVivo 12 following Braun and Clarke's (2006) theoretical framework. The programme OpenAI ChatGPT was used to check for grammar and language appropriateness at the writing stage (OpenAI, 2023). For the purpose of this chapter, we address the question: What are parents' hopes and concerns for their babies as they talk about attending online groups? Three themes have been identified: 'Hopes and fears for the babies' future'; 'Blissful and oblivious babies'; 'Babies as a perceived mirror of parents' abilities'. Pseudonyms have been used to protect the identity of the parents interviewed for this study.

Findings

We interviewed 13 mothers and one father. The participants' demographics reflected an average age of 33.9 years, with all responders being of White or White

British ethnicity, with household incomes surpassing £30,000 annually, averaging around £54,000; babies were aged 1–12 months at the time of the interview. Geographically, 12 participants lived in Scotland, while two lived in England. Interviews lasted up to 1 hour, exploring parents' experiences joining online groups and communities. Despite the limited diversity of the sample, likely due to participants' recruitment within networks known to the researchers, we acknowledged this limitation and aimed to enhance future sampling strategies.

Hopes and Fears for the Babies' Future

New parents were left with a sense of the unknown as they found it difficult to understand the impact of lockdown on their babies given their young age. Parents were concerned that their babies would miss out on opportunities for socialisation, and this could, in turn, affect their development.

> I want [the baby] to be quite sociable and be fine like meeting other people [...] I'm a bit worried about how long this lockdown's gonna go on for. (Jenny)

Mothers such as Jenny and Becca took their babies to online groups to foster their development, driven by concerns that not participating would hinder their child's growth. They were concerned that the level of stimulation at home was not sufficient, recognising the absence of various physical elements that their babies would experience at physical locations, such as different noises, lights and moving objects that typically contribute to a richer learning environment.

> I didnae want to make sure I was missing, you know an opportunity to help her wee brain. So again, I suppose there was a kind of a panic, like you know how is her development gonna be stunted because I'm not taking her to [group] on a Monday [slight laugh]. (Becca)

Online groups were welcome, but their effectiveness for babies was debatable, as parents struggled to make sense of their different reactions to screen time. Zoe shared with us that her child seemed engaged and happy during the online sessions, enjoying the colourful visuals and reacting positively to seeing other babies on screen. However, Jenny felt that her baby wasn't as engaged, only showing interest during specific moments, like when the teacher played music. Lily highlighted that her baby struggled with virtual interactions, attempting to interact physically with the laptop and becoming bored quickly. While some babies seemed to enjoy certain elements of the online sessions, others showed less interest or found it challenging to engage virtually.

> I was thinking is this worth it, 'cause he's not really getting anything, but I was still enjoying for the mum side, like getting to speak to everybody and having the chat. (Jenny)

Other parental worries about their babies included compromised immune responses and missed health checks from the dearth of social and professional contact. Hayley expressed concern about her baby missing developmental checks, considering them as valuable indicators of her child's progress, and Charlene shared that her baby, aged 8 weeks, had not undergone any checks, including an essential hearing assessment. Both mothers highlighted their worries about their babies missing crucial developmental assessments and tests. As will be highlighted in the following theme, some mothers worried about their babies growing up in unusual or unexpected ways.

> I don't know if [the development test] is gonna happen or not, but I'm assuming it even if it does happen, it might be over the phone rather than any physical meeting which is, which is a shame. [...] You know she's not been exposed to any other germs apart from just what we've got in our house. (Hayley)

Another important concern regarded the ability of children to distinguish between virtual spaces and reality, and becoming prematurely addicted to technology and screen time. Paul reflected on a recent conversation where he and his wife discussed their initial hopes of their newborn not becoming overly reliant on screens. However, within the first month, due to the lockdown circumstances, the only way their baby connected with their relatives was through screen time, mainly via phone or other digital devices. This sudden shift led Paul to recognise the unexpected reliance on screens for maintaining family connections, contrary to his initial intentions. There is evidence from further literature that online communication has been widely used as a strategy to achieve 'intimacy from afar' during the lockdown, striving to maintain close connections alive (Cascalheira et al., 2023; Lucas and Bellussi, 2023).

> Our kids are not going to be like totally dependent on screen'...and then within the first month, the only thing that they are seeing are their grandparents through screen time. (Paul)

On the other hand, parents also harboured hopes. For instance, they wished that hybrid methods of providing postnatal support would enhance long-term accessibility for new parents. Una expressed her aspiration for a substantial policy change that would enable parents to achieve a more balanced work-home life and wished for people to have more time to spend with their families. Una mentioned a study she read, indicating an increase in breastfeeding rates during lockdown: she attributed this rise to women not feeling compelled to constantly tidy their houses or attend various baby groups, allowing them more time and flexibility for breastfeeding. Some parents reflected on their experiences and transformed this into hopes for a post-pandemic setup in which they would maintain robust and close support networks.

> I think having spent this time in lockdown has made it more imperative to me how important it is to be together and have that support as we've had to become very much a family unit. (Maggie)

Peaceful and Oblivious Babies

As the previous findings illustrate, parents expressed hopes and fears about the impact of social distancing and reliance on digital technology on their babies. However, there was a further finding, about babies being oblivious to the challenging circumstances. Hayley expressed joy over her baby's well-being, emphasising the absence of health issues and describing her as a cheerful and talkative child with an emerging personality. Una remarked that the situation wasn't overly challenging for her, noting the baby's apparent resilience to the circumstances. Becca struggled with her transition from an active lifestyle to staying indoors but observed that her six-month-old displayed consistent behaviour; nonetheless, she expressed concerns about the potential lack of social interaction her baby might encounter in the future, due to the current situation.

> I found it really quite difficult, going from being out every day to not – sort of thing, but in terms of [the baby], she's, she seems absolutely fine. (Becca)

Parents enjoyed the increased bonding time with their children due to the higher availability of time at home, experiencing the joy of witnessing their development, to the point when they were apprehensive about returning to work, at the end of their parental leave, literally 'dreading' the end of this cherished time. Seeking ways to fill their days, parents created new play opportunities for their babies, such as daytime baths. Hayley expressed delight in the bonding between her partner and their baby, noting that this time allowed them to form a stronger connection which would not have been possible before lockdown. Rose highlighted the silver lining of having more family time during meals, mentioning that they could enjoy lunch together, which was not possible when her partner was at work; and Maggie emphasised the advantage of living near woods, allowing them to spend quality time outdoors daily, as she talked about her baby looking at the trees. There was a sense that these were cherished as magical, simple moments of bonding.

> We've got to know each other for the first time. (Hayley)

Some milestones of child development became seemingly slower, more private and intimate. Lily expressed her observations about her child's interactions, particularly noting how her baby engaged with the father and displayed efforts towards taking their first steps. She acknowledged the unique opportunity to closely observe her child's development, gaining insights as if she were, in her words, 'a child developmental psychologist'. On the other hand, Maggie shared her experience of spending prolonged periods simply observing and playing with her baby, believing it to be beneficial for her child: she found joy in witnessing her baby's evolving movements and improving dexterity, appreciating the opportunity to closely track these developmental milestones.

> I just kind of sit here for ages and just like keep playing and enjoying it and I think that's probably much better for her. [...] her dexterity is improving. (Maggie)

To some extent, the private nature of some of these milestones made some parents slightly unsettled. As a consequence of keeping their experience private or screened online only, they were concerned about not being able to compare their babies or show them to familiar or expert eyes, to be sure of what was considered to be 'normal' or not. Both Paul and Charlene articulated the challenges of remote interactions, with Paul highlighting the significance of in-person support to understand and address the baby's needs and behaviours, and Charlene expressing the desire to physically assess her child's growth compared to other infants, especially as their baby was born prematurely.

> And while it's like Zoom's fine, it's nice to see, oh the baby is smiling, the baby's moving or whatever...it is not the same as having your parents staying for the night and, and then seeing the baby crying. (Paul)

Some other milestones of 'normal' postnatal care were missed and grieved from the point of view of parents, as they expressed disappointment and longing. Jenny lamented the absence of the customary joy of displaying her baby to visitors and sharing those precious early moments with loved ones. Una voiced concern about her parents potentially missing significant moments in her baby's development, like witnessing first steps; Hayley conveyed a sense of loss, feeling deprived of the usual social connections and shared experiences that accompany maternity leave, yearning for outings and bonding moments with fellow mothers. However, she found solace in having her husband's support during this challenging period.

> ...[maternity leave is] meant to be an enjoyable time and you're not able to go and show off your baby and like people come to visit you and get your presents. (Jenny)

Only in a few cases, babies showed behaviours that were confusing to parents. Jenny shared her concerns about her baby's reactions during online interactions, noting that although he gazed at the screen due to the noises, he did not react visibly when her mother called his name while social distancing in the garden. She worried that this might affect his familiarity with relatives once the restrictions were lifted. Jenny hoped her baby would still recognise the voices of family members and friends and not be distant or uncomfortable around them when they were allowed to be physically closer. On the other hand, Lily expressed worry about her baby's behaviour and attachment, mentioning how her baby now 'associated Grandma with the phone'. She feared that this association might affect her baby's comfort in new environments like the nursery in the future, wondering if he would still adapt easily or potentially face challenges.

> It just makes me worried about him being strange. (Jenny)

Babies as a Perceived Mirror of Parents' Abilities

For some parents, there was a sense of nervousness that their babies would become unhealthy, or 'strange', or 'change their character', due to the effects of the pandemic and the lack of socialisation or stimulation, with recognition that their babies were indeed growing up 'differently' from other generations. Technology played a role in this alienating sensation, as babies grew up with a completely new relationship with screen time and virtual connections. It can be argued that the use of the term 'strange' might be connected to a fear that babies would grow up experiencing 'stranger anxiety', but the doubt remains (Bowlby, 1960). Not being able to compare their babies with other similarly aged babies while attending groups, was to some extent, a relief. Lily reflected on her experience before lockdown, as she struggled with comparing her baby's development with others and subsequently decided not to return to the classes. It is important not to adopt rose-tinted spectacles to in-person group activity attendance and, as Lily reminds us, attending groups can be a source of difficulty for some parents.

> All the [other] babies [in the class] [we]re sitting up… […] [my baby] couldn't sit up at that time. So he was lying on the floor. That to me was the ending point, like I was like: "I'm not coming back to this." (Lily)

The latter extract is particularly relevant, as it shows that there is evidence that some parents might withdraw from support at the time they might need it most, for fear of being judged, allegedly, of not being a 'good enough' parent (De Benedictis and Orgad, 2017; Hays, 1996). This might even prompt them to hide from the public eye altogether or fear this type of exposure intensely, as is evident in Charlene's words, with the potential for 'hiding' even greater during lockdown. Charlene expressed her anxiety about taking her baby out in public for the first time, as she hadn't experienced feeding her baby or dealing with his crying in a public setting yet. This lack of exposure to public outings left her uncertain about what essentials to pack in the baby's change bag because she hadn't encountered situations that would typically require these items outside the home. As such a sense of unfamiliarity and uncertainty added to Charlene's anxiety in transitioning from a new Covid-parent to a parent in the physical world, when the restrictions lifted.

> Another anxiety actually I have is I've never been out with [the baby] in public and so I've never like fed him in public. He's never cried in public. [...] I don't know what to pack in a change bag because I've never had to take him out. (Charlene)

Impression management is not only pertinent to public spaces, but it is a relevant issue in online environments, too, with parents fearing to show their living rooms on screen, or being wary of the insidious nature of social media that prompt people to compare themselves to others. Una reflected on the various barriers that prevent parents from participating in online activities, citing reasons like feeling self-conscious about their messy house, being judged about noisy children as well as the day-to-day juggle of responsibilities and social engagements. Hochschild's (1989) considerations of gender expectations and mothers' display work remain relevant to date.

> You don't even have to put clothes on you, just sit in in your [py]jamas, and yet people still can't make the groups, and I think it's telling about what we actually go through as stay-at-home parents or maternity leave parents. (Una)

Becca discussed her reasons for not using Facebook linked to the tendency for comparison that arises on social media, which can lead to feeling inadequate or uncomfortable. While recognising the challenges faced in managing impressions both online and offline, the findings of this study indicate that all parents perceived online support groups as welcoming and comfortable. Parents aimed to make these groups as reassuring as possible, offering feedback and suggestions for enhancement. Some parents noted that despite the potential benefits these groups could have for babies, particularly younger ones might not require extensive engagement with them, and this realisation made them question the necessity of joining these groups. However, parents still felt compelled to create a stimulating environment for their babies at home, similar to what they experienced in baby groups, leading to increased stress and pressure while confined with limited resources. Rose's sentiments captured this sense of frustration and helplessness.

> You know, you're working a lot harder and don't get as much out of it. [...] I can't really do all this stuff though, so we're not

> participating in the full activity as much. Because I haven't got the stuff or I don't have the time or the energy to do it. (Rose)

Claire shared her initial expectation of having to constantly engage in various activities and attend baby groups to stimulate her baby's development. However, due to the lockdown, she discovered that spending more time doing simple activities like 'tummy time' on the floor contributed to her baby's mobility progress. This realisation led her to believe in the significance of quality time with parents as crucial for a baby's development, equally if not more important than external stimuli from organised activities.

> I think that babies, their needs are just to be there with their mom and dad and they want to play and you know they don't want to be taken out doing things. (Claire)

Discussion

Parents made sense of their role and responsibility towards their babies without many reference markers or terms of comparison, to know if they were doing the 'right' thing or being 'good enough'. Their babies looked healthy; however, parents wanted validation and reassurance from professionals and other parents or family members. Parents' concerns for their babies' development and opportunities for socialisation were clear; however, this study unveiled how a proportion of their anxieties emerged from the role of this external gaze itself, or the way it was perceived to be, a tendency that seemed to be already existing and was 'digitalised' by the lockdown situation. Some parents were concerned about their parenting practices not being satisfactory, one of them tended to hide themselves or her baby because of perceived shame; some other parents were more open and able to share concerns for their or their children's health with friends, family or professionals, through the possibilities and limitations of online support.

Parents' usual support networks were consistently restricted during the pandemic, and mothers had to increase their labour at home to engage in activities that would have otherwise been reserved for other professions: from being receptive to any changes in the babies' health or behaviour, to entertaining them in activities normally reserved to class facilitators or play therapists. Such a situation seems to exacerbate the phenomenon that O'Brien Hallstein (2011) named 'now momism', described as the requirement for 'mothers to develop professional level skills, such as therapists, paediatricians, consumer product safety instructor, and teacher, in order to meet and treat the needs of their children'. In 2019, Lamb adopted feminist perspectives on the connections between gender and caregiving norms, and highlighted the challenging societal expectations that often unfairly blame mothers when anything goes wrong with their children. In this study, many mothers seemed to embody a sense of anxiety that their babies would grow up 'alien', especially as parents seemingly lost control of the circumstances that would normally enable them to, allegedly, enhance and steer their babies' development, due to the lockdown. Such circumstances included being able to take babies to classes and other opportunities for stimulation and socialisation.

It is arguable that, during lockdown, many mothers enjoyed their time at home as a protective cocoon to nurture their babies, and the babies referred to in this study were reported to thrive in this relatively low-intensity environment. On the other hand, the intensity and fatigue that parents experienced show the limitations of such an approach, which sees mothers (and fathers) providing continuous and 'intensive mothering' to their children while trying to cover all these roles by themselves (Hays, 1996). The pressure of expectations creates unrealistic models of what a standardised 'normal baby' should look like, and potentially takes away the pleasure of being a parent, while the risk of parental burnout is real and imminent in the absence of nurturing community-based support networks.

Transitioning to parenthood is a deeply transformative experience that has been defined as a metamorphosis – the name 'matrescence' was coined by the psychiatrists Sacks and Birndorf to define this highly impactful period, as similar to adolescence (Jones, 2023; Sacks and Birndorf, 2019). In this period of transformation, parents lack clear feedback from the baby on whether their actions are right or wrong, or good enough, and mostly rely on standardised milestones, and on what others define as right or wrong to assess their competence and consequently 'earn' their identity as parents. Participants in this study lacked opportunities for these moments of comparison.

There are considerations to make about social class, given the relatively high household income amongst the participants. It can be argued that social class defines parental involvement in their children's educational success from a very young age: in fact, obtaining access to parent/carer-baby classes might mark the beginning of a journey that seeks to provide children with 'the best opportunities', and how well babies respond to stimulation might be a marker to their success or failure in future life. The somewhat liminal spaces that the lockdown created, with increased reliance on technology and missed milestones, enhanced feelings of loss of control, with anxieties that babies might grow up non-conforming to a perceived standard. However, our study shows that some mothers saw the cracks in this unobtainable model, and expressed feelings of compassion towards other parents, emphasising the need for mothers to support each other and try not to judge, or feel judged; such findings are consistent with previous literature that showed how mothers started to rebel against traditional gender norms and unrealistic expectations of 'intensive mothering' during the pandemic, by sharing more compassionate, understanding definitions of what a good mother should be for their babies (Bailey, 2022; Handley, 2023).

Conclusion

In contemporary society, before and after lockdown, parents are seduced to consume and enrol their children in an increasing and varied number of groups, in order to maximise their children's development potential. In this study, the positive aspects of the pandemic were highlighted – there was less pressure and indeed options for parents to publicly socialise their babies, which for some parents led to their appreciation to just do the simple things. In conclusion, the need for socialisation, and, finally, of an empathetic and non-judgemental helpful community seems to be more urgent for parents, rather than for their babies.

References

Anderson, G. and Moore, J.G. 2014. "Doing it all… and making it look easy!": yummy mummies, mompreneurs and the North American neoliberal crises of the home. In *Mothering in the age of neoliberalism*, pp. 95-116, Demeter Press.

Bailey, L. 2022. Constructions of good mothering during lockdown learning. *Gender and Education* 34 (6), 674–689.

Blair-Loy, M., Hochschild, A., Pugh, A.J., Williams, J.C. and Hartmann, H. 2015. Stability and transformation in gender, work, and family: insights from the second shift for the next quarter century. *Community, Work & Family*, 18(4), 435–454.

Bowlby, J. 1960. Separation anxiety. *The International Journal of Psychoanalysis*, 41:1.

Braun, V. and Clarke, V. 2006. Using thematic analysis in psychology. *Qualitative Research in Psychology*, 3 (2), 77–101.

Brown, A. 2021. *Covid Babies: How Pandemic Health Measures Undermined Pregnancy, Birth and Early Parenting*, London, UK, Pinter & Martin.

Brown, H. 2013. *Marx on Gender and the Family: A Critical Study*, Haymarket.

Cascalheira, C.J., McCormack, M. and Wignall, L. 2023. Relationships, technology and the role of living arrangements during social lockdown related to COVID-19. *Families, Relationships and Societies*, pp. 1–19.

Chodorow, N. 1978. *The Reproduction of Mothering: Psychoanalysis and the Sociology of Gender*, Berkeley, CA, University of California Press.

Costantini, C., Joyce, A. and Britez, Y. 2021. Breastfeeding experiences during the COVID-19 lockdown in the United Kingdom: an exploratory study into maternal opinions and emotional states. *Journal of Human Lactation*, 37(4), 649–662.

De Benedictis, S. and Orgad, S. 2017. The escalating price of motherhood: aesthetic labour in popular representations of 'stay-at-home' mothers. In *Aesthetic Labour: Rethinking Beauty Politics in Neoliberalism*, pp. 101–116.

Demo, A.T., Borda, J.L., Kroløkke, C.H. (Eds.) 2015, *The Motherhood Business: Consumption, Communication, and Privilege*. University of Alabama Press.

Dib, S., Rougeaux, E., Vázquez-Vázquez, A., Wells, J. C. and Fewtrell, M. 2020. Maternal mental health and coping during the COVID-19 lockdown in the UK: data from the COVID-19 new mum study. *International Journal of Gynecology & Obstetrics*, 151(3), 407–414.

Dickerson, J., Kelly, B., Lockyer, B., Bridges, S., Cartwright, C., Willan, K., Shires, K., Crossley, K., Bryant, M., Siddiqi, N., Sheldon, T.A., Lawlor, D., Wright, J., McEachan, R. and Pickett, K.E. 2022. When will this end? Will it end?' The impact of the March–June 2020 UK COVID-19 lockdown response on mental health: a longitudinal survey of mothers in the born in Bradford study. *British Medical Journal*, 12(1), e047748.

Elson, D. 1998. The economic, the political and the domestic: businesses, states and households in the organisation of production. *New Political Economy*, 3(2), 189–208.

Emmott, E.H., Gilliland, A., Lakshmi Narasimhan, A. and Myers, S. 2023. The impact of COVID-19 lockdown on postpartum mothers in London, England: an online focus group study. *Journal of Public Health*, 1–13.

Fallon, V., Davies, S.M., Silverio, S.A., Jackson, L., De Pascalis, L. and Harrold, J.A. 2021. Psychosocial experiences of postnatal women during the COVID-19 pandemic. A UK-wide study of prevalence rates and risk factors for clinically relevant depression and anxiety. *Journal of Psychiatric Research*, 136, 157–166.

Federici, S. 2012. The unfinished feminist revolution. *The Commoner*, 15, 185–197.

Gray, A. and Barnett, J. 2022. Welcoming new life under lockdown: exploring the experiences of first-time mothers who gave birth during the COVID-19 pandemic. *British Journal of Health Psychology*, 27(2), 534–552.

Handley, K.M. 2023. Troubling gender norms on Mumsnet: working from home and parenting during the UK's first COVID lockdown. *Gender, Work and Organization*, 30(3), 999–1014.

Hays, S. 1996. *The Cultural Contradictions of Motherhood*, New Haven, CT, Yale University Press.

Heenan, C. 2002. The reproduction of mothering: psychoanalysis and the sociology of gender: a reappraisal. *Feminism & Psychology*, 12(1), 5–9.

Hochschild, A.R. 1989. *The Second Shift: Working Parents and the Revolution at Home*, New York, With Anne Machung, Viking Penguin.

Hochschild, A.R. 2022. The managed heart. In *Working in America*, pp. 40–48, Abingdon-on-Thames, Routledge.

Hochschild, A. and Machung, A. 2012. *The Second Shift: Working Families and the Revolution at Home*, Westminster, Penguin.

Jones, L. 2023. *Matrescence: On the Metamorphosis of Pregnancy, Childbirth and Motherhood*, New York, Random House.

Lamb, S. 2019. *The Not Good Enough Mother*, Boston, Beacon Press.

Lucas, S.E. and Bellussi, L. 2023. 'It is like talking to very good robots': experiences of online support groups for parents with babies during the COVID-19 lockdown in the United Kingdom. *Qualitative Social Work*, 14733250231185066.

O'Brien Hallstein, D.L. 2011. She gives birth, she's wearing a bikini: mobilizing the postpregnant celebrity mom body to manage the post–second wave crisis in femininity. *Women's Studies in Communication*, 34(2), 111–138.

OpenAI ChatGPT. November 2023. *ChatGPT Response to L. Bellussi Re Language Clarity and Readability of Findings*.

Reid, J. 2020. *Mothers, COVID-19 and Work at Home: Their account in words and portraits*, University of Huddersfield.

Rich, A. 2021. *Of Woman Born: Motherhood as Experience and Institution*, New York, WW Norton & Company.

Sacks, A. and Birndorf, C. 2019. *What No One Tells You: A Guide to Your Emotions from Pregnancy to Motherhood*, New York, Simon & Schuster.

Säilävaara, J. 2016. Imettämässä kaapissa?: Pitkään imettäneet äidit ja normatiiviset tilat. *Sukupuolentutkimus*, 29(2).

Thompson, L. and Walker, A.J. 1989. Gender in families: women and men in marriage, work, and parenthood. *Journal of Marriage and Family*, 845–871.

Turner, P.K. and Norwood, K. 2013. Unbounded motherhood: embodying a good working mother identity. *Management Communication Quarterly*, 27(3), 396–424.

Vazquez-Vazquez, A., Dib, S., Rougeaux, E., Wells, J.C. and Fewtrell, M.S. 2021. The impact of the COVID-19 lockdown on the experiences and feeding practices of new mothers in the UK: preliminary data from the COVID-19 New Mum Study. *Appetite*, 156, 104985.

Xue, B. and McMunn, A. 2021. Gender differences in unpaid care work and psychological distress in the UK COVID-19 lockdown. *PLoS One*, 16(3), e0247959.

Yoshida, A. 2012. Dads who do diapers: factors affecting care of young children by fathers. *Journal of Family Issues*, 33(4), 451–477.

Chapter 9

'I Don't Have a Lot of Choice … My Boss He Still Likes to Go to the Office Everyday Pretty Much' – Exploring the Impact of COVID-19 on Parents' Decision-Making When Planning Care During Their Child's First Year

Clare Matysova

University of Leeds, UK

Abstract

The closure of schools and nurseries during the COVID-19 lockdowns triggered the re-insourcing of childcare to the home, sparking extensive public debate and academic research on the pandemic's potential impact on gender equality (see, for example, Burgess and Goldman, 2021; Vandecasteele et al. 2022). My PhD research, which explores parents' decision-making influences when planning care during their child's first year in the UK context, coincided with COVID-19. The coinciding of my data collection with COVID-19 (seven online discussions with a total of 36 participants and 12 follow up interviews, 10 which include partners) created microcosms in which wider public debates were echoed. My research draws on the Capability Approach (CA) (Sen, 2009) to conceptualise parents' capabilities to share leave as they aspire to and employs dialogical narrative analysis (DNA) (Riessman, 2008) to explore how gendered parenting norms are constitutive of parents' care capabilities. In this chapter, I draw on feminist ethics of care to explore the disruption of gendered parenting norms, in the COVID-19 context, within parents' decision-making and a possible 'reimagining' of the value attributed to care (Ozkazanc-Pan and Pullen, 2021; Tronto, 2017). My findings support anticipation of what the promise of greater flexibility could bring as a result of increased visibility of caregiving during COVID-19. However, I also find evidence which supports the caution previously recommended of the need to reflect on work cultures and the predominance of masculine ideal worker norms in the UK (Chung et al. 2021).

Keywords: Capabilities; care; ethics of care; norms; parents; parental leave

Introduction

The closure of schools and nurseries during the COVID-19 lockdowns triggered the re-insourcing of childcare to the home. As a result, both mothers and fathers spent increased time caregiving (see Burgess and Goldman, 2021; Petts et al., 2021). This re-insourcing of childcare sparked extensive public debate and academic research on whether the increased time caregiving would be equally distributed between mothers and fathers and the pandemic's potential impact on gender equality (see, for example, Burgess and Goldman, 2021; Vandecasteele et al., 2022). On the one hand, there was concern that progress towards gender equality in employment witnessed over the last 40 years, in which women's participation in the labour market has increased (OECD, 2021), may be undone. On the other hand, questions were also asked about whether re-insourcing of childcare would create an 'exogeneous shock' and spark more egalitarian parenting norms (Vandecasteele et al., 2022, p. 2013). These questions asked whether increased fathers' participation in housework during the pandemic would advance gender equality at home (Burgess and Goldman, 2021), which has been slower to progress than gender equality within employment (Scarborough et al., 2019).

My PhD research explores how gendered parenting norms shape parents' decision-making when planning care for their child's first year. I focus on parents' planning in relation to take up of the UK's Shared Parental Leave (SPL) policy. My data collection coincided with COVID-19, creating microcosms in which wider public debates were echoed. In this chapter, I explore parents' reflections and draw insights on possible disruption of gendered parenting norms within parents' decision-making as arising from this pandemic 'shock'.

Exploring parents' choice (during a pandemic)

Parental leave policy provides possibilities to facilitate more equal sharing of care during a child's early years and contribute to progressing gender equality at home. A more equal sharing of leave creates opportunities for fathers to engage with their children, for children to be cared for by both parents (Javornik and Kurowska, 2017) and has potential to facilitate improved postnatal well-being (Goodman and Dumet Poma, 2023). The UK's SPL policy, introduced in 2015, enables parents to share up to 50 weeks of leave in their child's first year. A father's or partner's entitlement is based on the mother's commitment to curtail their maternity leave, and the length of available transferable leave depends on the extent of curtailment from the mother's maternity entitlement. Up to 37 of the total 50 weeks leave is paid at a statutory flat-rate. To be eligible to share parental leave, both parents must meet length of employment service criteria (Koslowski et al., 2022). In comparison to many European countries, the UK's provision of leave entitlement to fathers, and partners, and possibility for parents to share leave, was introduced relatively late (for an overview, see Kaufman, 2018). Introduction of SPL responded to fathers' aspiration for greater involvement and parents' aspiration to share care (Chung, 2021). Yet there has been limited take-up (approximately 4% of eligible parents) (Department for Business and Trade, 2023).

Explanations for low uptake of SPL, such as low wage replacement, restrictive eligibility criteria (Birkett and Forbes, 2019; Javornik and Oliver, 2019), poor and inconsistent employer implementation (Ndzi, 2017), highlight constraining structural policy features. However, less is known about how gendered parenting norms dynamically shape parents' capabilities to share parental leave – the focus of my PhD research. Evaluation of the effectiveness of social policies may focus on various value-laden policy aims and stakeholder objectives. Furthermore, the interaction between gendered parenting norms and parents' decision-making is variously accounted for by social justice positionalities, which also implicates how we attempt to examine the role of such norms.

A liberal gender equality of opportunities standpoint may discount the impact of gendered parenting norms and understand gendered take up of leave as arising from rational choice and the most effective household distribution of labour, based on aptitudes to be the homemaker or to be the breadwinner (see, for example, Beck and Beck-Gernsheim, 2002; Becker, 1993; Hakim, 1998). Indeed parents often refute the role of gendered parenting norms and rationalise their household division of labour as financially efficient – even when it is not (Zimmermann, 2023).

The Capability Approach (CA) has been employed as a multi-layered conceptual framework, which encapsulates personal choice, structural policy features and cultural factors such as the persistence of gendered parenting norms (Hobson, 2013). Utilising the CA to evaluate work-family policies aims to understand gaps between individual aspirations and their achieved capabilities (Hobson, 2013; Yerkes et al. 2019), to evaluate policy success in facilitating individuals' capabilities to live and make choices as they aspire to (Yerkes et al. 2019). Critically, the CA recognises that contexts such as gendered parenting norms, interpersonal relations and normative obligations to others impact on individual's opportunities; however, it does not prescribe how agency and social norms are conceptualised (Robeyns, 2017).

Feminist ethics of care contributes a lens through which to analyse parents' decision-making as dynamically mediated by gendered parenting norms (Held, 2006; Lynch et al. 2021; Tronto, 2017). A feminist ethics of care challenges a liberal and objectivist separation of rational and unencumbered individuals in the public sphere and care in the private sphere (Fineman, 2008). Furthermore, feminist ethics of care bring to the fore the differential value attributed by society between what is seen as feminine, reproductive work, and masculine, protection and production work in which (affective) care is 'backgrounded' and 'production as the proper pursuit and concern of individuals, the state and the market are so thoroughly foregrounded' (Tronto, 2013: 139). The COVID-19 pandemic lockdowns had potential to disrupt social norms and to foreground the value of care to society and to production (Bahn et al. 2020; Branicki, 2020), creating the opportunity to 'reimagine value' attributed to care as a feminist intervention (Ozkazanc-Pan and Pullen, 2021: 6). A feminist ethics of care provides a lens through which to examine this potential disruption to social norms.

Methodology and Research Methods

In my PhD thesis, I draw on the CA (Sen, 1993, 2009), as adapted within sociology and social policy (see, for example, Hobson, 2013; Yerkes et al. 2019), to conceptualise choice and evaluate parents' differential context-sensitive capabilities to access work family policies. From a social constructivist perspective, I explored *how* gendered parenting norms discursively shape parents' capabilities when planning care during their child's first year, in which it is recognised that what parents value is socially embedded and constituted by *normative* policy (macro) and workplace (meso) contexts.

I facilitated seven online discussions with approximately five to six participants in each (a total of 36 participants) between January and November 2020. I then interviewed 12 of the online discussion participants between April 2020 and January 2021. Ten interviews included a partner. All participants were asked to complete a pre-participation socio-demographic questionnaire. Table 9.1 provides a summary of participants' personal characteristics. Most participants had a higher education qualification, just over 50% had a household income of above £80,000 and various sectors were represented including higher education, education and private sector organisations. The sample reflected different career stages and contract statuses, as well as gender, ethnicity and sexual orientation.

Table 9.1. Summary of Online Discussion Participants Disclosed Personal Characteristics.

Online Discussion Participants	**Number**
Female	28
Male	5
Bisexual	3
Gay	3
Heterosexual	27
White	28
Ethnic minority	5
Total	**33**

While my original research questions predated and did not intend to focus on COVID-19 repercussions, my exploration of parents' decision-making during the COVID-19 pandemic provided the opportunity to explore how the 'shock' created by the re-insourcing of childcare disrupted (or not) gendered parenting expectations. Notwithstanding the importance of financial and policy constraints on parents' ability to share leave as they aspire to, as noted above, in this chapter I focus on gendered parenting norms. Specifically, I draw on feminist ethics of care to explore the disruption of gendered parenting norms, in the COVID-19 context, within parents' decision-making.

My analytical framework combined social constructivist thematic analysis, to identify what is valuable to parents when planning of care, and dialogical narrative analysis (DNA) (Riessman, 2008), to explore how gendered parenting norms shape parents' capabilities. Employing DNA enabled a focus on how normative expectations were articulated, resisted and evolved within 'small stories' as told in everyday conversations (Bamberg and Georgakopoulou, 2008); stories that are temporal and adaptable to audiences (De Fina and Georgakopoulou, 2015; Shuman, 2015). I also drew on Morison and Macleod's (2013) application of the concepts of positioning, trouble and repair to explore narrators' positioning of themselves or others in relation to gender norms or expectations, where this is troubled or 'negatively valued' or repaired to preserve 'positive positioning' (Morison and Macleod, 2013: 571).

Findings

I identified six main themes in the data regarding parents' articulation of what was valuable to them when planning care during a child's first year: shared parenting; spending time with baby; financial security; achieving career aspirations; postnatal well-being and gender equality. In this chapter, I focus on the second theme spending time with baby to reflect on the impact of COVID-19 in relation to valuing of time with baby. I present findings from thematic analysis, drawing out sub-themes in relation to COVID-19, and present narrative analysis of 'small stories' which exemplify or contrast these themes.

Value of Time with Baby

Spending time with baby was important to many participants, articulated as passing quickly yet important to value and embrace in the moment. The importance of 'treasuring time' was predominantly expressed by or about motherhood as exemplified in the following quotes:

> In terms of the first year I will do the main caring role and I am happy to do this as I feel this is precious time that you can never get back. (Sukhi – mother, maternity leave)

> I think you've always said to me you need to make sure that whatever happens [child's name] doesn't miss you... so yeah, it's time you'll never get back right. (Kiren, then Gregory – mother and father who shared parental leave)

The 'treasuring of time' created tensions for some couples when it came to choosing whether to share leave or not. While no (expectant) fathers directly expressed that they were not interested in taking leave, some (expectant) mothers reported that their partners were not interested in taking leave. For example, as expressed by Frances:

> I don't even think [my husband] spoke to his boss about it so I struggle a little to 'blame' this on outdated policies. (Frances – mother, maternity leave)

There was also tension between mothers' desire to share the time through transferable leave entitlement or to take their full entitlement. Consequently, some mothers questioned how they would have felt had their partner wanted to share leave. As Diana expressed:

> I really don't know how I would have felt had my partner wanted to share leave. ... Selfishly I just don't think I would have wanted to miss a second of it! (Diana – mother, maternity leave)

Some mothers, despite these conflicted feelings and not wanting to miss any precious time, described consciously sharing their leave not to deny their partner time to bond with their child. Other mothers described the negative impact that taking extended leave had on their own identity, alongside frustration at not being able to share leave and care more equally with their partner.

Increased family time at home created by COVID-19 (e.g. lockdowns, furlough, homeworking coinciding with parental leave, saved commuting time) was expressed as of value by some parents, both mothers and fathers, as illustrated by Gregory, who was working at home while his partner was on maternity leave:

> ... with COVID, ... as terrible as it is, I mean for me its amazing right cos I got another six months, I am working from home and I can see my kid every day ... (Gregory – father, shared parental leave)

In contrast, the balance of childcare responsibilities changed for some couples where one parent was a key worker, care shifting to a partner, who had not previously been very involved in caregiving. This was reported to have 'opened [fathers] eyes more to how hard the first few months are' (Catherine – mother, maternity leave). Florence, a frontline worker, witnessed her partner's increased confidence, which impacted on her opinion of his ability to care for their child:

> My opinions have definitely changed dramatically. I always thought he would struggle and would not cope but as time has gone on, he has really grown and coped so well considering my 3-year-old is used to going to nursery full time normally and is very busy! (Florence – expectant mother of one, undecided)

For others, especially mothers, COVID-19 exacerbated experiences of isolation.

Troubling the Preciousness of Time

There was recurrence in how time was expressed, through almost verbatim use of discursive resources such as 'time to be treasured' and 'time you can never get back'. Use of these discursive resources reinforced value attributed to time caregiving, conveying this value as something irrefutable. However, this irrefutability was contested in various ways, and it was through these interactions that we can see gendered parenting norms at play. This was exemplified in the following narrative, drawn from a couple interview with Rhonda and Michael (mother and father, shared parental leave).

> Rhonda: I would have happily returned to work about two months earlier than I did. (.) I'd really had enough ... It's true, most people say treasure every moment ... and you do treasure every moment, ... People say it passes really quickly and I completely disagree. I think there are some periods of time that pass incredibly slowly... I always feel like I need to prefix that with, I'm lucky to be able to afford to be off for this time you know, I'm lucky to have a child in the first place ... being on maternity leave was just never a great fit for me ...

Rhonda troubled the notion of 'treasuring of time', using reported speech to convey that 'most people ... treasure every moment' as the norm and contesting this norm by 'completely disagree[ing]' and suggesting that periods of time 'pass incredibly slowly'. The interview took place during COVID-19 possibly exacerbating Rhonda's experience of social isolation and Michael suggested that her maternity experience was 'a little bit warped by the whole lockdown'.

> Michael: 'I think the experience has been a little bit warped by the whole lockdown though as well'.
>
> Rhonda: 'I think so'.
>
> Michael: 'And I think certainly earlier on you were a lot happier when you could get out and about and you were seeing family on a regular basis ...'

> Rhonda: 'I think losing that interaction with a range of people is difficult (.) ... I think that was my coping strategy and I remember when lockdown started I thought I don't know what I'm going to do, because you don't sleep...'

However, there had been consistency in Rhonda's troubling of time throughout the interview. She expressed consciously feeling the need to prefix any negativity that she associated with time with baby by recognising that she is lucky: 'lucky to have a child in the first place'. This reflexivity and need to prefix, or repair any gender trouble caused by her negativity, illustrated the moral imperative and potential negative social repercussions she felt by troubling the 'treasuring' of every moment.

Michael's input on Rhonda's experience occurred following a period of quietness during which she had spoken at length about her experience. There had been a growing sense of discomfort on Michael's part when he attributed Rhonda's negative experience to her restrictions in being able to get 'out and about', loss of interaction activities, also suggesting his need to repair any gender trouble caused by Rhonda's narrative. She went on to refer to social interactions as a 'coping strategy', suggesting that she had already found maternity leave difficult, and the interactions were a way of coping with the 'same-y-ness' [sic] (Rhonda).

Rhonda illustrated the troubling of gendered assumptions that as mother she should treasure time, that maternity leave should be 'a great fit'. However, COVID-19 lockdowns appeared to have exacerbated her isolation rather than caused it.

Merging of Productive and Reproductive Work

In contrast, family time augmented by COVID-19 was reported as having a positive impact on family well-being by some participants. In relation to well-being, 'relish[ing] lockdown' in the COVID-19 context was described in one online discussion as reducing pressure to 'rush around and see people and go out and 'do' something every day'; being able to 'to pull up the drawbridge and just be with your little one' (Katie, Steve and Frances respectively). David and Katie exemplified this sub-theme that lockdown provided valued additional shared time. Katie expressed feeling better able to cope during her second maternity leave due to her partner working at home during COVID-19 lockdowns and David, who had previously taken relatively short periods of paternity leave for both children, shared the following:

> David: yeah, I mean I definitely enjoyed it because I got, got more time to see the kids. ... and it's kind of therapeutic sometimes (.) work's very stressful and err (.) you know Katie sometimes like 'oh go away from me', ... I'll go and grab her and she's like 'I don't know what she's talking about I've been an angel baby'

[mimicking the baby talking] [laughs]. Katie's stressing out and she's [baby] looking at me fluttering her eyelids …, and I forget everything that's going on on the computer for fifteen minutes. (David – father, paternity leave)

As well as being enjoyable, he describes the time with his children as being 'kind of therapeutic'. The stress Katie experienced looking after the baby contrasted the stress David experiences with 'work' and 'everything that's going on the computer'. For David, time with baby becomes an alleviator to stress arising from paid employment, through her purported innocence, which is emphasised through mimicking the child being 'an angel baby' and referring to 'fluttering her eyelids'.

A similar dynamic was described by Isobel and Ivy (birth and non-birth mothers – shared parental leave). Ivy, who was homeworking, described 'pop [ping] down' to hold the babies. In reverse, Isobel helped Ivy who 'came down cos I couldn't work out what to do with the spreadsheet this morning … and you helped me do the spreadsheet'.

This blurring of boundaries reflected an increased interrelatedness of care and work due to the shared physical proximity for those undertaking both care work and paid employment at home, that is, shared space in which both productive and social reproductive labour were undertaken due to COVID-19.

Visibility of Parents at Work

Merging of paid employment and care work also served to challenge and reinforce boundaries in paid employment workspaces. Reflections on discussions in the work context revealed parents' variable comfort with engaging their employers in relation to leave planning. Henry, for example, aspired to being involved in parenting 'relatively equally', yet described the possibility taking leave as '[n]ever going to be particularly realistic':

… well I didn't even talk to my boss about it but … we have talked about it more internally as a team (.) but I think it would be difficult because we're such a small team (..) umm (..) it would be expensive as well. (Henry – expectant father, paternity leave)

Guy, in the following extract drawn from an interview with him and his partner, Susan, felt similarly constrained by his employer:

Well, it feels substantially constrained by the company paternity policy … it doesn't seem a smart thing to rant about you know dads getting less time off umm when we're making redundancies and other things so I may fight that fight later or closer to the time. (Guy – expectant father, undecided)

Guy's focus on 'they' [the company], and the constraints of his employer's policy, positioned his employer as controlling the decision yet he was silent on his own preference. The increased precariousness of employment in the COVID-19 context is referenced as making raising concerns about limited paternity leave policy not 'a smart thing to rant about', remaining invisible to the employer felt a safer option. Other participants, expectant mothers, talked of hiding their pregnancy, remaining invisible as an expectant parent as long as possible. Wendy, for example, put off revealing her pregnancy, which she explained as follows:

> ... because I simply can't deal with the stress that this may bring and thankfully working from home has allowed me to put this off until I am truly ready. (Wendy – expectant mother, shared parental leave).

Susan, the partner of Guy quoted above, also spoke of not revealing her pregnancy in relation to going through a job application process:

> I'm waiting to find out whether I have an interview for a major fellowship (.) which would start six weeks before my baby's due. ... the interview I will be 25 weeks/24 weeks at interview. So, I don't have much of a bump yet and I'm hopeful that I don't have much of a bump ..., that I can get through the interview without anything. (Susan – expectant mother, undecided)

The following narrative is drawn from Susan and Guy's exchange about conversations within the workplace as expectant parents. Guy reflected that he and his male colleagues tend not to talk about family – 'the guys don't sit around and talk about family stuff particularly'. Guy spoke of knowing more about female colleagues' families, because 'the ladies are reaching an age where they are starting families'. We reflected on whether this had shifted at all due to the pandemic.

> Clare: 'and with everyone working from home would you? Would [discussing family at work] have changed at all?'

> Guy: 'umm yes it's happened on occasion but it (.) hasn't opened the flood gates... It's just you might occasionally see or hear one [child] in the background ... there's an American colleague who was working from ... kid's playroom so I got a brief tour, ... and he waved his laptop around at their kids Lego collection cos they like Lego too. ... but it didn't then trigger a twenty-minute conversation, so all I know is that particular guy has at least one child and they like Lego (.) but I still don't know name, gender, how many, age, nothing'.

By situating himself in the kid's playroom, 'the American colleague' became visible as a parent. Their intentionality is unknown. However, Guy's positioning of his colleague as an exemplar visible parent, acting contrary to (expectant) fathers or parents' visibility in the workplace, serves to reflect that the 'flood gates' have not been opened by the COVID-19 pandemic. The shift to online working during lockdown periods had not resulted, for Guy, in a new ideal worker norm in which parents, especially fathers, become more visible in the workplace. Rather boundaries of appropriate professional behaviour in the work context are retained and reinforced.

Fathers' reflections on being drawn back to the office suggested similar limited impact of COVID-19 on their workplace culture.

> ... it will be nice having those extra two days at home ... to do a lot more than I did ... before Covid ... I don't have a lot of choice (.) because [laughs] ... my boss he still likes to go to the office everyday pretty much. (Henry – father, paternity leave)

While Henry had enjoyed more family time at home because of COVID-19 lockdowns, his employer remained very much present in and driving his decision-making rationale.

Discussion

The COVID-19 pandemic lockdowns created potential for gendered parenting expectations to be disrupted, for example, by fathers and partners having additional family time at home and through increased visibility of caregiving in paid employment workspaces. It also created opportunities to reflect on what is of value to families and to society in particular in relation to care within the family (Chung et al., 2021). In the following paragraphs, I situate my findings within the academic literature and discuss the ways in which this differential value attributed to caregiving was disrupted by the blurring of boundaries due to COVID-19.

Firstly, parents' use of discursive resources, such as 'time you can never get back', illustrated how normative expectations were positioned, troubled and repaired, constitutive of parents' care capabilities. Desire to spend quality parenting time is associated in literature on intensive parenting with both mothers and fathers (see, for example, Andenæs, 2005; Faircloth, 2014). Yet, cultural expectations and obligations to care are more closely associated with mothers (Faircloth, 2021). This association of care with motherhood was reflected by parents in my study. The moral imperatives to 'treasure time' with baby and the idealisation of motherhood was predominantly invoked and enacted by or about mothers. It was through contesting 'treasuring time' that its gendering was highlighted, as was exemplified by Rhonda's 'time passes incredibly slowly' narrative. COVID-19 lockdowns were attributed to some extent, to have 'warped' experiences; exemplifying previous research on the negative impact of COVID-19 on parents' well-being (Chung et al., 2021). However, additionally, troubling of gendered assumptions that as a mother one should treasure time, and the need to prefix any negativity or maternal ambivalence, illustrated the moral obligations at play within gendered parenting expectations – which persisted during COVID-19 times.

Secondly, in contrast, for some, increased family time created by COVID-19 was seen as valuable – albeit with its challenges – suggesting the possibility of 're-imagining' value attributed to care (Ozkazanc-Pan and Pullen, 2021: 6). Fathers appreciated increased caregiving time and their demonstrable ability to care challenged previous gender essentialist assumptions about caregiving aptitudes. Fathers' increased confidence caring for their child/ren echoed findings in previous research focusing on fathers' experiences of COVID-19 (Burgess and Goldman, 2021). Furthermore, blurring of boundaries between reproductive and productive work, taking place in the same physical home space, was described as having a positive side-effect on postnatal well-being and provided potential to negate the foregrounding of either paid employment or care work (Tronto, 2013). These positive repercussions contrasted with the detrimental impact of the pandemic blurring of boundaries on well-being as reported in previous research (e.g. Chung et al., 2021; Petts et al., 2021).

Thirdly, however, the risks associated with being visible as (expectant) parents in (online) employment spaces were apparent. Fathers' reluctance to 'even talk to [their] boss' about the possibility of taking leave was potentially exacerbated in the pandemic context and deference to employer policy restrictions maintained their invisibility as parents in the workplace. Meanwhile, working from home created an ability for expectant mothers to maintain invisibility for longer than usual, which contrasted the hypervisibility of expectant mothers under normal circumstances and as found for existing parents working online during COVID-19 (França et al., 2023). My findings suggest that, for the parents involved in my study, the increased visibility of care during the pandemic did not alleviate concerns about risks associated with (discussing) leave taking. The 'American colleague' positioned to exemplify increased visibility in turn reinforced an ideal worker norm. This rejection of parenting as having a visible part to play in professional worker lives illustrates the insidiousness of gendered parenting norms as productive of parents care capabilities.

The risks associated with being a parent in the employment context contrasted the positioning of time with baby as paramount in the home context. In the emergency COVID-19 context in which the work and care were able to coincide, some parents experienced reprieve from the differential value and boundaries between reproductive and productive labour. However, once drawn back to the employer workspaces, the prioritising and physical location of productive work was articulated as driven by workplace and employer expectations rather than personal choice. As such, differential and temporal value was maintained between value attributed to the (masculine) non-relational aspects of care, such as protection and production (via breadwinning) and (feminine) relational aspects of care (Tronto, 2017).

Conclusion

In this chapter, I explored parents' care capabilities during their child's first year focusing on (sharing) time with baby and whether the 'shock' created by COVID-19 saw a 'reimagining' of the value attributed to care, or reproductive labour relative to productive labour (Ozkazanc-Pan and Pullen, 2021; Tronto, 2017). Within the literature, the increased visibility of caregiving during COVID-19, and the positive response of many employers and managers in supporting parents, has been noted as providing potential opportunities to expand flexible working (Chung et al., 2021). My findings support anticipation of what the promise of greater flexibility could bring as well as the caution recommended and the need to reflect on work cultures and the predominance of masculine ideal worker norms in the UK (Chung et al., 2021). Parents deference to employers as decision-makers shows that we cannot look to parents alone to create this shift and that there needs to be focus on policy, employers and society more widely.

References

Andenæs, A. 2005. Neutral claims - gendered meanings: parenthood and developmental psychology in a modern welfare state. *Feminism & Psychology*, 15(2), 209–226. doi:10.1177/0959353505051729

Bahn, K., Cohen, J. and van der Meulen Rodgers, Y. 2020. A feminist perspective on COVID-19 and the value of care work globally. *Gender, Work and Organization*, 27(5), 695–699. doi:10.1111/gwao.12459

Bamberg, M. and Georgakopoulou, A. 2008. Small stories as a new perspective in narrative and identity analysis 28 (3), 377-396. doi:10.1515/TEXT.2008.018

Beck, U. and Beck-Gernsheim, E. 2002. Individualization: institutionalized individualism and its social and political consequences. Available at: https://sk.sagepub.com/books/individualization. (Accessed 2023/02/03).

Becker, G.S. 1993. *A Treatise on the Family*, Cambridge, MA, Harvard University Press.

Birkett, H. and Forbes, S. 2019. Where's dad? Exploring the low take-up of inclusive parenting policies in the UK. *Policy Studies*, 40(2), 205–224. doi:10.1080/01442872.2019.1581160

Branicki, L.J. 2020. COVID-19, ethics of care and feminist crisis management. *Gender, Work and Organization*, 27(5), 872–883. doi:10.1111/gwao.12491

Burgess, A. and Goldman, R. 2021. *Lockdown fathers: The Untold Story*, London, Fatherhood Institute.

Chung, H. 2021. *Shared Care, Father's Involvement in Care and Family Well-Being Outcomes, A Literature Review*, Government Equalities Office. Available: https://assets.publishing.service.gov.uk/media/6017fd418fa8f53fc739255d/Shared_care_and_well-being_outcomes-_Literature_review.pdf.

Chung, H., Birkett, H., Forbes, S. and Seo, H. 2021. Covid-19, flexible working, and implications for gender equality in the United Kingdom. *Gender & Society*, 35(2), 218–232. doi:10.1177/08912432211001304

De Fina, A. and Georgakopoulou, A. 2015. Introduction. In *The Handbook of Narrative Analysis*, pp. 1–17.

Department for Business and Trade, 2023. Shared Parental Leave Evaluation Report. Available: https://assets.publishing.service.gov.uk/government/uploads/system/uploads/attachment_data/file/1166383/shared-parental-leave-evaluation-report-2023.pdf.

Faircloth, C. 2014. Intensive parenting and the expansion of parenting. In *Parenting culture studies*, Eds E. Lee, J. Bristow, C. Faircloth, J. Macvarish, pp. 25–50, London, Palgrave Macmillan UK.

Faircloth, C. 2021. When equal partners become unequal parents: Couple relationships and intensive parenting culture. *Families, Relationships and Societies*, 10(2), 231–248. doi:10.1332/204674319x15761552010506

Fineman, M.A. 2008. The vulnerable subject: anchoring equality in the human condition. *Yale JL & Feminism*, 20, 1.

França, T., Godinho, F., Padilla, B., Vicente, M., Amâncio, L. and Fernandes, A. 2023. "Having a family is the new normal": parenting in neoliberal academia during the COVID-19 pandemic. *Gender, Work and Organization*, 30(1), 35–51. doi:10.1111/gwao.12895

Goodman, J.M. and Dumet Poma, L. 2023. Paid parental leave and mental health: the importance of equitable policy design. *The Lancet Public Health*, 8(1), e2–e3. doi:10.1016/S2468-2667(22)00319-X

Hakim, C. 1998. Developing a sociology for the twenty-first century: preference theory. *British Journal of Sociology*, 49(1), 137–143. doi:10.2307/591267

Held, V. 2006. *The Ethics of Care: Personal, Political, and Global*, Oxford University Press.

Hobson, B. 2013. *Worklife Balance: The Agency and Capabilities Gap*, Oxford, UK, Oxford University Press.

Javornik, J. and Kurowska, A. 2017. Work and care opportunities under different parental leave systems: gender and class inequalities in northern Europe. *Social Policy and Administration*, 51(4), 617–637. doi:10.1111/spol.12316

Javornik, J. and Oliver, L. 2019. Converting shared parental leave into shared parenting: The role of employers and use of litigation by employees in the UK. In *Social Policy and the Capability Approach: Concepts, Measurements and Application*, Eds M.A. Yerkes, J. Javornik, A. Kurowska, pp. 61–82, Bristol, Policy Press.

Kaufman, G. 2018. Barriers to equality: Why British fathers do not use parental leave. *Community, Work & Family*, 21(3), 310–325. doi:10.1080/13668803.2017.1307806

Koslowski, A., Blum, S., Dobrotić, I., Kaufman, G. and Moss, P. 2022. 18th international review of leave policies and related research 2022. Available at: https://www.leavenetwork.org/annual-review-reports/review-2022/.

Lynch, K., Kalaitzake, M. and Crean, M. 2021. Care and affective relations: social justice and sociology. *The Sociological Review*, 69(1), 53–71. available: doi:10.1177/0038026120952744

Morison, T. and Macleod, C. 2013. When veiled silences speak: Reflexivity, trouble and repair as methodological tools for interpreting the unspoken in discourse-based data. *Qualitative Research*. doi:10.1177/1468794113488129

Ndzi, E. 2017. Shared parental leave: awareness is key. *International Journal of Law and Management*, 59(6), 1331–1336. doi:10.1108/IJLMA-07-2017-0160

OECD 2021. *Time Spent in Paid and Unpaid Work, By Sex [dataset]*.

Ozkazanc-Pan, B., Pullen, A. 2021. Reimagining value: a feminist commentary in the midst of the COVID-19 pandemic. *Gender, Work and Organization*, 28(1), 1–7. doi: 10.1111/gwao.12591

Petts, R.J., Carlson, D.L., Pepin, J.R. 2021. A gendered pandemic: childcare, homeschooling, and parents' employment during COVID-19. *Gender, Work and Organization*, 28(S2), 515–534. doi:10.1111/gwao.12614

Riessman, C.K. 2008. *Narrative Methods for the Human Sciences*, Thousand Oaks, Sage.

Robeyns, I. 2017. *Wellbeing, Freedom and Social Justice the Capability Approach Re-Examined*, 1st ed., Open Book Publishers.

Scarborough, W.J., Sin, R., and Risman, B. 2019. Attitudes and the stalled gender revolution: egalitarianism, traditionalism, and ambivalence from 1977 through 2016. *Gender & Society*, 33(2), 173–200. doi:10.1177/0891243218809604

Sen, A. 1993. Capability and well-being. In *The Quality of Life*, Eds M. Nussbaum, A. Sen, Oxford University Press.

Sen, A. 2009. Capability: reach and limit. In *Debating Global Society: Reach and limits of the Capability Approach*, Eds E.C. Martinetti, A. Sen, Fondazione Giangiacomo Feltrinelli.

Shuman, A. 2015. Story ownership and entitlement. In *The Handbook of Narrative Analysis*, pp. 38–56.

Tronto, J. 2013. *Caring Democracy: Markets, Equality, and Justice*, pp. 1–227.

Tronto, J. 2017. There is an alternative: homines curans and the limits of neoliberalism. *International Journal of care and caring*, 1(1), 27–43.

Vandecasteele, L., Ivanova, K., Sieben, I., and Reeskens, T. 2022. Changing attitudes about the impact of women's employment on families: the COVID-19 pandemic effect. *Gender, Work and Organization*, 29(6), 2012–2033. doi:10.1111/gwao.12874

Yerkes, M.A., Javornik, J. and Kurowska, A. 2019. *Social Policy and the Capability Approach: Concepts, measurements and application*, Policy Press, London.

Zimmermann, R. 2023. Do couples take financially rational decisions when they become parents? No, but they believe they do. *Gender & Society*, 08912432231189302. doi:10.1177/08912432231189302

Chapter 10

Family Life, Covid and Care: A Conversation Between Parent and Child

Fiona Ranson[a] and Cuong Nguyen[b]

[a]Northumbria University, UK
[b]Independent Scholar, UK

Abstract

In this chapter, we reflect together on the unfolding lockdowns in England. This reflection is presented as a conversation between foster parent (Fiona) and young person (Cuong), exploring the dynamics of care that marked that time period. Through our conversation we are able to point out the multi-directionality of the care we both gave and experienced during these times.

Keywords: Covid; care; lockdown; racism; trust; unaccompanied asylum-seeking children

In this reflection, we (Fiona and Cuong) provide an overview of our experience of care during Covid in conversation with each other.

Fiona

In the run up to and during the COVID-19 pandemic, I was a foster carer for two young people who had been separated from their parents, trafficked to the UK and were now seeking asylum. In the UK, young people in this situation become 'looked after' by local authorities' social services departments, who have a duty to safeguard and promote their welfare. Local authorities often place children into foster care, with foster carers who care for young people in their own homes, offering a family-like experience.

Cuong

I had been living with Fiona since I was 15, and was now over 18 (and designated a 'care-leaver'). Towards the end of 2019, Covid outbreaks occurred in Wuhan, China. I was worried. I had access to social media, which shared details of the pandemic in China that were not being shared or discussed by the UK media. My country of origin shared a border with China, and I was becoming increasingly worried about the people there. The first case of Covid in Vietnam occurred in January 2020. By February, I was becoming even more worried. I told Fiona that we should all be wearing masks. China and Vietnam had introduced this as a compulsory measure, yet mask wearing was not being discussed in the UK, except in media reports where Chinese students, who were wearing masks, had become the targets for racist attacks.

Fiona

I felt really conflicted. Cuong was already the recipient of racist microaggressions, and I was concerned that wearing a mask would make him even more of a target of racism. However, he was determined and so we bought masks and started to wear them in public places. Cuong was in college, wearing his mask, when a group of boys stopped him, asking if he was Chinese. He said he was from Vietnam, and they told him that Vietnam was in China and that he 'better not be bringing any diseases' with him. He shared this as a funny story. I told him that I thought this was racism and that we needed to report it. He said he didn't want to, reprimanded me, telling me he had shared the story because he thought it was funny. I reported it to his colleges' safeguarding lead. Later in February, we went to an Asian supermarket for a monthly 'big shop' of Asian produce. We wore masks and for the first time we were not unusual.

Cuong

Towards the end of February, my anxiety was rising. Coronavirus was spreading to Europe. I was tracking COVID-19's spread and concerned about the inaction of the UK government.

Fiona

It was becoming clear that Boris Johnson, Prime Minister at the time, and his government were not just ambivalent but were behaving flippantly.
We now know that the UK were treating this pandemic like a flu pandemic, rather than a SARs type pandemic and as such were ignoring the experiences, responsive approaches and measures being rolled out in Asian countries. Cuong, as it turned out, was giving us better advice than the UK government and its advisers.

By mid-March, Cuong was well aware of public health initiatives occurring in Asian countries and was becoming increasingly reluctant to go out in public, where there was no evidence of similar measures. I remember the whole nation was waiting for an announcement of a lockdown. On 12th March 2020, British Prime Minister Boris Johnson announced that he was considering prohibiting public gatherings for sporting fixtures/concerts, etc., and asked those households with symptoms to stay at home. Still, there were to be no school closures.

Cuong

Fiona picked me up from college. This was my last day in college. The next day I woke up and told Fiona that I was sure I had Covid.

Fiona

He had a cough (demonstrated a fake cough) and a sore tummy and smilingly announced that because of his symptoms, everyone needed to stay at home. Despite knowing that he was faking illness (and he knew that I knew), I contacted college and told them that I would not be bringing Cuong into class today, because he had a cough. He was visibly relieved. Our lockdown started on 13th March. Everyone else's was 10 days later.

The first period of our lockdown together was a positive experience. Cuong was buoyant at having achieved an earlier lockdown than the rest of the country. At that time, we thought lockdown would last only a few weeks, although this quickly increased to months.

Cuong

College organised approximately 6 weeks of online learning, which was very hit and miss. Once Microsoft Teams had been added to my iPad, I thought it would improve. However, online learning was problematic for me and my classmates. Online lessons were frustrating and tended to consist of late arrivals, students disappearing, cameras or audio not working and even lecturers, who were also new to online learning, not being able to share screens. I lost my interest in this very quickly and came up with excuses for not joining online lessons.

Instead, I took charge of our veggie garden and spent a lot of time outside preparing beds and tending to seed and seedlings that I had propagated in the greenhouse. This was where I was happy. Our neighbour gave me an incubator and I took eggs from our chickens and raised my own. I then spent a lot of time, with Allan (Fiona's husband), building and painting a new chicken coop for the chicks – I was busy during those first couple of months.

Fiona

Cuong actively conjured up 'plans' and activities in an attempt to keep his and our spirits high. One day, he appeared in the kitchen in sportswear, announcing that while I walked the dog, he was going to jog. He subsequently jogged on three consecutive days, provoking hilarity. However, slowly but surely, I could see him struggling to stay optimistic and positive, despite his own best efforts. He had had an active social life prior to the Covid pandemic and its disappearance was difficult for him.

Cuong

Before Covid, I would often meet friends after college in town, going out for a coffee, shopping, or going for a meal. At weekends, my friends would come to my house, and we would all cook together, enjoy a meal together and end the night with Karaoke and a dance. Sometimes, I would spend the weekend with my friends.

Fiona

One of the disadvantages of our 'early lockdown' was that freedom to socialise with friends had stopped at this time too. I was aware that Covid restrictions had removed his freedom and, in some ways, were beginning to mirror the control and restrictions he had experienced earlier in his life.

Towards the end of April, Cuong's mood had changed, and he was staying in bed for most of the day. This coincided with announcements that lockdown would not be over with as quickly as previously predicted. He was spending more time in his room alone and his behaviour was communicating a deep anxiety and unhappiness. As my husband and I attempted to lift him out of their low spirits, with suggestions of activities, asking him for help, or sharing funny stories; he sensed what we were trying to do and became irritated with us. This lockdown felt never ending. I would remind him that restrictions would eventually lift, and that scientists would eventually find a vaccine to keep everyone safe. However, there was no way of providing a time scale for any of these. Without this, I believe he felt trapped, out of control of his own life and even at times frightened for the future.

Cuong

I suggested that we organised to have meals at the same time as my friends and then called them on Facetime, so that we could have a meal together. We did this a couple of times and then I organised a party with my friends. My online parties became a regular activity. I would take my portable karaoke microphone, my meal (and maybe a beer) and party lights into my room, and Facetime a few friends, while we ate and sang together.

Fiona

By early May the government announced a phased plan for lifting lockdown, with specific ongoing and arguably unclear restrictions. As a phased reopening of schools took place in June 2020, colleges had reached the end of their terms, so there was no return to education for him. However, Cuong had 'leave to remain' (refugee status), which meant he had permission to work. As workplaces opened, he returned to his part time job, where he was still in training. This was exactly what he needed. He had a routine, had friends at work, felt safe – the Covid measures incorporated in his workplace were very robust.

Cuong

By the time the next full lockdown was announced, I wanted to try and find things to do. Fiona arranged to help me and my friends learn English for a food hygiene qualification. The online English lessons were only once a week, but after each session me and my friends continued to work together online, without Fiona. We all passed Food Hygiene Level 1 and then we began to look at Level 2.

Fiona

From this sprang an additional online group, organised by Cuong and his friends, where they revised for the driving theory test together. This led to lots of private study, independently from his friends. He also regularly spent time with me, looking at questions, determinedly trying to understand the quite technical, subject specific language. Later he failed his first driving theory test, but resiliently announced that he was very close to a pass and would try again (he did, and he passed). He thrived with a newfound purpose. He picked up his English textbooks, found online English learning videos and spent most of his time actively learning. Cuong read some adapted fiction books, collecting vocabulary and phrases he didn't yet understand and asking for support in understanding these. He then returned and re-read the books. I am not clear exactly what it was that kept him so motivated during this lockdown, except that we all knew that it would end and that we would come through it – it didn't feel endless.

Cuong

I also think doing the online studying with my friends really helped. I began to make plans to open my own business and decided that I needed to improve my English for this. Learning English that would help me in my business felt like a useful way to spend time – learning something that would be useful.

Fiona

By January 2022, the nation was now living with Covid, thanks to the roll out of mass immunisations. Cuong was unwell but had taken Covid tests for the previous 3 days, which came up as negative. However, he called me and asked me to pick him up from work because he felt dreadful. He came home and was very unwell for the remainder of that week – finally testing positive. As his health improved, he was desperate to test negative, because he was supposed to be attending a continuing professional development course in Sheffield. After about 10 days, his health improved, and he was ready to be dropped off at the railway station to go on his course. Later that day my husband and I took a Covid test only to find that we had Covid.

Cuong

When I heard that Fiona and Allan had Covid I cancelled the course and persuaded my friend to drop me off at home so that I could look after them.

Fiona

He couldn't be persuaded to catch a train to Sheffield. He stayed for the week, making us food, forcing us to eat, taking the dog out for walks and being generally bossy. He told us quite clearly that it was his job to do this, just as it was our job to look out and care for him.

During Covid, in many ways the young people I knew in care took charge of the care, using the information they had access to; ensuring we wore masks earlier than most and successfully securing an earlier lockdown than the one the government recommended. They rejected activities that frustrated them in favour of activities that brought them pleasure and allowed them a sense of ownership. They also found, as they experienced subsequent lockdowns, a sense of purpose through engagement with peers online, all working towards and supporting each other with the same aims. Lastly, the care we received from Cuong, when we had Covid, shone a light on our interdependence and support we all gave each other. We had Cuong's back and he had ours.

Section 4

Schooling as Care

Chapter 11

Caring and Schooling in the Time of COVID-19

Tom Disney[a], Lucy Grimshaw[a] and Judy Thomas[b]

[a]Northumbria University, UK
[b]Teesside University, UK

Abstract

This chapter presents a research study which explored the experiences of teenage secondary school girls in England whose schooling was disrupted by the pandemic and implementation of lockdowns. We begin by setting the context for school-based research with children and argue children and young people experience ever-increasing pressure to act as redemptive future agents and thus sites of capital accumulation. Despite this we go on to argue that there were important moments, practices and experiences of care during the lockdown periods that can be harnessed to help resist the capitalist logics that exert such pressures upon current school children. We explain the process of using arts-based methods to engage pupils in discussing their experiences and how these methods are based on caring practices which we argue are essential for research on care. Our findings suggest the girls had positive experiences of schooling and lockdowns and we present some significant examples of caring agency that young people demonstrated in contrast to the negative media discourses about home learning. We do not seek to obscure the difficulties that these young people experienced, but in highlighting their caring agency, we demonstrate the complexity of lockdown experiences and illustrate the role and importance of care in the unbounded space of the school.

Keywords: Arts-based methods; capitalism; caring agents; COVID; girls; school

Introduction

This chapter draws upon a creative mixed methods qualitative research study with girls in secondary school and their teacher, exploring their experiences and practices of care during the COVID-19 lockdowns in England. School is the de facto institution of everyday childhood for many children; it is presented as one of the central institutions of childhood socialisation (Wyness, 2012), yet an explicit focus on care within secondary school spaces is not as pronounced in academic or policy literature. There is a large, established area of academic study focussed on *early* childhood education and care but in relation to secondary schools a focus on care is less developed, which reflects dominant discourses of schooling that children become more competent with age and education, and thus less in need of care. Yet given increasing pressures on secondary school children in England as sites of accumulation to be viable future economic agents (Katz, 2018), and concerns about mental ill health amongst this group (Jerrim, 2022), the need for care has never been greater. This is powerfully demonstrated by the young people involved in our study.

The contribution of this chapter is twofold; firstly, to illustrate the role of care within secondary schools, highlighting what are often overlooked practices that are nonetheless vitally important caring practices and experiences. Amongst the overlooked elements of care, we demonstrate that these young people were themselves significantly involved in the giving or practice of care during the COVID-19 lockdown periods, a time when serious concerns were raised about the wellbeing of school children in the UK. Secondly, we introduce and emphasise the use and importance of an arts-based approach in not only revealing how care is experienced but also as a method of caring research practice. We begin our chapter with a discussion of the role of the school and its relationship to capital, before advocating for a greater attention to literature of care (noting concerns about teenage mental health). We then discuss our research context and methodological approach, which was grounded in participatory, arts-based methodologies. Finally, we present the experiences of the young people who generously contributed their time and experiences to help us better understand the dynamics of caring in schooling and the implications of this for future research, policy, and practice.

School and Care

The school is a central institution of childhood and a space that constitutes the everyday for most children in the Global North. Literatures in Childhood Studies have noted the role of compulsory schooling in shaping modern childhood and how it has contributed to the circulation of key discourses, such as children's incompetence and economic dependency on adults (Wyness, 2012). This has meant, however, that consideration of children's position within analysis of political economy has at times been overlooked in Childhood Studies (Spyrou et al., 2019); while schooling is central to the shaping of children's 'ambivalent futurities' (Moss and Petrie, 2002), it is also a means of generating future human capital (Ansell et al., 2020). Children in school have become sites of immense accumulation, with significant pressure placed upon them to work to become productive future neoliberal subjects. As Katz (2008: 5) argues childhood has 'become a spectacle – a site of accumulation and commodification – in whose name much is done'. In her work exploring the commodification of childhood, Katz (2018) explores the intense competition in the US school system and the pressure to succeed, with families and children haunted by the risk of potential 'wasted' futures. We live in an age of ontological anxiety, according to Katz (2008: 9–10), with pressure on children as potential economic agents to secure the future via accumulation of capital:

> ...[in] the current period, children are both an economic and psychic investment in the future. As such and exceeding it, children are a bulwark against ontological insecurity and other anxieties about the future, and it is here that the spectacular nature of children as an accumulation strategy can be seen most clearly. As the nature of the investment has shifted registers children themselves have been commodified to secure them. Each of these aspects of childhood as spectacle has particular consequences for children's lives and the material social practices of childhood as lived and imagined.

Running in tandem with this positioning of children as accumulation strategies and the pressure this exerts upon them, we note a rising concern around the mental health of secondary school aged children. The reasons for poorer mental health among secondary school students are complex and beyond the scope of this chapter, but it is important to note that while there is disagreement as to when mental ill health may be more prevalent in secondary school, many studies found that girls in particular were found to experience poorer mental health (see Jerrim, 2022). In Jerrim's (ibid: 331) recent research, we note that he queries initially whether the school might be a space that acts a 'background and precipitating factor for mental health concerns'. Our focus is aligned with this spatial approach but differs slightly from his focus on mental ill health; we note that space is not a backdrop to human behaviour, but a 'social structure in the ordering of social relations' (Nayak and Jeffrey, 2013: 86). We argue there is scope to look at the school as an unbounded space of care that may and should include practices and experiences that help to resist the pressures of being accumulation strategies and present means of promoting general wellbeing. Indeed, it is notable that the closure of schools during lockdowns has been associated with mental ill health among many young people (Ford et al., 2021). The pandemic marked a time where the need for care was particularly acute. We argue that the school is potentially a central space of care that is increasingly overlooked in academic and policy literature, with a role beyond processes such as safeguarding, which while important do not attend to the more everyday forms of vital care that sustain us. Although not discussing schools specifically, we find Power and Williams' (2019: 2) definition of spaces of care useful for our chapter. They define them as:

> ...'organisational spaces' ... [which] disclose care and facilitate practices of caring for, about, with others, both human and non-human ... [operating] within defined spatial settings such as homes and drop-in centres ... and are created through caring labour and intentions of users, including staff, residents and visitors in conjunction with the material environment within which they are located.

We use this definition because it broadens the context of care as something which crosses physical boundaries; caring practices that initiate in the school may expand beyond the physical space of the school into the home or neighbourhood and have implications for other actors, human and non-human. Such an approach emphasises the interdependency of care. This also foregrounds that young people are active agents in care themselves, something which is often overlooked (Horton and Pyer, 2017) and particularly so in relation to public health interventions (Spray, 2024). Finally, while we acknowledge that while school can represent an oppressive institution to some students, we find particular inspiration in the work of bell hooks in conceptualising it as a caring space. hooks (1994: 199) argues that care in schools is a rebuff to neoliberalism; she reminds us that capitalism informs the way we think about care, the way we are taught to compete and to imagine that a teacher cannot care for each individual student. Drawing on hooks, we seek to position schools as potential spaces of care to resist positioning children as accumulation strategies.

Schooling and COVID-19

In March 2020 schools in England were closed to all pupils, with the exception of those considered to be 'vulnerable' and those of parents who were designated as 'key workers' and thus able to go to work in person (Kim and Asbury, 2020). This meant a move to online learning for the majority of children in mainstream schooling in England. The shift to remote learning was not only jarring for many professionals and children (see Brown Chapter 13 and Burg Chapter 14 this volume) but also raised concerns about digital exclusion (Coleman, 2021), lost learning (UNICEF, 2021) and mental ill health (Ford et al., 2021). While such concerns were and remain important to explore, there is also a risk that the complexity of experiences during the lockdowns is missed. In reflecting on the diversity of lockdown schooling experiences, Breslin (2023) presents a typology of students during this time, which he suggests comprises 'lockdown strugglers' who found the lockdown period very difficult; 'lockdown survivors' who managed during lockdown, acquiring new skills but also experienced issues in relation to isolation and missed the social aspects of schooling; and finally, 'lockdown thrivers' who experienced the lockdown periods as positive and found these arrangements to work better for them than traditional in person schooling. It is important to qualify that these groups were stratified by phenomena such as poverty and other structural determinants, so it was likely that a 'lockdown thriver' would have good digital access and supportive housing conditions. Conversely, a 'lockdown struggler' might include children experiencing socio-economic marginalisation or even a home environment marked by abuse. Despite this, what is clear is that the notion that the lockdown periods necessarily constituted a comprehensively negative experience is to miss the opportunity to glean what positive moments of experience or practice there might be to support children and young people in future. As Breslin (88) notes:

> the lazy application of narratives of unmitigated loss to educational settings, and notably schools and colleges, belies the richly nuanced and intensely personal experiences of pupils, parents, and educational professionals who support these professionals in spheres such as school governance and system leadership.

We not only concur but also caution that the reproduction of the narrative of loss also risks exacerbating deficit conceptualisations of young people who have lived through this period. As Nxumalo (2019) warns, 'damage-orientated' research may unintentionally reproduce and facilitate self-fulfilling deficit approaches to youth. With this in mind, and the aforementioned diversity in lockdown experiences, we explore in this chapter some significant examples of caring agency that young people demonstrated in our study. We do not seek to obscure the difficulties that these young people experienced, but in highlighting their caring agency, we demonstrate the complexity of lockdown experiences and illustrate the role and importance of care in the unbounded space of the school.

Methodology

We define caring methodologies as an approach which prioritizes wellbeing, to build more equal relationships through playful approaches that make the experience of participating in research enjoyable and fun. We also argue that it is particularly appropriate to uncovering experiences and practices of care. In this section, we provide a detailed overview of our process as this has been noted as often lacking in arts-based participatory research with caution raised about approaches that may unwittingly reproduce harm (Coemans and Hannes, 2017). Additionally, this discussion is to demonstrate how we enacted care during our research processes.

We carried out a creative mixed methods qualitative research study with girls and their teacher in a large secondary school, located in a rural region of the North East of England. Driving the research process was the aim to address the limited understanding of young people's and teachers' experiences and practices of care during periods of lockdown and of changes to schooling norms and routines. Using participatory, art-based methods and working with a local school to capture young people's and teachers' experiences and activities of care during the lockdown periods, the study aimed to answer the questions:

- How was care experienced by school children during lockdown periods?
- How did teachers experience care in relation to children and young people during the lockdown periods?
- How might creative methodologies help us to understand the care experiences and activities of teachers and young people in relation to the lockdowns?

Ethical approval was granted by Northumbria University. The school was selected due to existing working relationships between the school and our university, in addition to its proximity to our location thus facilitating ease of access, essentially a form of convenience sampling (Punch, 2014). Following a call for an expression of interest in a research project around care and the lockdowns, a member of staff and her form class agreed to participate. Written, informed consent for participation and the sharing of images and artefacts was given by all parents or guardians. In addition, the school and the form tutor for this cohort also granted consent, and the young people assented to take part.

In total there were 12 participants, all aged 17 and 18 years; and their teacher. All participants were female. The students were all at school during the lockdown periods at a time when they would normally have been sitting mandatory state examinations, and thus had a shared experience to explore. In line with a caring methodology, the students' teacher also took part in the activities, not only to share their experiences and to breakdown hierarchies but also to safeguard wellbeing during the research process. The students were all studying Social and Childcare, they were not art students. From an inclusion perspective, it was important that we also engaged in all the sessions, as the research team, to foster a sense of ease, familiarity and to counter any lack of confidence regarding 'art making' or 'being creative'. The research took place after the end of lockdowns and the resumption of standard schooling routines, in November 2022. We held two arts-based workshops in their classroom, during school hours. The workshops were held one week apart from each other.

Central to our caring methodologies was the careful facilitation of workshops. Through facilitation and overt participant observation, we observed, and participated in playful, fun, art-based activities. We designed a series of inclusive activities and material encounters to create an inclusive caring space which helped students feel at ease. These were shared in advance with their teacher. This enabled us to collectively make observations, facilitate informal discussions and use the resulting artworks as creative tools of reflective inquiry. Engaging with the activities alongside the students and their teacher, we modelled reflection and creativity. Through our observations we reflected on the utility of the chosen arts-based methodologies for uncovering experiences of care during lockdown. The resulting data included field-notes and artefacts, facilitating opportunities to examine the students' experiences of care and schooling during lockdown.

The research was carefully framed and whilst we invited emotional responses, we did not want to elicit any distress and invited everyone to talk in general terms; there was also the opportunity to leave sessions if needed, although no participants did leave.

Process

Pseudonymisation: Using associations and colour to create pseudonyms, the first activity began with a packet of felt-tip pens. We all chose a pen and had to team up with our complimentary colour, for example: red and green, blue and orange, etc. Once in our complimentary pairs, we all gave positive 'compliments' to our partner, affirming generosity and kindness from the onset. Inviting everyone to describe their partner's colour, created a new name and identity for each participant, resulting in names such as iridescent blue, cobble grey, etc. These were used for reference and acted as safe pseudonyms during the research. We then asked everyone to place a paper plate onto their head and invited everyone to draw a very quick portrait of their colour partner on the plate. Serving as a useful icebreaker, as we drew our portraits the room filled with laughter and giggles; our portraits looked scribbly, wonky and funny; anxiety and tension quickly disappeared.

Slow breathing: Inhaling slowly, we all tried breathing out through paper straws, with the aim of slowing heart rates and bringing focus into the room. Resulting in more laughter, these moments of hilarity and togetherness helped the group ease; the atmosphere was relaxed and light, setting a tone of familiarity and support.

Freewriting: Open writing was used in both sessions; the only prescription was a 3-minute timeframe for everyone to write about their associations of schooling and care during lockdown experiences. With no expectation for the writing to be read out, this was a way of free thinking with words. Everyone selected and shared up to five words that held the most personal resonance. These words were written onto post-it notes and then ranked 1–5 in terms of significance for each author. Displayed on the whiteboard they were discussed, with the authors explaining why they choose specific words.

Creative making and metaphor: Each selecting two resonant words from the array of post-it notes, we undertook a couple of simple making activities to visually represent experiences. In session one, everyone was given a 30 cm square of foil to spontaneously sculpt with. In session two, covid masks became the basis of the work, or blank canvases, that could be transformed using a range of media. This was less impromptu, and everyone had the opportunity to plan what they might like to do or create. With the opportunity for preparation, some of the group came to the second session with photographs of pets, printed images, stickers, and beads. There was also a range of paints, clay, glue, and other media to choose from.

It is important to highlight the method was not art therapy; although the processes can be likened to therapeutic art, where artefacts create opportunities for 'self-expression and communication' (BAAT, 2023); the research team are not professional art therapists or psychotherapists. It is also essential to be aware that whilst the artefacts were openly discussed, aspects of transference will have occurred. In the Revealing Image (1992), art therapist Joy Schaverien describes transference as 'the transferring of emotion' (p13) and the 'framing' of experience. Schaverien suggests 'interpretation [...] is a matter of relationship' (Schaverien, 1992: 3) and whilst we aimed to be neutral in our response to the artefacts and as we listened to the young people, as a group of older adults and academics, our analysis of the creative responses will, inevitably, be influenced by our own life experiences, emotional responses, and academic context. Furthermore, as a part of the participatory approach, students and the teacher were active in the analysis of data. For example, students analysed their artwork and articulated the meanings behind the artefacts. Following the school sessions, the research team also met to analyse the observation notes. The findings were ultimately reviewed and agreed by the participants.

Students' Experiences of Care

The students displayed rich and complex experiences in relation to care practices during the lockdowns, closure and reopening of schools. Students expressed a range of emotions, too; experiences were diverse, encompassing a range of positive and negative feelings about the lockdowns. The overall experience captured in the first workshop about this time was a sense of uncertainty. One student reflected this by leaving one part of her sculpture virtually untouched, with just a section of the tinfoil left as a bare sheet to represent 'the unknown when it felt like no one knew what was happening'. A sense of a lack of control, was compounded by the news, and endless cycle represented by one student's tinfoil sculpture of a microphone, representing the news, which was confusing, as the student said:

> It was just a lot of posh words that we didn't understand
> (Workshop 1)

During the workshops and particularly the first workshop the students expressed their feelings and emotions, boredom, sadness; the most common set of words selected as most important was 'mental health'. A few students representing this by using the tinfoil to create a scrunched-up ball which symbolised the brain for one student (see Fig. 11.1).

The workshop triggered memories and changes in everyday lives and routines which were disrupted and reinvented for the lockdown periods. Our observation diaries note the teacher saying suddenly 'shops! How could you forget queuing in the shops?' (Workshop 1). Two students mentioned the NHS as a keyword,[1] and we all remembered the clapping on doorsteps then for health care workers (Workshop 2). Memories of sanitising tables in schools and hearing birds also triggered small conversations of collective remembrances. We noted in observation notes that:

> As a whole, it felt like an opportunity to reconnect with memories of lockdown, which triggered forgotten elements.... [of] just how fractured and stop start our return to normality was. (Workshop 2)

---

[1] The UK's National Health Service.

Fig. 11.1.   Example of Artefacts, Free Writing and Pseudonymisation Process.

The second workshop allowed the students the time to reflect and focus in more detail on their care practices and experiences. The negative aspects faded a little and more positive stories came to the fore with an overarching sense of repetition and routine highlighted by one student with repeated colours and stars on her mask.

Through the activities and discussions, we observed care practices emerged in three intertwining areas of the students' lives: school spaces; families and distance; and walking and movement.

School Spaces

The students discussed the initial shock of lockdown; it happened so suddenly and unexpectedly. One student remembered walking to school with a friend after the first case of a Covid-infected patient was reported at the hospital in Newcastle upon Tyne and she tried to comfort a worried friend unsuccessfully 'I remember saying to her, "calm down, don't worry, it's going to be fine!"'. The student laughed at her own reaction on reflection. Their initial reflections were that it was great to be off school, but then as time progressed, enthusiasm waned. The school became a skeleton school; open for a small number of children but for most, it became schooling at home, with online lesson lessons and new routines; they could stay at home, in bed, felt no pressure and one repeated three times 'I didn't have to put my camera on'. She had enjoyed staying in pyjamas and said: 'It just worked better for me'. However, the disjuncture and change to the caring spaces of school was not good for others who felt they lacked the usual support systems and felt unmotivated and worried about the impact on learning exams and qualifications. The school before lockdown provided access to care that students needed and when schools reopened, students were faced with the reality of new restrictions and rules enacted by both government and the school to keep students and staff safe. A visual example of this is presented below in Fig. 11.2.

Despite the best efforts of staff, the classroom could be a difficult space to be in. Students remembered being cold in classrooms with windows necessarily open for ventilation, which created 'a wind tunnel' and regardless of this they were not allowed to wear coats as one student remembered:

> Do you remember us sitting at the back of the classroom with me sitting with my scarf on my legs? (Workshop 2)

The school could feel like an uncaring space with students finding ways to cope with the experience. A student testing positive for COVID-19 could send 'a ripple through the classroom' (Workshop 2). The fear was still palpable when both students and teacher discussed classroom seating plans being requested, a senior teacher walking towards the classroom with an inevitable announcement of groups needing to be sent out of the classroom and they remembered:

> Waiting bored, the emptiness of the hall and silence. No one talked, just sat there waiting. (Workshop 2)

Caring and Schooling in the Time of COVID-19   155

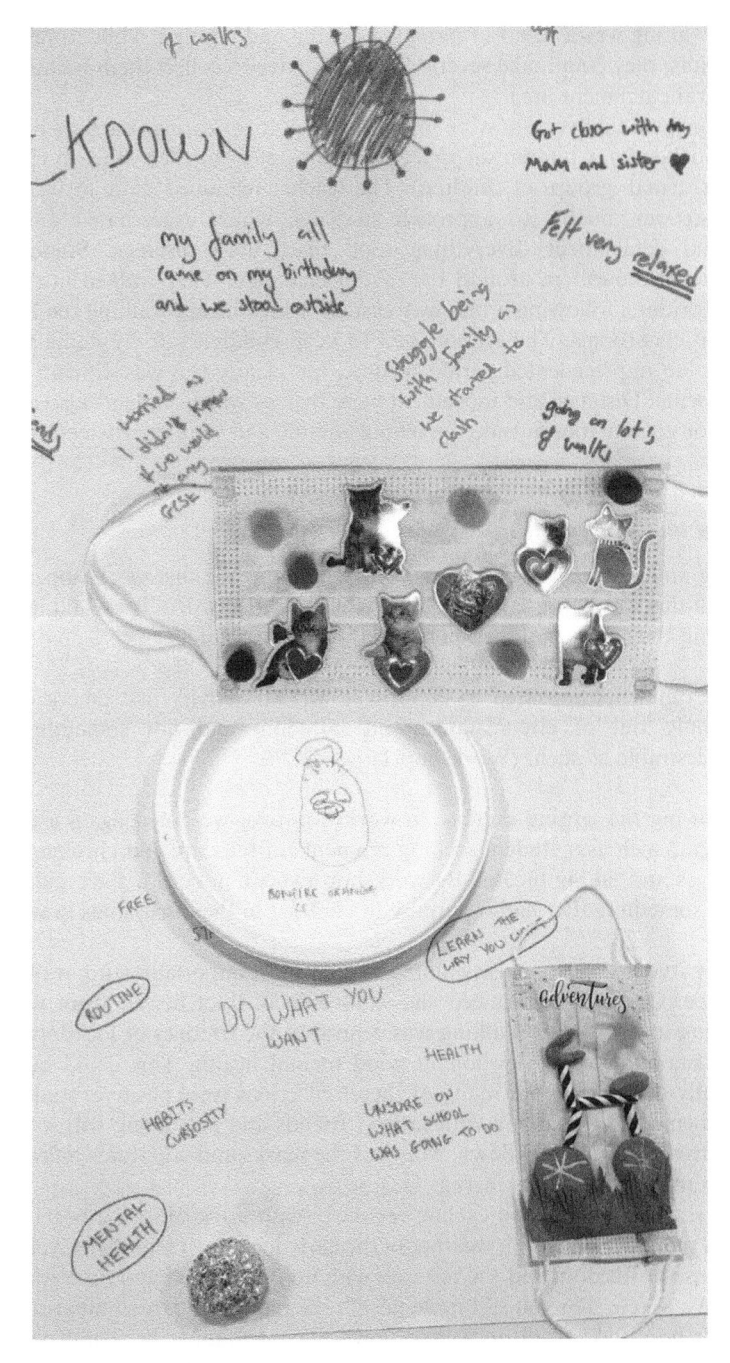

Fig. 11.2.   Example of Representations of Complexity of Schooling Experiences.

The waiting was a result of parents working and taking a while to respond to phone calls; they could take several hours to arrive to collect them because of the large rural catchment area.

Distance and movement were important aspects of caring practices in schools during lockdown. Children sat spaced out, distant from each other in classroom 'bubbles' (small groups of children). The teacher remained static at the front of the classroom, unable to approach students, which exacerbated a sense of emotional detachment. Everything took place at a distance. Students also remembered movement around the school changing. They walked in single file down corridors, following a one-way system, which meant walking the long way round to classrooms. The school tried to keep children safe by doing the right things in an unprecedented period of time, but clearly this was difficult for staff and students. Distance and movement were themes which students also discussed in relation to activities outside the school routine and were intertwined with care.

Walking and Movement

Walking and walks were common words chosen in the first workshop, and students felt this was because that was 'all you could really do'. They said it was not something they had continued post lockdown as we noted:

> Comments appeared to confirm it was an activity that emerged only out of circumstance and boredom and not something desirable as such. (Workshop 1)

Following the writing exercise in workshop two, we noted again a theme of movement, such as a student seeking moments of self-care and checking in with themselves and taking breaks. By workshop two we noticed a shift and walking became something that had a purpose in contrast to the discussions in workshop one.

Many students again chose walking as their most important word; walking was an escape. One student noticed she walked to distract herself from what was happening in the world. Walking was central to the routines of lockdown, a key part of maintaining or developing good mental health. This could be viewed potentially as negative but many of these reflections were positive; students had happy memories of walking with family, friends and pets along with other outdoor activities during lockdown. Many of the masks and sculptures reflected this. Some examples are shown in Fig. 11.3 below.

One student reflected on cycling regularly with a friend to the beach to sunbathe (a reminder of the hot weather in the early lockdown months). Cycling gave her a sense of freedom and she felt safe with no one around and no traffic on the roads. We asked, 'Do you still cycle now?', she replied 'No, too embarrassed... I wouldn't be caught dead on a bike now!'. These routines have not necessarily continued but they were enjoyable, important self-care activities during the lockdown period.

Fig. 11.3. Example of Complexity of Engagement with Lockdowns.

As a result of walking, many students said they felt closer to nature. Many of the artefacts, masks, sculptures created by the students contain trees, leaves, clouds, landscapes. Moments of moving and noticing the natural environment meant students became more aware of how nature contributed to their happiness and management of lockdowns. In creating new routines, they engaged in unanticipated or subtle practices of self-care.

Movement therefore was an act of self-care, and it was often carried out with others, family members, friends when possible and pets. It developed from being a way of filling time to becoming something that had purpose.

We end this section with perhaps the most impressive act of self-care unrelated to walking or the outdoors but a result of lockdown restrictions on movement and services and requiring quite skilled and precise movement: one student who learned online how to remove her own dental braces because she could not go to the dentist due to lockdown restrictions.

Family and Distance

Familial bonds grew stronger for some in their immediate families because of close proximity, spending more time together and being in almost constant contact. Some students were brought closer to their family through their acts of caring for others. One student explained how she and her dad both took care of her clinically vulnerable mum, including planning shopping trips with her dad and that this act of caring brought her closer to her dad. Another student talked about how her family worked together and took turns to look after a 92-year-old neighbour. Another student noted that she noticed when her mum came home stressed from work in the NHS too.

Students spoke of being unable to see and missing extended family members who were located further away and/or nearby. Whilst others found they became closer to extended family members as technology and regular zoom quizzes collapsed physical distance and created a sense of closeness. Family activities and traditions featured in reflections providing glimpses of the way in which families cared for each other: going for walks with parents and siblings; moments like putting a Christmas tree up early; missing a big family birthday party but celebrating instead at home with family gathered outside and distanced. As one student reflected when discussing her mask, it was with the care and love of her 'little circle of family... that helped get her through "this ride of emotions"'.

Caring for animals was central to the family unit for some, as shown below in Fig. 11.4. Dogs were central to self-care practices too and often accompanied students during their walks. One student cared for a horse, and another had a pet rabbit which was allowed to stay in the house during lockdown but promptly dispatched outside at their mum's insistence after lockdown.

There was a diversity of family experiences and the close proximity, inevitably, could be frustrating for some too but these aspects were not dwelt upon by students. Overall, the students focussed on happier experiences of caring practices that helped them get through perhaps best summarised by one student who said they were 'Better off than some – lucky'.

Fig. 11.4. Animals and Nature Appeared as Important Themes for Young People.

Discussion and Conclusion

The young people in our study certainly felt the pressures of the contemporary schooling system, exacerbated by the COVID-19 lockdowns; many of their artefacts hinted at fears and pressures about the need to be productive and develop into future economic agents (Katz, 2018). Yet, there was also significant hope and joy amongst the young people, in particular during workshop two; media discourse around school closures was generally negative in the UK (Crace, 2021), yet this different form of schooling was preferred by some students in our study reflecting the complexity of experiences (Breslin, 2023). Similarly, while the school attempted to put in place caring provision at times, such as implementing protective Covid regulations this could also be experienced as uncaring. This points to the complexity of care, that despite intention it can be felt as controlling and cold. As Puig de La Bellacasa (2017: 1) notes: 'To care can feel good; it can also feel awful. It can do good; it can oppress'.

Children and young people were largely sidelined in the pandemic, their agency severely restricted in the name of protection with little consultation. Such an approach could be thought of as largely uncaring. State and media communications powerfully represented this and left many young people feeling disconnected. This reflects concerns in Childhood Studies that children and young people are often disempowered in caring processes (Horton and Pyer, 2017). In contrast to this the young people recalled instances that demonstrated sophisticated and complex caring agency, such as looking after vulnerable parents, animals and frequently themselves. Movement, was clearly important to the young people in our study, and extant research within the mobilities paradigm has called for attention to the importance of children and young people's pedestrian practices (Horton et al., 2014). Our findings extend this through illustrating the agency of young people engaging in mobile self-care. These findings point to the importance of making space for everyday practices that do not feed the 'children as sites accumulation' discourse; taking time, engaging with nature and moving were important to the young people and helped to address anxiety and discomfort. Schools operating post-lockdown should consider the ability of young people to understand their own self-care needs, and structure in elements of everyday care that resists the pressures of contemporary schooling. It is important that we do not lose sight of the opportunities that appeared in the course of the lockdowns, and draw on these to shape a schooling system that can be caring and flexible in meeting young people's needs.

Finally, reflecting on the role of the caring methodological approach, we were struck by the way this facilitated the opening up of unheard stories, memories and emotions of care in a safe and supportive way. Many of these instances also took the teacher by surprise, who was unaware of these experiences, for us this highlights the power of this approach to unearth care experiences and practices. This also points to the fact that no space has really been provided to explore these experiences; perhaps we still need a space for caring reflection about this period, to consider what was lost and what was gained.

References

Ansell, N., Froerer, P., Huijsmans, R., Dungey, C., Dost, C. and Piti, C. 2020. Educating 'surplus population': uses and abuses of aspiration in the rural peripheries of a globalising world. *Fennia*, 198(1–2), 17–38.

BAAT 2023. Art therapy. Available at: https://baat.org/art-therapy/. (Accessed 23 July 2023)
Breslin, T. 2023. Schooling during lockdown: experiences, legacies, and implications. In *Pandemic Pedagogies: Teaching and Learning During the COVID-19 Pandemic*, Ed M. Ryan, pp. 88–103, London, Routledge.
Coemans, S. and Hannes, K. 2017. Researchers under the spell of the arts: two decades of using arts-based methods in community-based inquiry with vulnerable populations. *Educational Research Review*, 22, 34–49.
Coleman, V. 2021. *Digital Divide in UK Education During COVID-19 Pandemic: Literature Review*. Cambridge Assessment Research Report, Cambridge, UK, Cambridge Assessment.
Crace, J. 2021. The Guardian view on the pandemic's educational impact: make good learning losses. The Guardian available at: The Guardian view on the pandemic's educational impact: make good learning losses | Editorial | The Guardian. (Accessed 18 January 2024).
Ford, T., John, A. and Gunnell, D. 2021. Mental health of children and young people during the pandemic. *BMJ*, 372, n614. doi:10.1136/bmj.n614
hooks, B. 1994. *Teaching to Transgress*, New York, Routledge.
Horton, J., Christensen, P., Kraftl, P., Hadfield-Hill, S. and 2014. "Walking ... just walking": how children and young people's everyday pedestrian practices matter. *Social & Cultural Geography*, 15(1), 94–115.
Horton, J. and Pyer, M. 2017. Introduction: children, young people and 'care. In *Children, Young People and Care*, Eds J. Horton, M. Pyer, London, Routledge.
Jerrim, J. 2022. The mental health of adolescents in England: how does it vary during their time at school? *British Journal of Educational Research*, 48(2), 330–353.
Katz, C. 2008. Childhood as spectacle: relays of anxiety and the reconfiguration of the child. *Cultural Geographies*, 15(1), 5–17.
Katz, C. 2018. The angel of geography: superman, tiger mother, aspiration management, and the child as waste. *Progress in Human Geography*, 42(5), 723–740.
Kim, L. and Asbury, K. 2020. Like a rug had been pulled from under you': the impact of COVID-19 on teachers in England during the first six weeks of the UK lockdown. *British Journal of Educational Psychology*, 90(4), 1062–1083.
Moss, P. and Petrie, P. 2002. *From Children's Services to Children's Spaces: Public Policy, Children and Childhood*, London, Routledge.
Nayak, A. and Jeffrey, A. 2013. *Geographical Thought: An Introduction to Ideas in Human Geography*, London, Routledge.
Nxumalo, F. 2019. *Disrupting and Countering Deficits in Early Childhood Education*, London, Routledge.
Power, E. and Williams, M. 2019. Cities of care: a platform for urban geographical research. *Geography Compass*, 14, e12474.
Puig de La Bellacasa, M. 2017. *Matters of Care: Speculative Ethics in More than Human Worlds*, Minneapolis, MN, University of Minnesota Press.
Punch, K. 2014. *Introduction to Research Methods in Education*, London, Sage.
Schaverien, P. 1992. *The Revealing Image: Analytical Art Psychotherapy in Theory and Practice*, London, Routledge.
Spray, J. 2024. Children's care for public health and politically expedient care for children in Aotearoa New Zealand's COVID-19 pandemic. In *Care and Coronavirus: Perspectives on Childhood, Youth and Family (Emerald Studies in Child-Centred Practice)*, Eds T. Disney, L. Grimshaw, Bingley, Emerald.

Spyrou, S., Rosen, R. and Cook, D.T. 2019. In *Reimagining Childhood Studies*, Eds S. Spyrou, R. Rosen, D.T. Cook, New York, NY, Bloomsbury Academic.

UNICEF 2021. *The State of the Global Education Crisis: A Path to Recovery: A Joint UNESCO, UNICEF, and World Bank Report*, UNICEF.

Wyness, M.G. 2012. *Childhood and Society: An Introduction to the Sociology of Childhood*, London, Palgrave Macmillan.

Chapter 12

'Take Care Everyone!' Care Ethics at Work Whilst Homeschooling and Caring for Children During the COVID-19 Pandemic

Lucy Grimshaw, Kay Heslop, Kirstin Mulholland, Vikki Park, Jill Duncan, Jaden Allan, Cathryn Meredith and Christopher Warnock

Northumbria University, UK

Abstract

This chapter discusses the care experiences of a group of parents and a grandparent working at a Higher Education Institution in England and homeschooling during the pandemic. The group established an informal, work-based, online peer support group during and beyond the first COVID-19 lockdown. This chapter analyses a survey of group members and the group's online chat data to explore experiences of homeschooling and participating in the group. It represents a pioneering case study in how a group of parent-workers coped with the conditions brought about by the COVID-19 pandemic. We argue that the group was underpinned by an ethic of care, based on reciprocal care relationships. The group developed ways of caring together and sought to influence and create more caring working practices and cultures. Whilst it is possible to create small pockets of more inclusive, supportive and caring spaces within education workplaces, we conclude that the challenge to create supportive family-friendly working environments remains.

Keywords: COVID-19; ethics of care; homeschooling; online peer support; parents; work

Introduction

The global COVID-19 pandemic brought school closures for most children, changing family dynamics and educational and workplace practices. Like many countries, the United Kingdom (UK) government imposed lockdowns with the message of 'Stay home, save lives'. Home-life for families with children was transformed as homeschooling, once seen as an alternative form of education for only a minority of families, became the norm. For some in employment, working from home also became the norm. This chapter explores the experiences of care in relation to combining homeschooling, paid work and caring for children during the pandemic. We present the experiences of a group of parents and one grandparent who formed a weekly virtual parenting support group in a university during the pandemic. We begin by discussing the impact of the pandemic on school and work, children and families and the relevance of ethics of care to frame our case study findings. We then highlight the challenges encountered and the benefits of developing a caring community of colleagues. We conclude that challenges remain in creating more caring workplaces post-pandemic.

Context and Literature

Work, Homeschooling and Education During the Pandemic

As a global pandemic swept the nation in March 2020, schools, and nurseries closed (Hume et al., 2023) as part of a national 'lockdown'. Limited provision was offered for vulnerable children and for children of essential workers, but teachers, families and workplaces were unprepared (Bradbury et al., 2022). Government measures to protect the population posed challenges that affected health and wellbeing as well as education. Educators rapidly prepared online learning experiences (with little or no previous experience) and implemented COVID-19 policy overnight (Bradbury et al., 2022). With social networks curtailed and usual services reduced, balancing homeworking with homeschooling and childcare represented a particularly acute challenge for working parents of children with special educational needs or disabilities (Dobosz et al., 2022). Women inevitably took on more childcare responsibilities, but men also increased the amount of time they spent caring for children (Crook, 2020); grandparents also provided vital childcare when regulations permitted (Cantillon et al., 2021; Gilligan et al., 2020).

Unsurprisingly, Working Families (2021), the UK's work–life balance organisation, experienced increased demand for its legal advice helpline during the pandemic. Working Families (2021) estimated that one in seven parents had to change their working arrangements immediately following the government advice to work from home; some employers remained inflexible, failing to consider childcare needs and adapt. In some cases, parents had to take unpaid leave, reduce working hours, lost their jobs, or were furloughed (and then received state welfare benefits). For those able to work from home (mostly 'white-collar' workers), boundaries between work and non-work became blurred, bringing for some a negative impact on personal wellbeing (Adisa et al., 2022). A variety of coping strategies emerged as staff avoided meetings or took sick leave (Adisa et al., 2022). This chapter presents a more solidaristic strategy, neglected in the literature; the development of a work-based peer support group for staff caring for children and homeschooling.

The first lockdown in England lasted for 10 weeks, from March until June 2020, although some children were unable to return to school or nursery until September 2020 (and some could not return even then). Although social-distancing and safety measures were implemented to enable schools to remain open for some groups of children, staff absences were high, and not all parents were willing to take the risk and send their child. Some nurseries and schools remained completely closed due to staff shortages, exacerbating dilemmas about childcare, safety and working practices. In January 2021, with COVID-19 cases rising once more, there was a further nine-week lockdown, although 'essential workers' and vulnerable children could again (ordinarily) access schools and educational settings. The Institute for Fiscal Studies (2023) reported that the quality of home learning improved in this time, due to more access to laptops, planned learning and wider availability of online lessons. Yet, the Office for National Statistics (ONS, 2020) reported a lack of children's motivation affecting studies; and research also highlighted the significant levels of psychological distress for homeschooling parents at this time (Calear et al., 2022).

The edict of 'Stay home, save lives' also caused university campuses to close in March 2020. As students moved to online learning, academic staff were required to adjust their design and delivery overnight (Crook, 2020). This rapid work took place within their homes, while balancing family routines, care and new educational responsibilities for their own children. Some British universities reopened to students in September 2020, despite warnings about the risk of spreading infections (Yamey and Walensky, 2020). Universities were again closed after a few weeks as rates again increased and online teaching remained until September 2021.

Academia, Care and the Pandemic

Before the pandemic, negative accounts of the neo-liberal, marketised higher education system abounded in the UK and globally (Watermeyer et al., 2021). Universities were, for example, depicted as 'toxic' and 'care-less' institutions (Noddings, 2003). Working in universities can be a solitary experience, offering relatively few opportunities to interact with colleagues (Mulholland et al., 2023). This can be exacerbated by a 'publish or perish' culture within which 'support can be inconsistent, and a highly competitive research and funding climate may inadvertently create a setting conducive to feelings of self-doubt' (Hutchins, 2015: 4). This self-doubt fosters stress and depression; a lack of discussion about the effects of pressures in academia creates 'hostile atmospheres' (Smith and Ulus, 2020: 840). Exploitative working environments also exacerbate inequalities, particularly for those from marginalised groups such as working-class, minoritized ethnic and/or disabled academics (Watermeyer et al., 2021). The challenges to combining academic careers and caring were widely accepted pre-pandemic, and since caring is gendered, this has a detrimental impact on women, and especially on mothers (Crook, 2020; Miller, 2020). COVID-19 accentuated academia's deep seated gender inequality, with women researching and publishing less during the pandemic compared to prior (Crook, 2020; Fine and Tronto, 2020).

Whilst caring responsibilities abound and are intrinsic to the work of educators, care itself is often invisible. The pandemic further exposed (non)caring cultures in universities (Smith and Ulus, 2020). Evidently, there is something amiss in the cultures and practices of 'care-less' institutions (Noddings, 2003; Rogers, 2017) and as a counterbalance, accounts and suggestions for survival for those working in academia have emerged. Amongst these are the active rejection of neo-liberal norms and measures through feminist collectivism, collaboration and an ethics of care (Mountz et al., 2015; Miller, 2020; Rogers, 2017). We provide a pioneering example of how this happened during the pandemic.

Ethics of Care

An ethics of care approach emphasises care as relational, the basis of moral duty and central to human practice. Early care ethicists Carol Gilligan and Nel Noddings focussed on women's role as caregivers and the one-way nature of care between mother and child. More recent understandings view caring as a relational and reciprocal activity; a gendered and undervalued form of labour predominantly but not exclusively undertaken by women (Tronto, 2013). Necessary for sustaining life, the definition of care itself is complex, and embedded in social relations (Fisher and Tronto, 1990). An ethics of care approach suggests being cared for is not simply a passive activity; human vulnerability is something we all have in common, thus we should all recognise ourselves as care receivers (Tronto, 2013).

Joan Tronto's (2013) conceptualisation of an ethics of care is useful as it focusses on care as political, drawing attention to how neoliberalist emphasis on personal responsibility, individualism and the avoidance of dependency result in the undervaluing of care. For Tronto (2013), caring involves democracy, breaking down hierarchies and promoting equality. Tronto (2013: 34–35) suggests a framework for assessing care based on five phases and moral elements which can be used to judge the adequacy of care:

(1) Caring about: recognising people's needs and a need to care and being attentive to these needs (as opposed to being actively ignorant of those needs).
(2) Caring for: taking responsibility for meeting the needs linked to a counter-notion of privileged irresponsibility.
(3) Caregiving: someone or a group of people doing the actual caring and being competent in carrying out the caring tasks (as opposed to learned incompetence).

(4) Care-receiving: the care that is given by the caregiver and the responsiveness of this care to needs.
(5) Caring with: the process of care where habits and patterns of care emerge over time and trust and solidarity emerge.

The moral aspects of care – attentiveness, responsibility, competence, responsiveness and solidarity and trust – are the criteria by which we can judge care itself and also apply to institutions. Tronto (2013: 161), however, notes that this can be challenging since:

> ... in institutions of care there are many sets and levels of needs. The possibility of conflicting ends within institutions is a long-established problem with viewing institutions as single-purposed and single-minded. Just as all individuals have many ends, so too organizations and the individuals within them have many different ends.

The COVID-19 pandemic brought such complexities to the fore. The competing needs of institutions, individuals, organisations and families became exposed at macro, meso and micro levels. Lockdowns removed the social support networks families ordinarily relied on for practical and emotional help, guidance and care (as demonstrated in several chapters in this volume). Digitalised care and online peer groups became the only way for parents and carers of children to experience support during the pandemic (see also Chapter 8). In the workplace, caring for children can be rendered invisible, but as Fine and Tronto (2020: 304) suggest, care came out of the shadows during the pandemic and the 'political dimensions of caring were revealed afresh'. 'Political' here means that at all levels (macro to micro) the ways in which care was understood influenced how it was enabled, supported, managed and matched to needs (Fine and Tronto, 2020). We draw on the ideas around an ethics of care to understand the experiences of peer support groups, homeschooling, caring for children and working in education during the pandemic.

Methodology

In this qualitative case study, we draw on Yin (2018) to explore the experiences of our own peer support, which consisted of fifteen people; ten mothers, four fathers and one grandmother. Case study approaches produce a rich and nuanced understanding of a particular context, individual, or phenomena (Thomas, 2011). They offer a means of intense enquiry, facilitating the identification of novel insights (Flyvbjerg, 2006). While the aim is not to produce generalisable findings, we agree with Pring (2000: 258) that 'uniqueness in one respect does not entail uniqueness in every respect'. Therefore, this account can provide a starting point for similar research in different workplace settings. The project received ethical approval from Northumbria University. Participants (members of the group) signed consent forms assuring their anonymity and ability to withdraw data up to the research's publication. We have used pseudonyms as a mechanism of self-care, to not expose ourselves more than we are comfortable with; and to emphasise the collective rather than individual author/member experiences.

The study draws on written data produced by group members during the pandemic via the Microsoft Teams chat function. This was written during online weekly Teams meetings and continued in between meetings. This chat data (58,132 words) serves as a collective document and, more specifically, a digital diary (Jarrahi et al., 2021) presenting a contemporaneous historical record of interactions, experiences and immediate feelings from May 2020–May 2021. Twelve of the 15 members provided consent for their anonymised chat data to be analysed.

In addition, we conducted a short online survey of members in June 2021 to collect demographic information and ask about members' motivations for joining the group, their experiences within it and its impact. Eleven members responded to the survey; all were full-time academic staff and living with a partner, or husband or wife; 73% women and 27% men; no one identified as transgender or non-binary. Ten identified as White British and one identified as Other (self-reporting as British). Members each had caring responsibilities for one or two children, aged between 0–14 years.

As with case study approaches more broadly, we recognise the inextricability of our experiences and perceptions (Yin, 2018). We, the authors, were members of the group; we are insider researchers, academic parents and grandparent presenting an account of our and other members' lived experiences of caring during the pandemic. Our immersion in the context of this case perhaps means we are ideally situated to understand its complex realities, but we might also question the reliability of our interpretations of data. In our defence, we did not begin the group with the intention of using our experiences and the diary for research purposes. While we joked about, and were in awe of, others who found time to write about their experiences during the pandemic (see for example: Crook, 2020), this was not then our priority.

We approached the chat data and qualitative survey comments using Braun and Clarke's (2019) reflexive thematic analysis. Four authors carried out initial inductive analysis coding data individually, developing tentative themes and then collectively discussing analyses. Further deductive analysis was carried out by three authors drawing on the ethics of care literature which enabled a refining of the themes. Frequent communication between those carrying out analysis and all authors enabled the discussion of themes through a process of analytic triangulation (Given, 2008) to ensure that multiple possible interpretations and explanations were considered. Finally, returning to the diary data caused a certain amount of discomfort as we re-lived some awful moments. Our system for meeting and sharing during the pandemic helped us again as we met and shared our analysis and emotions online to regularly reflect on our analysis, experiences and to care for each other during this research process.

Findings: Experiences of Caring for Children, Homeschooling and Work During the Pandemic

This section tells the story of the group in mostly chronological order, albeit presenting our findings around four themes: (i) establishing a supportive group online; (ii) fitting in homeschooling and childcare; (iii) adapting to new work routines; (iv) accommodating care.

Establishing a Supportive Group Online

The group began on 22 May 2020. The group originated from an email exchange between two of the female chapter authors on the first day of lockdown (23 March 2020):

> Arghh! How are we supposed to work and be mums?!

The response:

> This is day 1, DAY 1!!!! I don't want to think about how hard it's going to be on day 21[sad face]

It took another 2 months of sporadic emails and struggle before the member posing the question above decided to establish a peer support group. Following management agreement, an email invitation to join a support group for parents went to all staff in two departments situated on the same university campus, with the additional intention of raising awareness amongst all colleagues of the need to support homeschooling parents. The group met online once a week at lunchtime via video and the written chat was available continuously. Initially, members did not all know each other well or in some cases at all. Group membership stayed fairly constant, with new members joining in the Summer of 2020 and January 2021.

In the survey most members said they joined the group for peer support, to connect with others and to talk to someone 'about the nightmare of homeschooling and working fulltime!' (as one participant wrote). Others mentioned joining as a coping strategy to reduce stress and share experiences. Survey analysis indicated that women members were more likely to do the majority of homeschooling and caring. Female members contributed more frequently to the chat too. However, the group was an inclusive space, as one father highlighted in the survey:

> As a Dad I was concerned it would be all about mum, but the diverse group has been amazing, emotional support, professional support or advice.... Just amazing group of people who have kept me going when things were very hard. One for all and all for each other...

Fathers can be reluctant to join parenting spaces where mothers are in the majority (Brooks and Hodkinson, 2020) but this group succeeded in including fathers. The chat facilitated inclusion, as another father wrote in the survey:

> I've not played a really active role, but have really enjoyed reading the threads on the Teams chat. More important, it's good to know that the group members are around if I was struggling and needed to vent/talk.

The chat served as a way of developing relationships and expressing care even if members could not attend weekly meetings. Well-wishing in the chat, as illustrated in the quote in the chapter title 'take care everyone!' were important. Similar phrases recurred: 'we missed you!' and 'hope you're all well!' if members could not attend weekly meetings. Members used emojis too as a quick way to demonstrate support. This is illustrated in quotes used in this section, where emojis are denoted by text in brackets, for example, hearts (love), thumbs up (like). The chat thus played a key role in enabling members to participate in the group and strengthen caring relationships alongside the weekly meetings.

Fitting in Homeschooling and Childcare

The group filled a gap and provided peer support when the implications of homeschooling on parents' lives was not completely understood, even after 2 months of schools being closed for most:

> Mel [22/05/2020 13:21] I've had an epiphany this morning. I've realized that many of my colleagues think that schools are operating like the university is, they think that our kids are being live taught and all we are doing as parents is checking in on them!

Members exchanged information about homeschooling and childcare. In one of the first conversations members shared experiences of the variations in practices amongst schools and nurseries:

> Mel [22/05/2020 13:24] I am having to actively direct my daughter's learning every subject, every lesson, every lesson, every day.
>
> Hannah [22/05/2020 13:25] ... my students with GCSE children are getting about an hour of work set per day. Maximum!
>
> Mary [22/05/2020 14:39] [my children] are in Nursery so the expectations aren't too bad, but obviously they can't do anything by themselves. Daily number writing, name writing, counting, a task around a story... Maybe takes 2 hours in total?

> But what really stresses me out is that [their teachers] monitor how much they're doing and mark it. And most parents post the stuff the kids are doing on Facebook and so it's led to some crazy competition between some of the parents.
>
> Gill [22/05/2020 14:48] That is too much Mel!.. And Mary the competitive parenting has to stop... There is loads of stuff on my daughters' elearning site but really they are choosing what they want to do sometimes with my help or me sitting with them.... Both need a lot of support for one reason and another (inc dyslexia).
>
> Mel [22/05/2020 14:53] I feel like when I was on maternity leave again – [my child] is 13 but I count the hours down until her dad gets home from work so that he can give me a break. [smiley face]

Sharing the challenge of seemingly competitive parents oversharing on social media in one of the first conversations revealed a collective desire to avoid this, establishing the tone and supportive ethos of the group early on. At each lockdown stage members wondered together about whether they should be worried about the lack of normal schooling and care practices. As seen above, experiences differed depending on age and ability of children and the school or nursery attended. Homeschooling children was not usual, and members felt pressured to manage and support their children's education, but they also came to understand the unprecedented nature of the situation and make sense of expectations.

When universities and schools reopened in September 2020 some members were expected to teach on campus. Members continued to share and support each other during times of uncertainty, when children could be sent home at any moment due to COVID-19 infections within their class, year and/or friendship groups; when not all schools and pre-schools returned at full capacity; when grandparent support was (in most cases) limited by COVID-19 restrictions and wraparound childcare was not available. Childcare support was complicated further for those whose partners had to return to work outside the home, and particularly for lone parents:

> Gail [17/09/2020 12:51] I have had my son in 2 weeks isolation and it is impossible to do the 4-5 lessons per day that school set alongside work and then drop offs pick up of other child. I cannot work if school shuts again. I have no external help from anyone [sad face]

Members shared an image of news on the chat that reported that even the Prime Minister struggled to explain lockdown rules (Murray, 2020) and Mel commented '... we are clearly expecting more of ourselves than he is...' It was helpful therefore that members could discuss and share the latest government guidance and for example, develop shared knowledge of what they need to do if our children were sent home with or without symptoms.

> Georgina [21/09/2020 14:14] Wow! Thanks for all replying. Its clear now why I'm so confused about it all [crying laughing face]

COVID-19 rates continued to rise after the easing of restrictions in summer 2020 when pubs and restaurants re-opened, and the nation was encouraged to 'Eat out to help out'. As group members predicted, by October university campuses had closed again. Schools stayed open but COVID-19 testing remained a frequent activity, as group members discussed:

> Will [06/10/2020 11:55] ... We've just had the homeschool scare... Our youngest had been awake most of the weekend with a cough and cold. ... went through the whole testing rigmarole... Trying to swab a baby properly is not the simplest of tasks. ... Yesterday was a complete right off [sic.] as a result, but the results came back as negative mid morning today. I've just got back from dropping them at school and nursery as a result.

> Mel [06/10/2020 11:56] Omg Will, I really feel for you - swabbing a 13 year old was hard enough!!

> [1 thumbs up]

> Paula [06/10/2020 11:57] Will, Mel, [sad face] take care.

It was helpful for members to share with each other the daily challenges and routines of looking after children and how this fitted (or not) with paid work.

Adapting to New Work Routines

The working day expanded, with paid work done in the early mornings, late at night and at weekends throughout the pandemic. In January 2021, the government classified university staff as 'essential workers' rendering them eligible to send their children to school. This confounded members who did not want or feel able to return their children to school. Members were particularly attuned to the situation in some schools and that there seemed to be confusion even within government:

> Will [11/01 14:18] Meanwhile, my wife's school have at least a third of their children in because of guidance's mixed messages. Some year groups/classes having 30 children in. The changes issued by DfE [Department for Education] late on Friday night just exacerbate the situation.

Members discussed the apparent carelessness in government and workplaces about the additional needs of staff parents/carers:

> Mel [25/02 09:35] I feel just like my teenager – no one genuinely listens, no one understands! And with schools about to return there is no incentive for engagement with us now, we'll be consigned to history.
>
> [5 thumbs up]
>
> Graham [25/02 12:19] ... our recent history has taught us that this government is uniquely talented at messing up the easing of lockdowns. I hope this is our last, but I have zero confidence.
>
> [2 thumbs up]

Members found new routines but it was challenging to maintain a clear working pattern as they seemed to lose 'all sense of working hours'. Multiple caring roles constantly challenged members:

> Paula [07/01 14:02] My working patterns are a bit strange and still settling into Lockdown v3. I've been mam/teacher/housewife until after lunch, then have been working on an afternoon, then again in the late evening into the early hours of the morning when the kids are in bed. Hope you're all well.

Members discussed responses from line managers about how to manage work. They found managers' suggestions were often either impossible due to COVID-19 restrictions; for example, 'get a childminder' [Will] or lacked understanding of our predicament: 'work early mornings and late at night' [Gill]. Members felt that individual solutions were unfair:

> Mel [11/01 14:13] I currently feel responsibilised for daring to have a child who can't go to school.

Members felt guilty for being unable to fulfil usual work commitments and, in rare circumstances, for having some tasks redistributed. Some, however, were angry or despondent at having to fight for changes:

> Amaka [26/01 20:55] I did negotiate with individual module leads to not allocate me for afternoon teaching sessions due to childcare constraints. I have to say, so far-so good, but very fragile negotiations. Failing that though..., I would not be able to work anymore. It is as simple as that for my situation.
>
> Paula [26/01 22:53] Reading the comments, it doesn't sound like any of us have managed to have team based approaches...

> Support seems very sporadic. I feel guilty for possibly getting marking help with 1–3 essays, which on balance is ludicrous given all I am juggling. Thanks again for your support everyone. It is making the world of difference for me (heart)

Children also changed their behaviour, impacting on members' routines:

> Georgina [04/02 16:51] Agree with all above. With less to do my kids are staying awake later which pushes my late nights into early mornings.

There are glimpses of children caring for adults too. Children who were old enough learnt to care about members' work, bringing cups of tea and knowing not to interrupt work (sometimes). Younger children played or did schoolwork next to members' sides whilst they worked, albeit not always successfully:

> Georgina [11/02/2021 10:09] This is why this group is fab-it's reassuring to know I'm not the only one cringing my way through meetings as [my childrens'] chaos reins [sic.] in the background. [2 thumbs up]

Group meetings were missed or interrupted by children's care needs; to paraphrase one member, 'parenting often got in the way of parent support'. The lack of private, child-free workspace also meant members missed group meetings. The chat however, allowed them to stay in the conversation.

Accommodating Care

As the emotional load of the pandemic took its toll, members found it difficult to care for themselves. Members cared for each other, providing encouragement and 'permission' to take breaks and have weekends off. Care also took the form of sharing and validating anxieties for example, about the rules for students returning to campus in September 2020 and the implications for our families if students in our classes tested positive for COVID-19. Members tended to feel better for sharing concerns, particularly when unsure about procedures at work:

> Maddy [29/09/2020 09:24] Okay, thanks both!! Feel better for getting my panicked thought out there!! Sorry if I have now stressed out anyone else!! [facepalm]

Members shared feeling stressed, working long hours and becoming exhausted at various points. Despite good intentions members worked through weekends mostly because, to paraphrase Hannah, members 'lived at work':

> Paula [17/09/2020 12:54] My stress levels are through the roof - so much to do!!!!!!!!!!!!!!!!!!!!!!

Members empathised with each other considerably during the second lockdown, as schools and teachers improved and increased their online teaching provision. The first months of 2021 seemed worse than the first lockdown: members did not cope well with university messaging that shifted from 'do what you can' to 'business as usual'.

Members discussed the benefits of using the group to raise the challenges of homeschooling, parenting and caring for children in other meetings rather than presenting these as individual issues. Working collectively, we raised issues with trade unions and supportive managers. For example, a few members met regularly with Human Resources and fed back to the group. We supported the university's Parents and Carers Network to improve our working and caring lives by writing emails and responses to university communications; something we could only do due to the trust and solidarity within the group.

> Mary [11/02 08:39] I would really like to get to today's group to discuss this but I'm teaching all day. I've not been about much lately but I get a lot of strength from reading this chat and knowing you are all there and going through similar things. I am so, so appreciative of all of the work members of the group have put into campaigning for our position to be understood and trying to secure some recognition and solution.

> Amaka [12/02 20:54] This group deserves an award for the spirit of collegiality.

The group collectively campaigned to raise awareness within the institution, successfully lobbying for a change in the tone of university communications, new policies and suggesting practical ways to facilitate a more caring approach. To be fair, the university did offer considerable information about wellbeing policies and self-care at this time; but there remained a lack of understanding about how some staff were failing to cope. Our group provided a space within the workplace for some parents and grandparents to share emotions and stress, the good and bad times often underpinned with wry humour. In a post which received a high number of emoji reactions Mel shared her unhealthy self-care strategy:

> Mel [04/02 16:21] After 15 years I've started smoking again, is that a welfare hack?
>
> [1 thumbs up][1 heart][1 smiley face][1 surprised face][2 sad faces]

Humour played a constant part of the chat from the start (and during weekly meetings we have memories of laughing a lot); members kept their sense of humour amongst the exhaustion:

> Paula [06/10/2020 12:57] What is this thing you speak of??? rest?? I may have to google this unfamiliar term [3 sad faces]

Members encountered troubling situations at work due to multiple caring roles. Although we sympathised with students, particularly those with caring responsibilities, care for students did not always go as planned despite members' best intentions. Care was sacrificed in multiple ways and sometimes inadvertently:

> Gail [05/02 14:04] ... One example from last week, I was on a call with a recently bereaved student - so concerned ... about ensuring she had my full attention I asked the kids to play outside (9 and 6).... - it ended in them screaming at each other, at the window directly in front of my workstation, crying and fighting with each other.... My immediate reaction afterwards was to tell them off for disturbing me when they knew it was important, but then I thought about it, and realised, they are 9 and 6, they have no concept of what is happening. They were upset, I was upset, it was just awful. [3 hearts][1 surprised face][3 sad faces]

Members were constantly exhausted; some said they could not share the full extent of their emotions. Members also recognised that their difficulties and the accompanying negative impacts on mental health were far from unique to the group. As schools re-opened for all children in March 2021, members shared feelings and offered support:

> Gill [11/03 12:21] Sorry I won't make it today, feeling emotionally exhausted today to be honest - second daughter went back to school today. I feel the need to sleep! Hope you are all okay this week.

> Mel [11/03 12:24] My daughter went back yesterday and I felt (feel) exactly the same Gill. I'm constantly on the verge of bursting into tears through tiredness/weird emotional dimensions that I can't articulate! Take care.

Concluding Discussion

We have presented a novel case study of how workers responded to COVID-19 in the workplace when faced with homeschooling and caring for children and demonstrated how membership of a peer support group enabled us to cope. The findings demonstrate the importance of online peer support for working parents during the pandemic and the benefits of bringing together a small group of staff with a common need to care for and homeschool children. Those involved in the research were overwhelmingly positive about the group. Within the group we experienced 'good care' relating to Tronto's (2013) five phases and elements of care outlined above; members recognised and cared about each other's needs on a weekly and at times daily basis; cared for each other by collectively taking responsibility for the group (and its chat and meetings); giving care to each other by demonstrating caring skills including compassion, empathy and humour; and receiving care from each other in response to member's needs. Finally, the group cared with each other, the group worked because care became habitual and enabled the formation of strong, enduring relationships of trust and solidarity. The group's collective care meant that members could do better than they might otherwise have done to care for their children; summarised by one member's declaration: 'Without... this group I would have drowned by now!'

Our case study demonstrates how peer support provided a way of surviving working, homeschooling and/or childcare throughout the pandemic. The group provided an inclusive, supportive and caring space within the context of 'care-less' institutions where inequalities exist due to caring responsibilities. The ethic of care highlights first the gendered nature of care that contributes to its undervaluing within institutions and, second, the political nature of care (Tronto, 2013). The group successfully attracted a gender mix, which is uncommon in parenting groups (Brooks and Hodkinson, 2020). Perhaps it was male members' increased involvement in childcare during the pandemic (Ferguson, 2020) and common professional bonds that facilitated this inclusion. Despite increased media attention and research on gendered inequalities during the pandemic (Crook, 2020; Ferguson, 2020), the group was established because of the invisibility and unresponsiveness within the workplace to homeschooling and increased childcare. Tronto (2013) refers to this as 'privileged irresponsibility'; those not having to care (for children in this case) absenting themselves from discussions about responsibilities (Zembylas et al., 2014). This could be framed as unintended harm and lack of care from institutions during this time. We need to recognise, however, that this phenomenon pre-existed the pandemic (Askins and Blazek, 2017; Smith and Ulus, 2020) and is perhaps a genuine result of ignorance of other people's lives (Rogers, 2017). For the group, this meant that care became a form of activism and everyday resistance (Wood et al., 2024) and the source of additional practical and emotional labour to raise awareness and change organisational cultures.

Having a supportive network was essential in helping us to manage stress. It did not, however, always work for us. During the pandemic and lockdowns, caring relationships could be joyful but they could also be overwhelming, particularly when combined with paid employment (Miller, 2020). Pressure points were heightened during times of school closure (Khan, 2022), but even when schools reopened, there was a fear of children being sent home at any moment; children and their care seemed to be an afterthought. Our case study provides evidence of how difficult this period could be for working parents at a university, even though we were a relatively privileged group, able to work flexibly and at home for most of the pandemic.

Fine and Tronto (2020: 302) contend that during the pandemic 'care has "come out," emerging from the shadows as a taken-for-granted afterthought in public life'. There was hope that the pandemic would change understandings and practice of care in society in radical ways; that care would remain visible (Miller, 2020). Our experiences and exhaustion meant that we were perhaps not so hopeful about this at the end of the pandemic. Consequently, we urge universities and education institutions to find the space and time to allow for reflection on pandemic care experiences, to consider what 'good care' might entail, to develop more positive cultures of care (Askins and Blazek, 2017) and to address the inequalities resulting from caring both during and after the pandemic.

References

Adisa, T.A., Antonacopouou, T., Beauregard, A., Dickmann, M. and Adekoya, D. 2022. Exploring the impact of COVID-19 on employees' boundary management and work–life balance. *British Journal of Management*. doi:10.1111/1467-8551. 12643

Askins, K. and Blazek, M. 2017. Feeling our way: academia, emotions and a politics of care. *Social & Cultural Geography*, 18(8), 1086–1105.

Bradbury, A., Braun, A., Duncan, S., Harmey, S., Levy, R. and Moss, G. 2022. Crisis policy enactment: primary school leaders' responses to the covid-19 pandemic in England, *Journal of Education Policy*. 10.1080/02680939.2022.2097316. (Accessed 9 August 2023).

Braun, V. and Clarke, V. 2019. Reflecting on reflexive thematic analysis, *Qualitative Research in Sport, Exercise and Health*, 11(4), 589–597, 10.1080/2159676X.2019. 1628806

Brooks, R. and Hodkinson, P. 2020. Out-of-place: The lack of engagement with parent networks of caregiving fathers of young children, *Families, Relationships and Societies*, 9(2), 201–216.

Calear, A.L., Morse, A.R., Banfield, M., Gulliver, A., Cherbuin, N., Farrer, L.M., Murray, K., Rodney Harris, R.M. and Batterham, P.J. 2022. Psychosocial impacts of home-schooling on parents and caregivers during the COVID-19 pandemic. *BMC Public Health*, 22, 1–8. DOI.10.1186/s12889-022-12532-2

Cantillon, S., Moore, E. and Teasdale, N. 2021. COVID-19 and the pivotal role of grandparents: childcare and income support in the UK and South Africa, *Feminist Economics*, 27(1–2), 188–202.

Crook, S. 2020. Parenting during the covid-19 pandemic of 2020: Academia, labour and care work, *Women's History Review*. 10.1080/09612025.2020.1807690

Dobosz, D., Gierczyk, M. and Hornby, G. 2022. Parental perspectives of home-schooling of children with special educational needs and disabilities during the COVID-19 pandemic: a review. *Journal of Research in Special Educational Needs*, 23(1) 3–11.

Ferguson, D. 2020. "I feel like a 1950s housewife": how lockdown has exposed the gender divide. *The Guardian*, 3rd May. Available at: https://www.theguardian.com/world/2020/may/03/i-feel-like-a-1950s-housewife-how-lockdown-has-exposed-the-gender-divide?CMP=Share_iOSApp_Other. (Accessed 24 October 2023)

Fine, M. and Tronto, J. 2020. Care goes viral: Care theory and research confront the global COVID-19 pandemic. *International Journal of Care and Caring*, 4(3), 301–309.

Fisher, B. and Tronto, J. 1990. Toward a feminist theory of caring. In *Circles of Care*, Eds E. Abel, M. Nelson, pp. 36–54, Albany, NY, SUNY Press.

Flyvbjerg, B. 2006. Five misunderstandings about case-study research. *Qualitative Inquiry*, 12(2), 219–245.

Gilligan, M., Suitor, J.J. and Rurka, M. 2020. Multigenerational social support in the face of the COVID-19 pandemic. *Journal of Family Theory and Review*, 12(4), 431–447.

Given, L. 2008. *The SAGE Encyclopaedia of Qualitative Research Methods*, London, Sage.

Hume, S., Brown, S.R. and Mahtani, K.R. 2023. School closures during COVID-19: an overview of systematic reviews. *BMJ Evidence-Based Medicine*, 28, 164–174 Available from: https://ebm.bmj.com/content/ebmed/28/3/164.full.pdf. (Accessed 8 August 2023).

Hutchins, H.M. 2015. Outing the imposter: a study exploring imposter phenomenon among higher education faculty. *New Horizons in Adult Education and Human Resource Development*, 27(2), 3–12.

Institute for Fiscal Studies 2023. Home learning experiences through the COVID19 pandemic. Available from: https://ifs.org.uk/sites/default/files/output_url_files/R195-Home-learning-experiences-through-the-COVID-19-pandemic.pdf. (Accessed 8 August 2023)

Jarrahi, M.H., Goay, C., Zirker, S. and Zhang, Y. 2021. Using digital diaries as a research method for capturing practices in situ. In *Research Methods for Digital Work and Organization: Investigating Distributed, Multi-Modal, and Mobile Work*, Eds G. Symon, K. Prichard, C. Hine, Oxford, Oxford University Press.

Khan, T. 2022. Parents' experiences of home-schooling amid Covid-19 school closures, in London, England. *Journal of Early Childhood Research*, 20(4), 580–594.

Miller, K. 2020. The ethics of care and academic motherhood amid COVID-19. *Gender Work and Organisation*, 28(51), 260-265.

Mountz, A., Bonds, A., Mansfield, B., Loyd, J., Hyndman, J., Walton-Roberts, M., Basu, R., Whitson, R., Hawkins, R., Hamilton, T. and Curran, W. 2015. For slow scholarship: a feminist politics of resistance through collective action in the neoliberal university. *ACME: An International Journal for Critical Geographies*, 14(4), 1235–1259. Available at: https://acme-journal.org/index.php/acme/article/view/1058

Mulholland, K., Nichol, D. and Gillespie, A. 2023. 'It feels like you're going back to the beginning…': addressing imposter feelings in early career academics through the creation of communities of practice. *Journal of Further and Higher Education*, 47(1), pp. 89–104.

Murray, J. 2020. Boris Johnson's bluster comes unstuck over lockdown rules. *The Guardian, 29th September, 2020*. Available at: https://www.theguardian.com/politics/2020/sep/29/boris-johnsons-bluster-comes-unstuck-over-lockdown-rules. (Accessed 27 October, 2023)

Noddings, N. 2003. *Educating Moral People: A Caring Alternative to Character Education*, Vermont, Teachers College Press.

Office for National Statistics (ONS) 2020. *Coronavirus and Homeschooling in Great Britain: April to June 2020*. Available from: https://www.ons.gov.uk/peoplepopulationandcommunity/educationandchildcare/articles/coronavirusandhomeschoolingingreatbritain/apriltojune2020. (Accessed 8 August 2023).

Pring, R. 2000. The false duality of educational research. *Journal of Philosophy of Education*, 34(2), 247–260.

Rogers, C. 2017. "I'm complicit and I'm ambivalent and that's crazy": care-less spaces for women in the academy. *Women's Studies International Forum*, 61, 115–122.

Smith, C. and Ulus, E. 2020. Who cares for academics? We need to talk about emotional well-being including what we avoid and intellectualise through macro-discourses. *Organization*, 27(6), 840–857. https://doi.org/10.1177/1350508419867201

Thomas, G. 2011. *How to do your Case Study. A Guide for Students and Researchers*, London, Sage.

Tronto, J.C. 2013. *Caring Democracy: Markets, Equality and Justice*, New York, New York Press.

Watermeyer, R., Shankar, K., Crick, T., Knight, C., McGaughey, F., Hardman, J., Suri, V.R., Chung, R. and Phelan, D. 2021. 'Pandemia': a reckoning of UK universities' corporate response to COVID-19 and its academic fallout. *British Journal of Sociology of Education*, 42(5–6), 651–666. doi:10.1080/01425692.2021.1937058

Wood, B.E., Black, R., Walsh, L., Garrard, K.A., Bearman, M., Thomas, M.K.E., Ryan, J. and Infantes, N. 2024. Resisting neoliberalism: teacher education academics navigating precarious times. *Teaching in Higher Education*, 29(3), 707–722. doi:10.1080/13562517.2023.2300950

Working Families 2021. *Working Families Impact 2020-21*. Available from: https://workingfamilies.org.uk/wp-content/uploads/2020/09/2019-2020-impact-report-FINAL.pdf. (Accessed 8 August 2023).

Yamey, G. and Walensky, R.P. 2020. Covid-19: Re-opening universities is high risk. *BMJ (Clinical Research Ed.)*, 370, m3365. doi:10.1136/bmj.m3365

Yin, R.K. 2018. *Case Study Research and Applications*, London, Sage.

Zembylas, M., Bozalek, V. and Shefer, T. 2014. Tronto's notion of privileged irresponsibility and the reconceptualisation of care: implications for critical pedagogies of emotion in higher education. *Gender and Education*, 26(3), 200–214. https://doi.org/10.1080/09540253.2014.901718

Chapter 13

Teaching During Lockdowns

Linzi Brown

The Duchess's Community High School, UK

Abstract

This reflective chapter draws upon my experiences as a secondary school teacher in England during the COVID-19 lockdowns. I reflect on the difficulties of teaching and providing care towards the young people at our school, who were trying to navigate their education at such a difficult time. In this piece, I conclude that education is intertwined with all aspects of wellbeing and that through care for this wellbeing, education can flourish.

Keywords: Care; COVID-19; education; secondary school; teaching; wellbeing

I initially worked as an Early Years Practitioner for several years in various rural settings before retraining to teach Secondary School. I have worked as a teacher for 17 years, focussing on child development and care. I'm now head of faculty at a large rural school that serves 1500 students from ages 11 to 18. The faculty I lead covers the subjects Food and Nutrition, Health and Social Care, Childcare, and Hair and Beauty. I am also a Form Tutor, which involves providing pastoral support to students, so care features as a central part of my everyday work and is important to me. The school has one of the largest catchment areas in the UK, which means that some students can be travelling over an hour to get to school. Similarly, some of our students may be involved in rural employment, which can shape their education and the school accommodates this.

In March 2020, it was announced that schools would close, and we had two days to try to plan and put in place measures for what was initially envisaged to be three weeks of lockdown; clearly this extended for a much longer period. Paramount concerns were how will we maintain students' welfare during this time and maintain our obligation to provide an education? We began the first set of lockdowns using Google Classroom to teach online, and we always had a skeleton classroom for potentially vulnerable students to attend in person. By the time

Easter had passed, it was clear we were going to have to develop more approaches, as some students were exhausted by their situation; this was impacting their wellbeing, increasing their anxiety. By the time the second lockdown occurred, we built in flexibility to when and how students engaged; flexibility and reassurance was key to safeguarding students' wellbeing at this time. So, accepting that some may not have done aspects of the work but reassuring them that this was okay and managing my own expectations as a teacher about what was achievable at home. This has fed forward to today; when a student is absent, we don't flag this as a negative, instead we provide the information missed with a sticker that says: 'while you were away'. It has the date, and all the material gets posted on Google Classroom and we will just put which lesson it was on, so they can catch up if they can.

After a while, the written feedback just felt too robotic and we made sure to provide audio feedback to students so that they could hear their teacher's voice; this is so important, down to the tone, to help them to feel connected to me and their education. I tried to get them to do this back, and some of them did, which humanised the whole process somewhat. We would talk and get to know each other a bit more, talk about hobbies and goals, like me clearing out a wardrobe and them learning new skills and we would hold each other accountable. We just had to work out the best way to do things.

Lockdown education was mentally exhausting for teachers too; at one point I think I averaged possibly 90 hours of screen time a week working. It was relentless. You felt like you had just cleared the decks and then there would be another email. Or there would be a message to send because a student was accessing the online work at 9 p.m. who hadn't accessed it all day because they were sharing computers with siblings and this was their allocated time, but I wouldn't want to let them down, especially for the student who hadn't engaged for a week, or had just started to engage I would think 'Oh my goodness, I've got them, I can't leave them now'. As teachers we all tried to support each other too; tried to allow people to work at their own pace, to not have unrealistic expectations of each other. Everyone had different pressures, including some caring for their own children. I learnt I never want to work from home. We work from home now of course but it is not the same, at least when you are leaving the school building, you can leave it behind; during the lockdowns it was constant, the balance just went out of the window.

The students experienced the lockdowns in different ways; while it was certainly very difficult for some of our students, some of them thrived in their online learning. Some have found it difficult to come back to the classroom as a result; more socially anxious, they find it hard to communicate and that is no surprise – they were in small bubbles for a significant amount of time. So, we have some school refusers now. It makes me think that in an ideal world, we would offer a more flexible education system for students to learn in ways that really suit them.

Being back in the classroom when restrictions eased was a relief, but this brought additional challenges; we could not move from the front of the classroom. You could give them verbal feedback, but all you really wanted to do was go and sit beside them, and really support them with things. It highlighted to me how important it was to be physically present in the room and how that can support students.

Some students need that structure of being at school where they feel safe and secure; home is not always a safe place for children. Some were never going to access education at home; some families were unable to afford meals at home. The return to school has meant more of an appreciation of that and an example of this is we now have regular breakfast clubs as a result to support students, to enhance school provision and the learning opportunities.

Fundamentally, this really highlighted that school is so much more than education. An education cannot start until all the other social needs are provided for.

Chapter 14

Precarious Schooling and COVID-19

Jason Burg

The Duchess's Community High School, UK

Abstract

This short reflection considers experiences of providing care as an education professional during the lockdown periods in England. My experiences as a trainee teacher and then as an hourly paid teaching assistant highlight how often the many important caring professionals were also left in particularly precarious situations during the COVID-19 pandemic.

Keywords: Care; COVID-19; precarity; secondary school; teaching; zero hours

I am a secondary school history teacher in a school in the North East of England, but during Covid I was initially a student teacher and then precariously employed as a teaching assistant at two schools.

I began my initial teacher training (ITT) in September 2019 as a salaried trainee, teaching classes by myself, learning on the job while I also studied remotely for my Postgraduate Certificate in Education. At the time of my training, all trainee teachers were expected to complete two practice placements as part of their course before qualifying as an Early Career Teacher. In March 2020, as the then UK Prime Minister Boris Johnson was announcing the closure of schools to 'flatten the curve', I was three weeks into my second placement, before returning to complete my placement at my first (and main) school, an all-girls, independent school. Initially, it felt unclear what the closures would mean for student teachers. My department in the school where I was based primarily, split responsibility for planning lessons by year groups, and I was assigned Year 10 (ages 14–15). Remote teaching at my school was not done with any live element, but rather just PowerPoints with voice notes sent out via our virtual learning environment (VLE). This made me feel remote from everything, as though I had left my students to flounder.

Upon completing my ITT I looked for jobs and could find none that I could travel to; I did not have a car and many schools were unreachable by public transport. I eventually registered with an agency and was offered a temporary, hourly paid position at a city-centre school in September 2020 as a teaching assistant (TA) and cover supervisor (to cover lessons for sick or absent colleagues) when schools reopened in September. I had no real understanding of these roles beyond what I had seen in my classes, and Covid restrictions meant that my natural instincts to adopt a formal teaching role had to mostly be curtailed.

I was given a rota of one-to-one, in class support for Special Educational Needs and Disabled students. It was very difficult at first, as I was receiving mixed messages: teaching staff were told to stay at the front of the class and not sit next to students, but I was expected to be in amongst the students, sitting close by/next to them to offer help, and moving between them in the classroom. In some ways, the TAs were freer than the teaching staff; we could move away from the front of the room and therefore took on more of a whole-class role, in contrast to the teachers who stood at the front of the class. In some respects, this was unnerving; I was closer to people and felt more exposed to the virus, but I also appreciated that I was able to do my work in supporting the students, which also supported and enabled the teacher in their role. As a teacher now, I reflect on this, how TAs are often doing that 'care' work in amongst the students and how important that is, even while they are often paid poorly and precariously employed (my pay was £65 per day, but nothing if I could not attend as I experienced when I was off work with suspected Covid).

After a few months, in November 2020 I got a position at another city-centre high school, but this time as an English-specific TA. My remit was to plan and deliver interventions for year elevens, as at that time the Government had not yet decided that exams would not go ahead in May/June 2021.[1] All of that was thrown off course when schools were again closed in January 2021. At first, I was asked to come into school to supervise classes of students who were coming in. I was given students who were children of key workers, while more experienced staff supervised vulnerable students who were coming in because it was safer for them to be at school than at home. I was taken off supervising rather quickly, and given the job of phoning home to a year group to check how students were doing in their online lessons. The most persistent concern from parents was the perceived lack of live lessons (this school had a system of one live lesson per subject per week, then independent work in the rest of the lessons). Many parents compared their high school children to their primary school children, not understanding why the former were not getting eight live lessons a day, as the latter were. It was difficult to get many parents to understand that I was not a decision maker, or even a classroom teacher, and that all I could do was pass on

---

[1] In England and Wales, students take a set of exams called General Certificate of Secondary Education (GCSE) at age 15–16 (in Year 11). The qualification is offered in specific subjects, such as English, Mathematics, Sciences, History, Geography, etc.

their message to the Head of Year. It quickly felt hopeless. Looking back, it makes me think how exhausting some of this caring work could be.

I was then moved from this role by the Head of English, who asked me to cover for an ill colleague. I was given three, Year 11 classes organised by ability; a top, a mid, and a bottom set, as well as a Year 9 class. I had never met these students before, and they had never met me. I followed the school policy of one live lesson a week per class, but found these incredibly difficult; I didn't receive any specific training in online teaching, attendance was low in live lessons (often zero), and I got the feeling that many logged in and left. The bottom set class was often empty except for me. I soon realized that the Virtual Learning Environment used in the school allowed me to give recorded audio feedback on work, and I began doing this. To my surprise, some students began responding to the audio feedback with their own recordings; this made me feel more connected to the students I had never seen in person and made live lessons easier as I was able to put a voice to a name on the screen.

When the school reopened after Easter in April 2021, I had a connection to those students who recorded audio feedback that I may not otherwise have had. Students who never spoke in live lessons would speak on the feedback. I think the pressure of speaking in front of others during a lesson was eased by the private nature of the feedback notes. When I was in the classroom with them later in the year, I knew which 'quiet' students I could talk to if I approached them independently, rather than in front of the class. Having built those relationships meant that I was able to embed care into my teaching more effectively.

Reflecting on that period, I gained particular awareness of the important caring work that TAs do in the classroom and how vital that can be to facilitating education. I am also conscious of how digital approaches can both enable caring teaching and also impede, depending on how they are used.

Section 5

Young People Navigating Care and Control Beyond the School

Chapter 15

Virtual Hearings and Their Impact on Children's Participation in Decisions About Their Care and Protection

Catherine Nixon[a], Kirsty Deacon[a], Andrew James[b], Ciara Waugh[b], Zodie[b] and Sarah McGarrol[c]

[a]Scottish Children's Reporter Administration, UK
[b]Our Hearings, Our Voice, UK
[c]NIHR Health Determinants Research Collaboration Aberdeen, Aberdeen City Council, UK

Abstract

The Children's Hearings System is a Scottish welfare-based tribunal-based system in which decisions are made about the care and protection of children in conflict with the law and/or in need of additional care and protection. The Covid-19 pandemic resulted in the rapid implementation of a virtual Children's Hearings System. This system, which operated as the sole mechanism through which decisions were made between March and July 2020, continued to be used alongside in-person and hybrid Hearing formats for the duration of the pandemic. Early research into the use of virtual Hearings identified that their use presented significant barriers to participation, particularly in relation to the impacts of digital literacy and digital poverty. However, much of this research focused upon the experiences of adult participants in Hearings and failed to capture the experiences of children. In this chapter, we present findings from a qualitative study designed to explore the impact of virtual Hearings upon the participation and rights of children. In doing so, we demonstrate that virtual Hearings acted as both a barrier and facilitator of children's participation.

Keywords: Children's participation; children's rights; covid-19 pandemic; decision-making; social care and justice; virtual hearings

Introduction: Background to Scotland's Children's Hearings System

In 1964, Lord Kilbrandon recommended that a national system of legal tribunals (known as Children's Hearings) be established. These would make decisions about the need for compulsory state intervention in the lives of children who were: in conflict with the law; persistently truanting from school; in need of additional care or protection due to maltreatment, neglect or living with somebody who poses a threat to their welfare. The underlying ethos would be that the 'needs, not deeds' of children would be considered within the context of a welfare-based tribunal rather than in the criminal courts. For children in conflict with the law, this meant recognising that children who commit offences often share the same histories of trauma, neglect and adversity as maltreated children, and therefore require similar levels of care and protection (Kilbrandon, 1964; McGarrol et al., 2022).

The Children's Hearings System was established in 1971. Its current remit and function is outlined in the 2011 Children's Hearings (Scotland) Act which specifies that children in need of compulsory measures of supervision should be referred to the Scottish Children's Reporter Administration (SCRA). After a child has been referred, a Children's Reporter investigates and determines whether there are legal grounds to pursue compulsory measures. If there are grounds, then a Children's Hearing is arranged. Hearings are conducted by trained volunteers known as Panel Members. Their role is to decide whether to place the child onto a Compulsory Supervision Order (CSO). This is a legal order that instructs social work services to provide support and supervision to the child. It also states whether the child will be looked after at home by their parents with social work support or looked after away from home in kinship, foster, residential or secure care. The views of children, their parents and any relevant professionals or caregivers will be sought during the Hearing to help the Panel make this decision. A Children's Reporter will also be present to ensure the Hearing is conducted lawfully. Between 1st April 2022 and 31st March 2023, 10,981 children were referred to SCRA. Of these, 10,128 had Hearings arranged. CSOs were made for 1897 children (SCRA, 2023).

What role do children play in making decisions about their care and protection?

Article 12 of the United Nations Convention on the Rights of the Child (UNCRC) states that every child has the right to express their views, feelings and wishes in all matters affecting them, and to have their views considered and taken seriously. The Children's Hearings System provides a number of ways for children to share their views with the Panel, namely: being allowed to meet privately with Panel Members during Hearings; children's views being shared by social workers, solicitors, advocacy-workers and safeguarders; children writing to the Reporter to say what they would like to happen and through the self-completion of 'Hearing

About Me' forms (McDiarmid et al., 2017; Porter et al., 2016, 2020). In addition, Scottish Law states that all children should attend their Hearings unless they are deemed by the Panel to have insufficient capacity to understand the proceedings. Most children under the age of eight are excused from their Hearings.

Kilbrandon's vision of Children's Hearings was that they would be a non-adversarial space in which children can feel supported to share their views. However, the evidence shows that Hearings have become increasingly adversarial spaces in which children do not always feel emotionally safe and empowered to share their views (Children's Parliament, 2010; Mackie, 2023). Qualitative data gathered from children indicate that they often feel that their views do not carry the same weight as those of adults participating in Hearings (Children's Parliament, 2010; Duncan, 2020; Kurlus et al., 2016; Porter et al., 2020; SCRA, 2016; Who Cares? Scotland, 2020). A number of reasons are given for this, including children: not being invited or encouraged to share their views by Panel Members during the Hearing; feeling that they had to wait until all the adults had spoken until they were asked their views; perceiving that decisions about their care and protection had already been made prior to the Hearing. Children who feel that their views are dismissed by Panel Members often choose to stop sharing their views.

Lack of control over what information is shared within Hearings has been identified as a barrier to children's participation in the decision-making process. This is because the information discussed at Hearings can result in children feeling stigmatised, shamed and (re)traumatised (Our Hearings, Our Voice, 2020). Choosing not to share thoughts and feelings with Panel Members can therefore be an active choice to help children (re)gain control over what information is shared; particularly if they consider the information to be personal, private or irrelevant to proceedings (Who Cares? Scotland, 2020).

Finally, the environment that Hearings are held in can affect participation. Children's participation is adversely affected by the presence of board-room style tables in Hearings rooms, along with the use of 'big words', formal language and formal titles. Participation is also hindered by the presence of windows on Hearing room doors and the presence of communal corridors outside Hearings rooms as these leave children feeling that their Hearings are not private (Children's Parliament, 2010; Kurlus et al., 2016; Our Hearings, Our Voice, 2020; Who Cares? Scotland, 2020).

In February 2020, Scotland's Independent Care Review (The Promise) was published. It states:

> ... children must be listened to and meaningfully and appropriately involved in decision-making about their care, with all those involved properly listening and responding to what children want and need (Duncan, 2020, p .9)

To support this, The Promise recommended that the Children's Hearings System should explore how digital technologies, particularly those that children regularly use to communicate, could be used to ensure that children's views were better heard and reflected within the decision-making process.

The Covid-19 Pandemic and Its Impact on How Children's Hearings Were Conducted

On 11th March 2020, the World Health Organization declared Covid-19 to be a global pandemic. The implementation of a UK-wide lockdown on March 23rd presented a significant challenge to incorporating children's voices in the decision-making process as all Children's Hearings Centres were forcibly closed. This resulted in the need to rapidly develop, test and implement a virtual Hearings system (see Nixon et al., 2023).

Between 23rd March and 4th May 2020, all Hearings were conducted as administrative Hearings with only the Children's Reporter, Panel Members and Solicitors in attendance. From May 4th, participation in Hearings was extended to parents, health and social care professionals and any other relevant persons (e.g. foster carers). Although children remained able to attend their Hearings from May 4th, the Coronavirus (Scotland) Act 2020 allowed all children to be excused from attending Hearings until 30th September 2022. Until 10th July 2020, all Hearings were conducted using video-conferencing technology. After this point, a hybrid model for conducting Hearings was implemented. This allowed fully virtual Hearings to operate alongside fully in-person Hearings, hybrid Hearings (where some people attended in-person and others attended virtually) and digital hub Hearings (where video-conferencing software was used to connect two or more rooms of socially distanced participants). The use of fully virtual and hybrid Hearings has continued since the end of the pandemic.

SCRA monitored the impact of introducing virtual Hearings during the first three months of the pandemic. This included online surveys completed by Hearings participants and formal written feedback from Children's Reporters, illustrating barriers to fair and effective participation in Hearings. The findings highlighted that digital poverty and digital inequity significantly impacted participation. Children and families did not have sufficient digital literacy skills or access to appropriate devices, lacked high-speed internet access or were reliant on mobile data, and experienced regular connectivity difficulties. These findings were corroborated by a rapid evidence review undertaken by Porter et al. (2020). How SCRA addressed these issues is described in detail in Nixon et al. (2023).

Porter et al. (2020, 2021) also highlighted the wider emotional impacts that participating in Hearings from home could have on children and families. Their research illustrated that the pandemic removed many of the usual pastoral and legal supports that families received from social workers, legal representatives and advocacy/rights workers before, during and after Hearings. They also highlighted that participants in Hearings felt that they did not receive sufficient information from SCRA about virtual Hearings. All of these issues, combined with the technological barriers, resulted in concerns being raised about the fairness of virtual Hearings.

Including the Voices of Children

Research on the impact of virtual Hearings is limited in three ways: (1) The data provide a snapshot of what participation looked like during an emergent period where virtual Hearings had just been implemented and tested, and choices had been made to deliberately exclude individuals from Hearings. (2) The data do not reflect changes made during the course of the pandemic to try to address the impact of digital inequity and technological challenges on participation. (3) The research presents an adult-centric view of the impact of virtual Hearings, with only 2 of the 276 voices recorded in Porter et al. (2020) and only 10 of the 1200+ views recorded by SCRA (Nixon et al., 2023) coming from young people who had attended virtual Hearings. This means that there is a significant gap in our understanding not only of children's experiences of virtual Hearings but also their experiences of these within an embedded and tested system.

To assess the impact that virtual Hearings had upon children's participation in decisions about their own care and protection, a mixed methods study was designed with Our Hearings, Our Voice (OHOV). This is an independent Board of Hearings-experienced young people that exists to make improvements to the Children's Hearings System. Members of OHOV, including those listed as authors of this chapter, met with the research team in July 2020 to explore ways of measuring the impact that the pandemic was having on Hearings-experienced children. Through discussion with the young people, it quickly became apparent that there were concerns around the impact that virtual Hearings was having upon children's participation and well-being. The research questions for the study were designed based on these discussions.

Ethical approval for the study was granted by SCRA's Research Ethics Committee. The study combined a realist-inspired synthesis of all published and non-published data about the implementation of virtual Hearings, an analysis of routinely collected administrative data on Hearings attendance during the pandemic, and the collection of both qualitative and quantitative data from children and their caregivers in order to explore how the use of virtual Hearings impacted children's participation and rights. Members of OHOV met with the research team on two occasions to inform the content of the materials that would be used for the study, including the proposed topic guides and wording of information sheets and consent forms. In this chapter, we present findings from the qualitative elements of the study. These data were collected from 15 Hearings-experienced young people, 8 foster carers and 18 residential and secure care workers between March and December 2022. The decision to include the voices of caregivers reflected the fact that the provisions made by the Coronavirus (Scotland) Act 2020 meant that less than a third of children attended Hearings during the pandemic (Nixon et al., 2023). Their voices are presented here as a means of capturing how the voices of children were shared in Hearings when they were not present, either physically or virtually.

Data were collected using a range of methods, including: one-to-one or paired interviews, group discussions and participatory workshops. The methods were designed in conjunction with OHOV, and reflected requests from young people to provide children and young people with choice over how their voices were shared. Requests from OHOV members to provide children and young people with frequent breaks and sensory inputs such as fidget toys during interviews were incorporated into the approach taken. Interviews with adult caregivers were conducted either in-person or via video-conferencing software depending upon the preferences of participants and the public health protection measures in place. All of the qualitative work conducted with children was done in-person. Social distancing and masking regulations were adhered to during data collection with adults but relaxed when speaking to children. Rapid antigen testing was used to minimise the risk of transmission.

The collected data were analysed thematically using the framework method (Ritchie and Spencer, 2002). The analysis of data was undertaken by SCRA researchers, with sense checking of findings and implications for policy and practice gathered through meetings with the OHOV members listed as authors. During these sense checking sessions, Ciara and Zodie asked if they could illustrate how virtual Hearings made children feel in order to ensure that the findings were more accessible. These illustrations can be found in Figs. 15.1 and 15.2.

The Negative Effects of Virtual Hearings on Children's Participation and Well-being

The organisation and conduct of virtual Hearings acted as a barrier to some children having their voices included in the decision-making process. Four main reasons were given for this. First, connectivity issues, such as poor connectivity, adversely affected participation. Second, the way virtual Hearings had been set up removed the opportunity for children to meet privately with Panel Members:

> Hearings that are virtual are difficult as you do not have the ability to privately speak to a panel member to convey anything you don't want to say in front of other people. (Chris, Hearings-experienced young person)

Third, young people felt that issues that they had experienced during in-person Hearings, such as feeling that they weren't being listened to, were amplified in the digital space:

> ... it is easier to disregard the child's opinion as it is easy to talk over them' (James, Hearings-experienced young person)

Fourth, how the digital space was managed by Panel Members, including how technological features such as the mute button were used, was highlighted as a way of intentionally or unintentionally shutting down children's voices:

> I have seen a Panel Chair mute a child... Now ok, they were maybe talking over people and being disruptive, and maybe they

were causing the meeting to slow down, but it is their meeting. Panel Members have to understand that the kids are going to swear, they are going to get emotional, maybe they will shout at somebody, but when we were in-person we just dealt with that. We never gagged children (Mark, Secure Care Worker).

Having to raise your hand to indicate you wanted to speak was challenging for children:

> You have to raise your hand to speak. The child just wants to jump in and say something, but I'm having to press to put the hand up and then they'll be like "oh forget it" (Claire, Secure Care Worker).

In addition to feeling unheard, some young people worried about the privacy and safety of virtual Hearings. The biggest concern was whether other individuals were present who shouldn't be. This concern was amplified when hearings participants couldn't see everyone who was in attendance on their screen. There were two key ways this occurred. First, individuals switching their cameras off to improve connectivity appeared as 'little black boxes' on the screen (Jennie, Hearings-experienced young person). Second, the use of mobile phones and networked computers that had local area settings that restricted the number of video connections that could be made prevented all participants being shown in gallery view. Young people also worried that electronic links to meetings could be shared with individuals who were not supposed to be present. These concerns were echoed by caregivers:

> You can't trust the people will send the link on to someone who is not supposed to be there (Annie, Foster Carer).

> We suspected that one of the parents, who was quite dangerous and not supposed to go near the other parent, was living in their house (Claire, Foster Carer)

Privacy for young people to freely participate in Hearings was also raised, particularly in relation to the challenges faced by young people living independently, or in group-care environments:

> I live with 8 flat mates. I could have done it in the kitchen, but that was not private. My bedroom was not ok as the walls aren't soundproofed (Laura, Hearings-experienced young person)

> At a physical Hearing you are in a place specifically designed for a Hearing. There is no exterior noise or people walking by. You don't get the external factors that affect [Microsoft] Teams such as doors banging, young people walking down the corridor, or staff coming in and out of the room to get medication (Andy, Secure Care Worker).

Some residential and secure care staff told us that they had resorted to locking doors to prevent other children walking into Hearings being held in shared spaces. They wondered how this felt to children:

> We tend to lock the door when we come in... it is that kind of, it is already a big enough day as it is so that could be enough to make a young person feel really, really uncomfortable (Mary, Residential Care Worker)

The other major barrier to participation that was highlighted was the negative impact that virtual Hearings had upon relational practice. In particular, it was identified that virtual Hearings lacked the rapport building and social interactions that some children needed in order to be able to share their views.

> I keywork a wee girl who really, really struggled with it. She would hide off the screen, would hardly say anything. Whereas if you met her in person she is dead bubbly and would get her point across rather than hiding from the screen and lying on my shoulder and grabbing onto me because she was so nervous because it has not got that personal touch (Andy, Secure Care Worker)

The lack of a 'personal touch' resulted in young people and caregivers frequently describing virtual Hearings as 'cold', 'clinical', 'formal' and 'court-like'. The main explanation given for the use of these adjectives was that many of the more subtle parts of human interaction could not be replicated on a screen.

> When you are in person you get a lot more than just the visual of a flat screen. In virtual Hearings you can't judge the body language. You lose the social cues (Alistair, Residential Care Worker)

The loss of these social cues was succinctly summed up by Amy (*Hearings-experienced young person*) who said:

> ... because you can't see them, you don't know if they are a robot person and not a real person.

Young people with negative experiences of participating in virtual Hearings told us that they had found their Hearings to be 'stressful', 'frustrating' and 'anger-inducing' events. They also told us that virtual Hearings had left them feeling 'isolated', 'alone' and 'worried' during their Hearings. Some of the young people questioned the fairness of proceedings, and the decisions taken by Panel Members. These feelings were amplified when technological issues such as connectivity issues or poor audio-visual signals occurred. For some, having to invite trauma into their homes affected their emotional security:

... my bedroom is supposed to be my safe space. Discussing the issues that come up in Hearings in that space makes me feel unsafe (Laura, Hearings-experienced young person).

For others, their emotional security was threatened by virtual Hearings acting as a barrier to their voice being heard:

I was fighting for my life and not able to say anything. It left me feeling really bad. It was the first Hearing [in 3 years] that I felt scared and anxious (Tom, Hearings-experienced young person).

The impersonal nature of virtual Hearings, along with the feelings of anxiety and disempowerment they provoked are exemplified in the illustration created by Ciara in Fig. 15.1.

The Positive Effects of Virtual Hearings on Children's Participation and Well-being

Although virtual Hearings were a negative experience for some children, for others, being able to attend their Hearings remotely from 'safe spaces' improved their emotional well-being. Removing the need to travel to and from Hearings reduced children's stress and anxiety prior to the Hearing. It also allowed caregivers more time and space to help children emotionally regulate if they became upset or distressed as a result of the Hearing.

It is a very daunting experience where decisions are being made about their lives. Having watched it from both sides it just seems that virtual Hearings are a little bit more relaxed for them. It is like 'here is the time, here is the link'. You are just waiting for people to logon so it takes away that whole kind of anticipation (Margaret, Residential Care Worker).

... with virtual Hearings you can contain the distress better. It is more manageable because you are able to be there and support it within their home rather than being miles away and having to drive back with a really upset child (Pam, Foster Carer).

Not having to travel to Hearings Centres also reduced the potential for (re)traumatisation, particularly for children in secure care who needed to be transported under escort, children who were not permitted or did not want to share a room with their parent(s), and children who might be exposed to acrimonious and adversarial behaviour between family members.

Fig. 15.1. The Negative Emotions Associated with Virtual Hearings.

> ... we've got young girls in here with lots of trauma... and they're sitting in the middle of two guys, handcuffed in the back of a secure transport. You are saving that kid a journey which could be quite traumatising for them (Mark, Secure Care Worker).

> ... they're able to avoid difficult situations like having to witness family members in the car park screaming dogs abuse at each other (Joanne, Residential Care Worker).

Some of the young people we spoke to reinforced this idea, stating that the use of virtual Hearings was protective as it meant that they did not have to sit in the same room as their parent(s). Virtual hearings were also seen as 'less intimidating' and 'less traumatic' because children can 'feel more protected being behind a screen'.

Virtual Hearings provided children with more autonomy around their Hearings, including when they wanted their Hearings to happen, being able to choose who they wanted to attend their Hearings with, where they wanted to sit and what they wanted to bring to their Hearings with them. Being able to choose when Hearings occurred was considered particularly beneficial as not having to travel to a Hearings centre meant that Hearings could be more easily scheduled around young people's education, employment and extracurricular activities. It also allowed children to attend their Hearing in private; something that was considered to improve their participation as they were able to share their views without other people being in the room with them.

> He will sit in his room on his computer. He feels more comfortable there. Even though he is in the same house, he feels he can speak clearly, freer if you like, if he is not sat next to me (Iain, Foster Carer).

Virtual Hearings were identified as means of bringing the Hearing into the child's space; allowing them to participate from an environment that was familiar and comfortable. This can be seen in Zodie's illustration (Fig. 15.2) showing what participating in a Hearing from home can look like. Being able to participate from a familiar environment reduced children's anxiety around attending Hearings. It also allowed them to seek comfort and reassurance more readily.

> ... doing it at home was better because I [could] have my cat with me (Stephanie, Hearings-experienced young person).

> It feels safer and less stressful at home and I can get a hug from my grandma straight away, cause when you're in the Hearing room I need to wait till everyone has left the room before I can get a hug (Claire, Hearings-experienced young person).

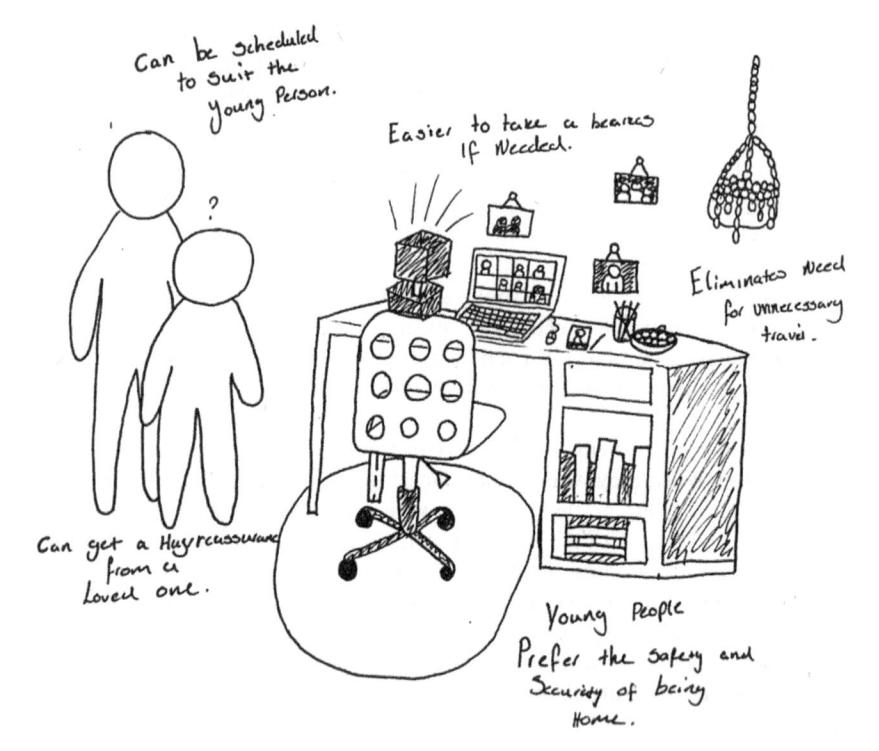

Fig. 15.2. Inviting the Hearing Into the Child's Space.

In addition to feeling more protected, virtual Hearings allowed children the opportunity to temporarily disengage from their Hearings without feeling like they had to ask permission to leave or becoming so distressed that they were no longer able to participate. Being able to take breaks and use a mobile phone were all identified as distraction tools used to help children remain in their Hearings.

> I muted the camera and said 'it looks like you are struggling to concentrate. Would you like to go and make a cup of tea and then come back so you are not missing out on stuff and I can inform you about what you miss?'. She then said 'can I go and get my mobile phone and have my mobile phone in the room with me so that I can be present but maybe not 100% listening?' (Anna, Residential Care Worker).

They also presented caregivers, particularly residential and secure care workers, with the opportunity to find new ways to support the inclusion of children's voices in the decision-making process. There were several examples given of the creative ways that caregivers had worked to include voice. These included: supporting children to use mobile devices to take panel members on tours of where they were living; encouraging children to show their favourite toys to panel members; using creative and therapeutic approaches to help children articulate their thoughts and feelings; and actively encouraging children to use the chat box and emojis during their Hearings.

> I got some pens out on the table and we were just colouring in, and I said as the meeting goes along do you want to write things down and then you can either say them or ask can you bring this up? (Sarah, Residential Care Worker).

What Does the Learning From Virtual Hearings Tell Us About the Impact That the Virtual Space Had Upon Emotional Security, Sense of Agency and Participation?

Our findings indicate that the extent to which children were able to meaningfully participate in virtual Hearings was related to: (1) perceptions around the safety of the virtual space; (2) the sense of agency and control that children and their caregivers were able to exert around virtual Hearings.

Looking at the first of these issues, it has been argued that remote participation in legal proceedings, particularly for victims, can reduce the psychological burden of testifying and alleviate the potential for distress and re-traumatisation (Yamagata and Fox, 2017). Our study shows that allowing children to participate in their Hearings from safe and familiar environments can engender a sense of safety and security that promotes meaningful participation. Similar findings have been reported in relation to the use of remote testimony for victims of domestic and family violence, and remote family conflict resolution services (Heard et al., 2022; Reeves et al., 2023).

Children's Hearings are known to be scary, distressing and unsettling experiences for children (Children's Parliament, 2010; Mackie, 2023). Our findings suggest that providing children with a sense of agency and control over where, with whom and to what extent they engaged with their Hearings can increase their emotional safety during Hearings. The importance of agency in remote legal proceedings was also highlighted by Reeves et al. (2023) who concluded that victims of domestic and family violence felt safer if they were able to: sit in a different room to the accused; turn off cameras; change screen angles and video settings to prevent the accused being seen; and disengage from proceedings without having to ask permission to do so.

Childhood adversity and maltreatment are known to adversely affect children's ability to emotionally regulate; resulting in the need for additional support from caregivers to manage their reactions to stressful life events (Essau et al., 2017; McCrory et al., 2017). Our results indicate that allowing children to participate from familiar places provided caregivers with more opportunities to support children's well-being through: offering creative methods to support children to express their views; respecting and facilitating choices around participation; introducing homely touches into Hearings through the provision of drinks and snacks and promoting regular breaks for children. Not having to travel to and from Hearings Centres also allowed caregivers the time to focus solely upon helping children to emotionally regulate.

Those children who were distressed by virtual Hearings described experiencing a lack of agency and control, particularly in relation to how private their Hearings were. Concerns around privacy are not unique to this study, with Heard et al. (2022) identifying similar concerns in relation to participation in remote family resolution services. Addressing privacy concerns in remote proceedings is challenging. While it is possible to minimise risk through establishing standards for participation, including rules around who should be in attendance, the lack of control SCRA has over these spaces can make it difficult to guarantee that children's privacy will be maintained. This contrasts with in-person Hearings where both the management and design of the space can be controlled to maximise privacy.

Lack of agency and control in the virtual space adversely affected children's ability to share their views with panel members. One particular area of concern was the use of digital behaviour management tools and the impact that they had on children's voice. Although the use of digital tools can be beneficial for managing the flow of legal proceedings, their use can reinforce power imbalances (Bannon and Keith, 2020). Given that some children already perceive that their voice does not carry the same weight as adults, the use of these tools to intentionally or unintentionally silence their voices is likely to amplify the barriers and harms associated with their Article 12 rights not being realised. At present there is a lack of evidence around the use of digital behaviour management tools in legal proceedings. Given the implications for children's voice, we believe that further research is needed to identify the circumstances in which they are used. In relation to enforced muting, this should include exploring whether those running proceedings have different tolerance thresholds for disruptive behaviour during virtual and in-person proceedings, and how de-escalation processes differ in the virtual and physical space.

Lack of voice within legal proceedings can result in questions being raised about the fairness of proceedings. This is something we saw within our data, with some young people who felt that they lacked a voice in virtual Hearings questioning the decisions made by Panel Members. Unfortunately, findings around lack of voice are not restricted to virtual Hearings, with the wider evidence on in-person Hearings repeatedly highlighting that children do not feel heard within their Hearings (Children's Parliament, 2010; Duncan, 2020; Kurlus et al., 2016; Porter et al., 2020; SCRA, 2016; Who Cares? Scotland, 2020). Better provision of advocacy for children has previously been identified as a means of amplifying children's voices. For instance, Section 122 of the Children's Hearings (Scotland) Act 2011 places a duty on the chair of every children's Hearing to inform children about the availability of children's advocacy services. These provisions were fully enacted in November 2020. Early findings from the evaluation of advocacy provision indicate that the provision of advocacy during Hearings was considered beneficial by children as it provided them with a named individual who could share their views, explain legal processes and help them to appoint and instruct solicitors (Scottish Government, 2022a, 2022b). Future evaluations of advocacy provision should explore how this service can be used to support children's voice in the virtual space.

Conclusion

Virtual Hearings were introduced during the Covid-19 pandemic as an emergency measure to allow Hearings to continue during the enforced closure of public buildings. Our results indicate that for some children, virtual Hearings can be emotionally protective and promote the participation of children in the decision-making process. They also show that for other children, they can be a frightening, disempowering experience. Alleviating the distress and trauma associated with children's Hearings is a key underlying theme within the Hearings for Children Report, which outlines how the children's Hearings system needs to be reformed in order for Scotland to 'Keep The Promise' (Mackie, 2023). Our findings highlight that the key way of doing this is to provide children with control and agency around their Hearings; irrespective of whether these are held virtually or in-person. To that end, SCRA has been working with Our Hearings, Our Voice to test a number of initiatives designed to give children more control over the timing and location of their hearings, the ways they can share information with Reporters and Panel Members, and providing children with control over things like the seating arrangements in physical hearings (OHOV, 2023; SCRA, 2023). The continued use of virtual Hearings for those children who wish to participate in this manner is part of this approach.

References

Bannon, A.L. and Keith, D. 2020. Remote court: principles for virtual proceedings during the COVID-19 pandemic and beyond. *Northwest University Law Review*, 115, 1875.

Children's Parliament 2010. *Children's Hearings Reform: The Views of Children*, Edinburgh, Children's Parliament.

Duncan, F. 2020. *The Independent Care Review: The Promise*, Glasgow, The Independent Care Review.

Essau, C., LeBlanc, S. S. and Ollendick, T. H. (Eds.) 2017. *Emotional Regulation and Psychopathology in Children and Adolescents*, Oxford, Oxford University Press.

Heard, G., Bickerdike, A. and Opoku, S. 2022. Remote family dispute resolution services for COVID and post-COVID times: client and practitioner perspectives. *Family Court Review*, 60(2), 220–240.

Kilbrandon, L. 1964. *Report on the Committee on Children and Young Persons, Scotland (Cmnd 2306)*, Scottish Home and Health Department/Scottish Education Department, Edinburgh.

Kurlus, I., Henderson, G. and Brechin, G. 2016. *The Next Steps Towards Better Hearings*, Stirling, Scottish Children's Reporter Administration.

Mackie, D. 2023. *Hearings for Children*. The Promise Scotland. https://thepromise. scot/resources/2023/hearings-for-children-the-redesign-report.pdf

McCrory, E., Gerin, M.L. and Viding, E. 2017. Annual research review: childhood maltreatment, latent vulnerability and the shift to preventative psychiatry—the contribution of functional brain imaging. *Journal of Child Psychology and Psychiatry*, 58(4), 338–357.

McDiarmid, C., Barry, M., Donnelly, M. and Corson, S. 2017. *The Role of the Safeguarder in the Children's Hearing System*, Edinburgh, The Scottish Government.

McGarrol, S., Henderson, G., Deacon, K., McNiven, G., Baird, N. and Cairns, C. 2022. *Children Aged 12 to 15 Years Involved in Offending and Referred to the children's reporter and Procurator Fiscal in Scotland*, Stirling, Scottish Children's Reporter Administration.

Nixon, C., Kurlus, I., Hunt, M., Deacon, K., McGarrol, S., Lamb, D., Etchells, H., McNaughton, L. and Henderson, G. 2023. The rapid development of a virtual children's hearings system in Scotland: a realist-inspired synthesis assessing the impact of the covid-19 pandemic on the participation and rights of children. *Adoption and Fostering*, 47(3), 347–372.

OHOV 2023. *Helping Children Take Control of Their Hearings*, Stirling, Our Hearings, Our Voice. Available at: https://www.ohov.co.uk/2023/12/07/helping-children-take-control-of-their-hearings/

Our Hearings, Our Voice (OHOV) 2020. *40 Calls to Action*. Stirling: Our Hearings, Our Voice. Available via: https://www.ohov.co.uk/wp-content/uploads/2021/09/Inside-Page.png

Porter, R.B., Gillon, F., Mitchell, F., Vaswanu, N. and Young, E. 2021. Children's rights in Children's Hearings: the impact of Covid-19. *The International Journal of Children's Rights*, 29, 426–446.

Porter, R.B., Mitchell, F., Gillon, F., Young, E. and Vaswani, N. 2020. *Experiences of Virtual Children's Hearings: A Rapid Consultation Report*, Glasgow, CELCIS.

Porter, R., Welch, V. and Mitchell, F. 2016. *The Role of the Solicitor in the Children's Hearings System: A Study Commissioned by the Scottish Legal Aid Board*, Glasgow, CELCIS.

Reeves, E., Iliadis, M. and Pfitzner, N. 2023. LGBTQ+ domestic and family violence victim-survivors' experiences of remote court hearings during the COVID-19 pandemic: the gendered dimensions of safety, independence and visibility. *Criminology and Criminal Justice*, 17488958231216561.

Ritchie, J. and Spencer, L. 2002. Qualitative data analysis for applied policy research. In *The Qualitative Researcher's Companion*, Eds A.M. Huberman, M.B. Miles, pp. 305–329, London, SAGE.

Scottish Children's Reporter Administration (SCRA) 2016. *National Survey of Children and Families*, Stirling, Scottish Children's Reporter Administration.

Scottish Government 2022a. *Children's Advocacy in Children's Hearings National Scheme – Good Practice and Issues Arising*. Available at: https://www.gov.scot/publications/childrens-advocacy-childrens-hearings-national-scheme-good-practice-issues-arising/

Scottish Government 2022b. *Children's Advocacy in Children's Hearings – National Scheme: Good Practice and Issues Arising. Part 2 Children and Young People's Feedback and Demonstrating Outcomes*. Available at: https://www.gov.scot/

publications/childrens-advocacy-childrens-hearings-national-scheme-good-practice-issues-arising/pages/2/

SCRA 2023. *Child Friendly Scheduling Project*, Stirling, Scottish Children's Reporter Administration. Available at: https://www.scra.gov.uk/2023/09/child-friendly-scheduling-project/

Who Cares? Scotland 2020. *Young People and Parents' Views on Privacy and How This Affects Their Participation in the Children's Hearings System*, Glasgow, Who Cares? Scotland.

Yamagata, H. and Fox, D. 2017. Evaluating the use of videoconferencing technology in domestic violence ex parte hearings: assessing procedural consistency. *Justice System Journal*, 38(2), 135–148.

Chapter 16

Everyday Life, Informal Care and Grassroots Sports Clubs

Stephen Crossley

Durham University, UK

Abstract

Millions of children participate in community sports clubs and leagues each weekend across the UK, and other countries. The rates of participation and the cultural significance of these sports in different countries are not always matched by recognition or support from governments. Policy interest in sport in the UK has, in recent years at least, tended to focus on elite performance and the hosting of events such as the Olympics and the UEFA European Championships. Commitment to grassroots and community sports has waned, or been limited to how sport and/or physical activity can help to deliver other policy goals. The lack of funding provided to community sports clubs can lead to young people with limited resources being excluded from clubs. Inequalities in participation in sport and physical activity were exacerbated during lockdowns and restrictions imposed during the coronavirus pandemic. This chapter explores some of the contemporary challenges facing grassroots youth sports clubs and highlights the possible advantages of adopting a different approach to them, including consideration of the informal care provided by sports clubs and the role that they can play during critical moments in children and families' everyday lives.

Keywords: Community sport; grassroots sports clubs; physical activity; shadow infrastructures of care; welfare state

Introduction

Despite the cultural significance of sports such as football, cricket and rugby, government interest in this area has often been limited, or focused on ways that it can help deliver other policy goals. This chapter draws on a range of literature exploring the value, or lack of it, attached to grassroots and community sports clubs at different times by policymakers, and a small number of research studies that were undertaken with community sports organisations in the UK during the pandemic. It uses the concept of shadow care infrastructures to highlight the important role that these clubs can play in the lives of players, families and volunteers, and suggests that more attention should be paid to the benefits that membership of these clubs can bring. Grassroots sports clubs are not often associated with care practices, often for good reason, but I argue that the everyday routines involved with grassroots clubs enable and encourage care practices to flourish across and between players, parents, coaches and volunteers.

Despite its relative wealth, the UK, in recent years at least, has not appeared to value investment in children and young people. Since the early days of the New Labour government (1997–2010), when they 'discovered early childhood' (Eisenstadt, 2011), and made bold commitments to 'end child poverty forever' (Blair, 1999), children and young people have rarely been a political priority for UK governments. Childhood and youth services suffered under the Coalition government's programme of austerity, as did education and school budgets. Welfare 'reforms', such as the two-child limit on child benefit and the overall cap on household benefits, resulted in an estimated annual loss of £10.7 billion to families with dependent children (Beatty and Fothergill, 2016). It is estimated that 29% of children in the UK are living in poverty (DWP, 2023), and the number of children in mental health crisis has soared in the period following the pandemic (Bawden, 2023), with many children going untreated for mental health issues as a result of 'buckling' services (Hall, 2023a, 2023b). Childhood policy in the UK has been described as 'fragmented, inconsistent and uneven' (British Academy, 2022: 11). At the time of writing, there is similarly no discernible overarching youth policy in the UK.

During the COVID-19 pandemic, schools and colleges 'locked down', and all education moved online, with little consideration of many children's difficulty in engaging with this format. Advisors on the government's Scientific Advisory Group for Emergencies (Sage) which fed into government decision-making processes warned of a 'lost generation' of children who could be 'scarred for life' as a result of the government's response to the pandemic. They 'warned ministers "several" times about the risks to people in this age group [those aged 7 to 24] but believed they were "brushed aside"' (Hill, 2020). There have since been calls for bold and radical interventions to support children and young people, especially the already marginalised or disadvantaged groups who have been disproportionately affected by the virus and/or by the policy responses to it. Thus far, policy attention has focused on educational attainment and addressing and improving mental health through innovative interventions, and improved service provision and coverage, usually within schools. There appears to have been little appetite to look at things afresh following the pandemic, especially in relation to children's physical health.

For a variety of historical and contemporary reasons, UK welfare and/or health policies towards children have often focused on physical activity, usually in schools, to the neglect of participation in sports or opportunities for joining clubs.

Community and grassroots youth sports clubs receive almost no direct support from central government in the UK, with funding allocated via local government, arms-length bodies such as Sport England and through National Governing Bodies (NGBs). Targeted programmes and time-limited interventions, often delivered by social enterprises or private companies, and funded via local authorities through competitive commissioning processes, have proliferated, as a 'mixed economy' of grassroots sports provision has emerged.

This chapter examines some of the challenges facing grassroots youth sports clubs at the current time and highlights the possible advantages of adopting a different approach to them, including consideration of the informal care provided by sports clubs and the role that they can play during critical moments in children and families everyday lives. The following section explores the valuing and devaluing of youth sports clubs, in the UK and beyond. The attention then turns to the situation during the pandemic and the processes of 'lockdowns' being implemented in response to the pandemic, followed by a discussion of everyday care practices and sports clubs as 'shadow care infrastructures' (Power et al., 2022). The chapter concludes with a discussion of how the situation could improve.

(De)valuing Grassroots Sports?

There are an estimated 50,000 sports clubs across England and Wales, with an average of 90 young junior members under the age of 18 (Sport and Recreation Alliance, 2013). Sport England (2023:37) estimates that 65% of children aged 7–11 participate in a team sport at least once a week, with around 60% of 11–16-year-olds participating in team sports. The number is slightly smaller for participation in predominantly individual sports such as athletics/running, swimming and gymnastics. According to the English Football Association (The FA), nearly 4.5 million children, aged 5-18 play football each week.

Despite the levels of participation amongst children and young people mentioned above, there has been a relative lack of interest in them from politicians, policymakers and researchers. Increased interest in different political and sociological aspects of elite level and professional sport has not been matched by an equivalent interest in the more mundane, taken for granted, prosaic activities that can be found in villages, towns and cities across the country each weekend (Green, 2006).

Grassroots and community sports clubs are run largely by volunteers in the UK. NGBs such as The Football Association, the Rugby Football Union, the British Boxing Board of Control and the Marylebone Cricket Club long predated the establishment of a welfare state. As such, grassroots sport in the UK, including governance arrangements and sourcing of financial support, is tied up with ideas of 'the gentleman amateur' (Parnell et al., 2021: 180). The administration and leadership arrangements of sporting organisations mirrored those of the country more generally:

> This 'amateur ideal' was embedded in the corridors of Whitehall, where the imagery of the 'non-specialist' or 'all-rounder' resonated as much as in the clubhouses and boardrooms of British sport. Historically, the administrative elite in Britain has been disproportionately represented by men from a narrow social and educational background, particularly Oxbridge and the major public schools, which was steeped in the late Victorian belief in amateurism, in government as well as sport. Parnell et al. (2021: 180)

The Beveridge report, widely recognised as the catalyst for the establishment of a welfare state in the UK, mentions sport just once, in the context of accidents and injuries (Beveridge, 1942: 38). Children and young people were also generally overlooked in the original vision of the welfare state, which believed that they would receive all the support they required from their families and through expanded educational provision.

A later but lesser-known report by Beveridge on Voluntary Action, published in 1948, recognised the role of voluntary and community organisations in promoting 'social advance', but failed to mention sports at all. There was, however, a greater focus on leisure, including a section on the redistribution of leisure. Beveridge makes known his contempt for the idea of state involvement in the planning of leisure activities, arguing that the 'last stage in totalitarianism would be reached if the use of his leisure were being arranged for each citizen by the State' (Beveridge, 1948: 286). He does, however, recognise that the state has a role to play in encouraging people to pursue 'active leisure' opportunities:

> ... the main attack on wasteful or harmful use of leisure cannot, in a free society, be made by direct action of the State. It must depend on the development of alternative: it depends on education, in the widest sense of the term, at all stages of life, but above all in adolescence and after ... This is an interest of the State but should not be undertaken by the State. Here is a limitless field for Voluntary Action, assisted so far as is necessary but not controlled by the power of the State. Beveridge (1948: 286)

The intervening years have seen government interest in sport and community and grassroots sport ebb and flow. A commitment to 'Sport for All' was launched in 1966 and ran until 1984, with an evaluation of the programme noting that 'aid from central government is essential, but has been parsimonious' (McIntosh and Charlton, 1985: 156). The Sports Council (later to become Sport England) was inaugurated as an independent body under the Department of National Heritage, by Royal Charter in 1972. Also in the 1970s, local government expanded the leisure services and facilities they provided, with a significant increase in the number of public sector swimming pools and leisure centres. Leisure provision was 'rolled back' in the 1980s and 1990s under Conservative governments, along with many other public sector services (Sugden and Knox, 1992).

Under the New Labour government (1997–2010), with its communitarian perspective and with the help of funding available through the National Lottery, grassroots sport projects enjoyed slightly greater political support, especially if they helped to achieve related policy goals. The government also saw the hosting of major events as an opportunity to support and increase participation in sport, with London successfully bidding to host the 2012 Olympics with government support. A core element of the London 2012 Olympic legacy was participation in grassroots sport, and physical activity more widely. However, a National Audit Office report found that, under a new Coalition government (2010–15) and subsequent Conservative administrations, the proportion of adults participating in sport declined in the three years following the Olympic and Paralympic Games, and government attention to its legacy waned significantly:

> The Olympic and Paralympic Legacy Cabinet Committee was disbanded in 2015 and the Department published what was to be its last legacy monitoring report in 2016. The Department did not complete a promised evaluation of the long-term impact of the Games in 2020 and so does not know the full extent of any sporting legacy delivered from the £8.8 billion that the government spent on the Games. NAO (2022: 7)

The situation described above is not to be found in all countries. Most governments recognise that sport can be beneficial and that it can be used for a variety of political, social and economic ends (Coalter, 2007), but there are a range of approaches to supporting and acknowledging participation in grassroots sports, and the role that the welfare state plays in this support. In some countries, such as Switzerland, Poland and Spain, sporting participation is a 'right' or a goal enshrined in the constitution, sports acts or decrees (Ibsen et al., 2022: 10), although state support can vary in upholding that right. Persson (2022): 1) notes that in Scandinavian countries, 'sport is largely publicly funded and closely connected to the welfare state' and 'voluntary community sports clubs are the most prominent organisations for children and youth'. State support for community clubs and leisure facilities can be expansive, compared to the UK:

> In Denmark, most sports facilities are owned by the municipalities, which are obliged to give sports clubs access to facilities free of charge. Municipalities are also obliged to pay most of the expenses for the use of private sports facilities. The public financial support is primarily 'basic grants'. Sports clubs have a statutory right to public support for activities for members under 25 years of age, but the public funding accounts for a small share of the economy in most clubs. Ibsen et al. (2022: 10)

These are not recent developments either. Just as the 1960s and 70s saw an increase in public sector sports provision in the UK, the same period saw other countries develop their approach to sport and leisure. In France, the Mille Clubs

Programme, aimed at increasing young people's participation in sport and a range of other leisure activities and 'one of the largest programmes that the French government developed for its citizens during the post-war years' (Avermaete, 2013: 633) was launched in 1966. At around the same time, the concept of 'leisure planning' began to emerge in Sweden, which saw 'a remarkable expansion of leisure infrastructure in Sweden, with the steady expansion of public swimming pools, indoor arenas for various sports, and facilities for outdoor recreation and play' (Pries and Qvistrom, 2021: 926). Accompanying the increase in facilities were government inquiries into related fields, such as organised sport, the outdoor environment of children and the leisure activities of young people.

COVID-19, Lockdowns and Grassroots Sports

On 23 March 2020, the UK Prime Minister Boris Johnson announced the first UK 'lockdown', ordering people to stay at home. Two days later the Coronavirus Act (2020) received Royal Assent and the measures introduced in the Act formally came into force on 26 March 2020. They required most households to stay at home as much as possible, with people only allowed to leave the house for specific reasons, including: one period of exercise per day; shopping for essentials; visiting or helping a vulnerable person; medical need and travelling to work if employed as a designated 'key worker'. Households were not allowed to mix and therefore all forms of leisure and social activities involving more than one household were banned, including grassroots and community sports. Schools, colleges and universities also closed (although many colleges and universities had already stopped or reduced in-person teaching activities), with efforts made to shift all education provision online.

Reopening schools and supporting children and young people in their education was presented as a priority for the government, with concerns expressed about the damage caused by prolonged periods without contact with peers and friendship groups. There was also the potential for already disadvantaged groups to 'fall further behind' with unequal access to educational resources and support in different households. Another consideration was the economic impact of children being at home: if children were able to return to schools and in-person teaching, then their parents would be more likely to be able to return to work on a full-time basis, and possibly move back to working from an office or a workplace outside the home.

Although lockdown restrictions, including a phased re-opening of schools, began to ease across the UK at the end of May and the beginning of June (the four devolved administrations eased lockdown restrictions across three different dates), it was not until the middle of July that outdoor community sport and play provision reopened across the UK, and it was not until August that indoor facilities such as leisure centres were able to re-open, albeit with some restrictions and regulations still in place on both occasions. Spectators and participants were supposed to limit the amount of car sharing or travelling on public transport as much as was practicable and, where possible, players were expected to arrive changed and ready to warm up, limiting the amount of time spent waiting around, socialising or in changing rooms (DCMS, 2020). The traditional handshake at the end of many matches was replaced with elbow or fist 'bumps'.

Perhaps understandably, given the context of a global pandemic which many countries were struggling to contain, there was little prominent focus on grassroots and community sport during discussions about how best to support people and communities affected both by the virus and by the restrictive policies aimed at stopping its spread. The same was not necessarily true of elite sport, however, with a recognition of the cultural (and perhaps economic) importance of large-scale spectator sports and significant government interventions were made to support some professional sports and leagues. The English Premier League was suspended on 13 March 2020, but a government-supported 'Project Restart' saw the league restart on 17 June, with all league games being televised as fans were not allowed in stadiums, to 'lift the spirits of the nation' (Dunn, 2020). The UK government also pledged support for other elite support, with the Rugby Football League receiving £16 million in May 2020 to safeguard the future of the sport, and a further £300 million support package (mainly comprising low-interest loans) for a range of sports affected by the lack of fans announced in November 2020.

On 5 November 2020, a second national lockdown was announced, affecting England only, which lasted four weeks. At this point, in response to a question about the impact of COVID-19 on non-league football clubs, the Culture Minister Oliver Dowden stated:

> I know that football clubs large and small make a huge contribution to their community on and off the pitch, and I can assure my hon. Friend that they will not be forgotten. As soon as we are in a position to start lifting restrictions, grassroots sports will be among the first to return, but until then, we have made sure that families can keep exercising throughout this lockdown, and I urge people to get out and get fit. Hansard (2020)

A third national lockdown was announced on 6 January 2021. On 29 March 2021, as part of the second step on the 'roadmap' for exiting the third lockdown, outdoor sports facilities were allowed to reopen, with the re-opening of indoor leisure facilities such as gyms, leisure centres, theatres and libraries following on 12 April 2021.

Research conducted by Sport England during the pandemic highlighted the already well-established link between sport, physical activity and mental health, as well as identifying some trends relating to the impact of the pandemic on young people's participation in sport and physical activity. The Active Lives Children and Young People Survey Coronavirus report (Sport England, 2021a) suggested that participation in sporting activities decreased (understandably so given lockdowns and the cessation of grassroots sport for long periods), but other types of activity such as cycling, walking and fitness workouts increased. Positive attitudes towards physical activities (competence, confidence and enjoyment) decreased the most for children from the least affluent families, Black children and young people, and for boys more than girls. Boys' activity levels dropped on average, whilst girls' participation increased on average. The Annual Report of the Active Lives (Sport England, 2021b) survey noted that 'physically literate' children (those with fundamental movement skills such as throwing, catching, running, jumping, etc.) and those who are more active tend to be happier and have higher levels of individual development (such as improving soft and social skills, and increasing persistence and perseverance) and community development (such as increased trust and reduced isolation).

In keeping with much research activity undertaken during the pandemic, a small number of research projects examining grassroots sports clubs relied largely on online interviews and survey responses for data collection and were often 'rapid responses' to the developing situation. Research carried out by the Sports Volunteering Research Network highlighted the range of impacts on different sports clubs, with clubs providing weekly activities for large number of young people potentially hardest hit:

> The worst affected club in our sample was a gymnastics club which would normally have 750 junior participants per week and maintained its own facility. The least affected was a mountaineering club with 83 members paying an annual subscription of £35 and a peppercorn rent for a meeting room. Findlay-King et al. (2020: 2)

The researchers also noted the social bonds that existed between members and the 'social rewards of membership', highlighting the difficulty of sustaining these during periods of lockdown and restrictions on gatherings. Other research has shown how some sports clubs quickly changed tack during the pandemic and supported members online, often with 'challenges' for members to undertake, and many used their limited resources to provide services such as food deliveries and shopping collection for vulnerable groups (Sported, 2021: 5). Perhaps understandably, it was also acknowledged that few of the clubs saw the aftermath of the pandemic as an opportunity to develop these or other services, to recruit new members or to align themselves with new policy agendas focusing on improving the health of the nation. The focus tended to be much more on 'returning as close as possible to what was there before' (Findlay-King et al., 2020: 25), which, again, is understandable given the reliance on volunteers and the increased demands on their time. The authors note that to do more than getting clubs back on their feet would 'need inspiration and help' (2020: 25). A short report by the charity Sported (2021: 7) found similar views, stating that 'Despite the need for increased collaboration, groups found that organisations had turned inwards, focussing on their own survival rather than supporting and building the network'. Mackintosh et al. (2021: 51) highlighted an 'increasingly disconnected delivery system' within sports provision, emphasising again the lack of co-ordinated work to support the community sector and the fragmented nature of policy.

The Sported report explored how grassroots sports clubs 'survived' the pandemic, highlighting the precarious nature of the clubs themselves, and also the structural vulnerabilities and disadvantages experienced by many young people who access sports clubs, including disabled groups, minoritised communities, women and girls and people experiencing poverty (Sported, 2021: 3). Community sports clubs and groups experienced 'more difficulty in engaging young people in activities' and noticed their 'low morale' as a result on Covid restrictions (2021: 4). Concerns were raised about the 'deepening negative impact of COVID-19 on young people's mental health', a lowering of participation levels and volunteer engagement as a result of increased health risks and financial challenges (Sported, 2021: 6–7).

A survey commissioned by the energy provider Utilita in August 2020 highlighted how important football is for many children and young people and their families. Some headline statistics from the survey and accompanying report include:

- Nearly two-thirds of parents encourage their children to play football because of the mental and physical health benefits and the social element – making friends and being part of the local community.
- 75% of parents said their children had really missed playing football with their teams.
- 74% of parents whose children play grassroots football had experienced a reduced income during the pandemic.

(Utilita, 2020: 4)

Few of the research projects or other texts relating to grassroots sports provision mention care in the context of the relations that exist between club members, their families and volunteers. A legal 'duty of care' was mentioned, as was the increase in care within families, that the pandemic necessitated. Issues that link with the concept of care, such as trust, vulnerability, identity and so on were discussed, but there was little explicit mention of care that takes place within the clubs, and that was affected by restrictions associated with the pandemic.

'In the Middle of Things'

In an often quoted passage, the football historian James Walvin argues that, away from the attention paid to the professional game, 'there is another football story to tell', that remains 'generally untold because it is part and parcel of the world we live in' and 'embedded deep in the routines and habits of ordinary people' (Walvin, 2001: 251–252). The same can be said of many other sports, where weekly training sessions and matches or competitions at weekends shape, if not dictate, the weekly routines of millions of families across the country. Joan Tronto (2015: 4) has suggested that care must 'start in the middle of things', with the everyday practices of offering and receiving of help. Small gestures can help people to cope with and/or adapt to changing circumstances and times of individual or social crisis. Grassroots, community-based youth sports clubs are often in 'the middle of things' for families, and minor connections and offers of help at training, on game days or at social events can help to sustain and nourish everyday life for those involved. Time spent at such clubs, away from the more formal arenas of school and/or work, provide ample opportunities for 'small gestures' as part of the everyday rhythms and routines of daily life: chatting with other players or coaches whilst waiting for training to start; or for parents watching training; offering or receiving lifts to games; loans or passing on of equipment; buying cups of tea or coffee and/or arranging social activities beyond the club.

There is limited research literature examining the relations between youth players, parents and coaches in youth sport. Children's voices are rarely heard in sports-related research, especially at the non-elite level (Messner and Musto, 2014), and there is also limited literature in relation to parents (Bjork and Hoynes, 2022). A relatively small number of studies have explored the relationships parents form as a result of their child's participation in youth sport (Gottzen and Kremer-Sadlik, 2012; Warner et al., 2015; Brown, 2017; Stefansen et al., 2016), but these rarely focus on the concept of 'care'. Bjork and Hoynes (2022: 2292), for example, barely discuss care, but highlight the 'connections' between parents, the 'positive bonds' they form and note that:

> Parents also chat regularly during practices and games, often about much more than their kids and sports. With these regular, somewhat structured opportunities to socialise, they have the chance to get to know each other fairly well.

Cronin and Armour (2019: 1) have argued that, despite a lack of academic literature in the area, 'coaching needs to be repositioned as an activity with caring at its very core', noting that many coaches support players and athletes through hard times and help with their personal and social development. They also note that such work often goes under the radar:

> The media rarely documents these instances. Thus, it is that coaching as a profession can be described as having a paradoxical care crisis. The crisis is characterised by the simultaneous presence of abusive, uncaring coaching practice and the unheralded, often-unseen caring practice that is at the core of a coach's duty to care. (2019: 2)

Care is generally viewed as taking place in settings where there is more of an explicit focus on the practice. The spaces and practices of care in the UK have, however, changed dramatically in recent years as a result of an increased role for private sector providers, austerity measures that affected the reach and depth of public and charitable sector provision, and the COVID-19 pandemic. Youth clubs and Children's Centres have been affected by austerity measures, with consequences for the health and well-being of those individuals and families that accessed these services. Where care provision still exists, higher caseloads for workers, higher thresholds for 'interventions', longer waiting lists, fewer resources to support the work and often low-paid insecure employment opportunities have affected the relations between care workers and recipients (Disney et al., 2022; Hall, 2023a, 2023b; Topping, 2023). Welfare reforms have made it more and more difficult for a wide variety of groups to claim or to remain on out-of-work benefits, changing the home life and arrangements of many families. The prevalence of low-paid part-time jobs mean that many people on low-incomes work multiple or unpredictable jobs which, again, affect the potential for care within family settings.

In an insightful article focusing predominantly on foodbanks, Power et al., 2022: 3) argue that 'new care infrastructures have emerged as a result of austerity and societal changes and crises' and that understanding the intersections between the state and other, often new, or emerging, care infrastructures will become even more vital in post-COVID times. They advance the concept of 'shadow care infrastructures' to describe overlooked, often neglected or misrecognised spaces where care takes place:

> Shadow care infrastructures mobilise the shadows as metaphor to direct attention to spaces, practices and resources that are obscured within dominant welfare discourse ... when light is shone on phenomena ... certain features are foregrounded, while others fall into the shadows, unseen, or appearing differently to how they might if light were directed toward them. Power et al. (2022: 8)

Jupp (2021: 12) also highlights the distinction between notions of the 'visible' and the 'invisible' in society acknowledging that 'that which is visible in society might be considered a matter for political and media debate' whilst that which is rendered 'invisible' can feel marginalised or easier to ignore. There is therefore value in looking into the shadows in an effort to understand people's lives and to 'foreground the vital, yet less visible, spaces and practices that underpin them' (Power et al., 2022: 9) and which are often taken for granted and/or devalued.

Grassroots sports clubs can be viewed as 'vital, yet less visible spaces' where care can and does take place. Clubs are often rooted in local communities, sometimes with long histories, and are able to provide stability at a time when precarity appears to be the 'new normal'. Weekly routines of training and playing provide safety and familiarity for millions of children and their families, especially at 'critical moments' (Thomson et al., 2002) in children's lives such as the transition from primary school to secondary school and when family circumstances change.

The informal relations between coaches and players contrast with an increasingly strict education system, with a strong emphasis on discipline and behaviour (see, for example, Bennett, 2017). The loss of youth clubs, and the closure of or reduced services offered by other local spaces such as libraries, children's centres and community centres mean that grassroots sports clubs are potentially increasingly important organisations in their local areas. It is, perhaps, a paradox that the lack of support offered to such clubs in the UK by the government may have aided their survival, as they have been forced to ensure they are self-sufficient by looking for support from other sources. This situation, however, is less than ideal, especially when players and their families are often required to pay subscriptions to clubs and to meet other costs associated with their participation. Given that these costs will exclude some children from joining clubs and/or pursuing sports that they enjoy, change would be welcome.

Conclusion

To date, in the UK at least, little value has been attached to grassroots youth sports clubs and the role they play in the everyday lives of their members and their families, and the caring practices they facilitate. Academic research in this area is limited, and we know little about care in youth sports clubs. This chapter has suggested that the concept of shadow care infrastructures, which argues for the foregrounding of 'spaces, practices and resources that are obscured within dominant welfare discourse' (Power et al., 2022: 8), provides an opportunity to reassess the contribution that these clubs play, especially at the current time. In times of crisis, and rapid social change, neighbourhood clubs can offer stability, security, friendships and routine that are in short supply elsewhere. The chapter does not advocate for sports clubs to be used to deliver government policies or priorities, or to replace other spaces of care, but instead hopes that their existing work and remit can be properly acknowledged, supported and resourced.

Findlay-King et al. (2020: 25) argue that as 'the capacity of the state to meet society's needs is stretched, and local government is forced to focus even more on providing essential services ... the network of [sports] clubs can be regarded as a valuable national resource'. Other countries have recognised the value and importance of community-based sports clubs and supported them through the welfare state. Such a situation in the UK feels a long way off at the current time, but the response to the pandemic has shown us that unexpected policies can be pursued and implemented with little warning. All that is required is the little 'inspiration and help' that Findlay-King et al. (2020: 25) spoke of, and for policymakers and politicians to recognise the value of grassroots and community sports clubs.

References

Avermaete, T. 2013. A thousand youth clubs: architecture, mass leisure and the rejuvenation of post-war France, *The Journal of Architecture* 18 (5), 632–646.

Bawden, A. 2023. Number of children in mental health crisis at record high in England, *The Guardian*, 15 August. Available at: https://www.theguardian.com/society/2023/aug/15/number-children-mental-health-crisis-record-high-england

Beatty, C. and Fothergill, S. 2016. *The Uneven Impact of Welfare Reform: The Financial Losses to Places and People*, JRF/Oxfam, Sheffield.

Bennett, T. 2017. *Creating a Culture: How school leaders can optimise behaviour, Independent review of behaviour in schools.* Available at: https://www.gov.uk/government/publications/behaviour-in-schools

Beveridge, W. 1942. *Social Insurance and Allied Services, Cmd 6404.* HMSO, London.

Beveridge, W. 1948. *Voluntary Action: A Report on Methods of Social Advance,* George Allen &Unwin Ltd, London.

Bjork, C. and Hoynes, W. 2022. Parents find community: youth sports as a mobile neighborhood, *Sport in Society* 25 (11), 2284–2302.

Blair, T. 1999. *Beveridge Lecture.* Available at: https://www.bristol.ac.uk/poverty/downloads/background/Tony%20Blair%20Child%20Poverty%20Speech.doc

British Academy. 2022. *Reframing Childhood: Final Report of the Childhood Policy Programme.* British Academy, London.

Brown, S.F. 2017. Mechanisms of social capital creation and consumption in a youth baseball league. *Sport in Society* 21 (10), 1517–1543.

Coalter, F. 2007. *A Wider Role for Sport: Who's Keeping the Score?* Routledge, Abingdon.

Cronin, C. and Armour, K. 2019. *Care in Sport Coaching: Pedagogical Cases.* Routledge, Abingdon.

DCMS. 2020. *Recreational Team Sport to Return Safely this Summer, 9 July.* Available at: https://www.gov.uk/government/news/recreational-team-sport-to-return-safely-this-summer

Disney, T., Crossley, S., King, H., Phillips, J., Robson, I. and Smith, R. 2022. Family Hubs and the vulnerable care ecologies of child and family welfare in austerity, *The Geographical Journal.* doi:10.1111/geoj.12505

Dunn, A. 2020. Government responds to Premier League Project Restart plans, *The Mirror, 5 May.* Available at: https://www.mirror.co.uk/sport/football/news/government-responds-premier-league-project-21978998

DWP. 2023. *Households below average income: An analysis of the UK income distribution: FYE 1995 to FYE 2022.* Available at: https://www.gov.uk/government/statistics/households-below-average-income-for-financial-years-ending-1995-to-2022/households-below-average-income-an-analysis-of-the-uk-income-distribution-fye-1995-to-fye-2022#children-in-low-income-households

Eisenstadt, N. 2011. *Providing a Sure Start: How Government Discovered Early Childhood.* Policy Press, Bristol.

Findlay-King, L., Reid, F. and Nichols, G. 2020. *Community Sports Clubs' response to COVID-19.* Sports Volunteering Research Network, Northumbria University, University of Sheffield.

Gottzen, L. and Kremer-Sadlik, T. 2012. Fatherhood and youth sports: a balancing act between care and expectations, *Gender & Society* 26 (4), 639-664.

Green. 2006. From 'sport for all' to not about 'sport' at all?: interrogating sport policy interventions in the United Kingdom, *European Sport Management Quarterly* 6 (3), 217-238.

Hall, R. 2023a. 'Buckling' NHS fails to treat 250,000 children with mental health problems, *The Guardian, 16 April.* Available at: https://www.theguardian.com/education/2023/apr/16/buckling-nhs-fails-to-treat-250000-children-with-mental-health-problems

Hall, R. 2023b. Social workers in England quitting in record numbers, *The Guardian, 23 February*. Available at: https://www.theguardian.com/society/2023/feb/23/social-workers-in-england-quitting-in-record-numbers

Hansard. 2020. *National League Football: COVID-19 Support Volume 683, 5 November*. Available at: https://hansard.parliament.uk/Commons/2020-11-05/debates/0E701A66-BBFC-4A9B-B833-4A215549EFEA/NationalLeagueFootballCOVID-19Support?highlight=grassroots%20sports#contribution-F70A146C-F73B-465E-87D5-3ECC146D973E

Hill, A. 2020. 'Scarred for life': Sage experts warn of impact of Covid policies on the young. *The Guardian, 20 October*. Available at: https://www.theguardian.com/uk-news/2020/oct/20/sage-experts-warn-of-impact-of-covid-policies-on-young-generation-z-harm-pandemic-coronavirus

Ibsen, B., Nichols, G., Piątkowska, M., Nagel, S., Llopis-Goig, R. and Elmose-Østerlund, K. 2022. What can explain the differences between European countries' public policies for sports clubs? *International Journal of Sport Policy and Politics*, 13 (3), 435–451. doi:10.1080/19406940.2022.2052148

Jupp, E. (2021). *Care, Crisis and Activism: The Politics of Everyday Life*. Policy Press, Bristol.

Mackintosh, C., Ives, B., Staniford, L., Gale, L., Thompson, A., Sims, D., Daniels, J., Oldfield, S. and Kolic, P. (2021). *COVID-19 Research Report: The impact of the Pandemic on Community Sport provision and participation*. Available at: https://www.mmu.ac.uk/media/mmuacuk/content/documents/research/COVID-19-RESEARCH-REPORT-The-impact-of-the-Pandemic-on-Community-Sport-provision-and-participation.pdf

McIntosh, P. and Charlton, V. 1985. *The Impact of Sport for All Policy 1966-1984. And a Way Forward*. The Sports Council, London.

Messner, M.A. and Musto, M. (2014). Where are the kids? *Sociology of Sport Journal* 31 (1), 102–122.

NAO. 2022. *Grassroots Participation in Sport and Physical Activity, HC 72*. Available at: https://www.nao.org.uk/reports/grassroots-participation-in-sport-and-physical-activity/

Parnell, D., Fitzpatrick, D., May, A. and Widdop, P. 2021. The political economoy of grassroots football: from obscurity to austerity. In:.Carr, J, Parnell, D., Widdop, P., Power, M.J., Millar, S.R. (Eds.), *Football, Politics and Identity*. Routledge, London, pp. 177–192.

Persson, M. 2022. Playing without goals: gendered practices in recreational youth football. *Journal of Youth Studies*. 10.1080/13676261.2021.2022641

Power, E.R., Wiesel, I., Mitchell, E., and Mee, K.J. 2022. Shadow care infrastructures: sustaining life in post-welfare cities, *Progress in Human Geography*, 46 (5), 1165–1184. doi:10.1177/03091325221109837

Pries, J. and Qvistrom, M. 2021. The patchwork planning of a welfare landscape: Reappraising the role of leisure planning in the Swedish welfare state, *Planning Perspectives*, 36:5, 923–948.

Sport and Recreation Alliance. 2013. Sports Club Survey 2013:*A review of clubs including membership, facility access, finances, challenges and opportunities*. Sport and Recreation Alliance, London.

Sport England. 2021a. *Active Lives Children and Young People Survey Coronavirus (COVID-19) Report: Mid-May to late-July 2020 (the summer term)*. Available at: https://sportengland-production-files.s3.eu-west-2.amazonaws.com/s3fs-public/2021-01/Active%20Lives%20Children%20Survey%20Academic%20Year%2019-20%20Coronavirus%20report.pdf?VersionId=2yHCzeG_iDUxK.qegt1GQdOmLiQcgThJ

Sport England. 2021b. *Active Lives Children and Young People Survey: Academic year 2019/20*. Available at: https://sportengland-production-files.s3.eu-west-2.amazonaws.com/s3fs-public/2021-01/Active%20Lives%20Children%20Survey%20Academic%20Year%2019-20%20report.pdf?VersionId=4Ti_0V0m9sYy5HwQjSiJN7Xj.VInpjV6

Sport England. 2023. *Active Lives Children and Young People Survey: Academic year 2022-23*. Available at: https://sportengland-production-files.s3.eu-west-2.amazonaws.com/s3fs-public/2023-12/Active%20Lives%20Children%20and%20Young%20People%20Survey%20-%20academic%20year%202022-23%20report.pdf?VersionId=3N7GGWZMKy88UPsGfnJVUZkaTklLwB_L

Sported. 2021. *Surviving a Pandemic: Community sports groups and COVID-19*. Sported, London.

Stefansen, K., Smette, I. and Strandbu, A. 2016. *Understanding the Increase in Parents' Involvement in Organized Youth Sports. Sport, Education, and Society* 23 (2), 1–11.

Sugden, J. and Knox, C. 1992 *Leisure in the 1990s: Rolling Back the Welfare State.* LSA Publications, Eastbourne.

Thomson, R., Bell, R., Holland, J., Henderson, S., McGrellis, S. and Sharpe, S. 2002. Critical moments: choice, chance and opportunity in young people's narratives of transition, *Sociology* 36 (2), 335–354.

Topping, A. 2023. 'Invisible, endless, relentless': The reality of care work in England. *The Guardian, 29 August*. Available at: https://www.theguardian.com/society/2023/aug/29/invisible-endless-relentless-the-reality-of-care-work-in-england

Tronto, J. 2015. *Who Cares? How to Reshape a Democratic Politics*. Cornell University Press, Ithaca.

Utilita. 2020. *State of Play Report: How COVID-19 has impacted grassroots football in the United Kingdom*. Utilita, London.

Walvin, J. 2001. *The Only Game: Football in Our Times*. Longman, London.

Warner, S., Dixon, M. and Leierer, S. 2015. Using youth sport to Enhance parents' sense of Community. *Journal of Applied Sport Management* 7 (1), 45–63.

Chapter 17

Youth Work During Covid Lockdowns

Alison Ní Charraighe[a], Kelly Coates[b], Shannon Devine[b] and Elisha Sanchez[b]

[a]Northumbria University, UK
[b]Projects4Change, UK

Abstract

In this chapter, we reflect collectively on the role of Youth Work during the COVID-19 lockdowns in England. Our contribution, presented as a conversation about practice during this time, reflects on the status of Youth Work and argues for its critical role in providing care for young people.

Keywords: Austerity; care; covid; key workers; young people; youth work

Introduction

Youth Work is often misunderstood by those outside of the profession. Fundamentally it is a relational activity (Ranahan, 2018) foregrounding the social interactions between the worker and the young person as the basis of all professional interactions. Youth work aims to support young people (11–25 years) during adolescence in developing their sense of self, autonomy, and social, emotional, spiritual and political growth. Youth Workers begin from the premise that each young person is worthy of regard, has potential to succeed in whatever they are interested in, and has a right to have a voice in the society and neighbourhoods that they belong to.

Youth Workers often work with young people that other services may have labelled 'challenging'. On the Estate we are discussing, many of the young people have difficulties at school, and within the community itself; they can be viewed as 'troublesome'. They often come from families that are facing multiple hardships and risks, and during the Covid pandemic, the lockdowns exacerbated those situations.

This practice orientated contribution is presented as a conversation between Alison, a Senior Lecturer at Northumbria University and former Youth Worker, and Kelly, Shannon and Elisha, three current Youth Workers from Projects4Change.

Alison:

What was your role prior to the pandemic and did it change at all during Covid?

Kelly:

So, I run a small local charity in an area of high deprivation, we're very small, our income is around £100,000 a year. The Charity at the time that Covid hit was three years old ... We are a youth-led charity working with young people along themes chosen by young people, giving young people a voice; the environment; feeling safe; and mental health. We work with quite a diverse, broad range of young people, about 300 a year. We also engage with the local school twice a week. We have excellent partnerships with local arts organisations.

Shannon:

Prior to Covid I was a youth worker working for the Project. We engage with young people and try to help them get off the streets, see their creative side and just support them with any needs they have. During Covid it was an experience because we had to change our delivery of the project and we had to adapt to what the rules and regulations were.

Elisha:

I was still a student in sixth form; 2020 was the year I left sixth form, so that September is when I was employed to be a support youth worker.

Alison:

When Covid hit and particularly during lockdown, certain professions were granted 'key worker' status... did youth workers?

Kelly:

I do think that we were overlooked. And I think that the important role that we provide to the community, especially some extremely vulnerable young people who were left without any contact with any professionals at all. These were young people who I felt people needed to have eyes upon, and that made me incredibly frustrated. So, I think that was the hardest period for me and the lowest period was the first lockdown, when we couldn't do anything.

Shannon:

And you didn't want to get the young people in trouble by going and seeing them, and you didn't want to get yourself in trouble, against ... the rules. We didn't do a lot of online work, because these young people are in such high poverty, they can't access the things to be online ... So, us not being key workers was just another kick in the face to youth work because again, it's not being recognized as a necessity.

Kelly:

Because we do work with quite a diverse bunch of young people, we did a couple of online sessions - But I felt that those that were really struggling couldn't access the online work.

Shannon:

A lot of these kids that we work with have hard family problems ... it's not just them, the family can't just focus on these young people. They have other family members that they've got to look after, which is difficult and it's probably no one's fault, but these young people needed the attention and support and unfortunately, they just didn't get it.

Kelly:

So as soon as we got the green light to do face-to-face work, we really homed-in on those young people who needed the service the most; and those young people actually weren't having a lockdown. They were running riot around the estate. They were very visible in the community by the police during that period and they were left unchecked, really enjoying lockdown, being unsupervised in the community when everyone else was indoors; and they were getting fined and their parents were getting fined and it was in not a great situation. They weren't doing any homeschooling whatsoever and the houses really weren't even set up for it, there was nowhere to study. There was no Internet, there was no functioning equipment, there was no support. There was no quiet, there wasn't a desk. They just were completely unequipped to even consider homeschooling.

Shannon:

I think as well because the housing where they live, some of them in high rise flats, so they couldn't even get in a garden to burn their energy out.

Alison:

Thinking about the concept of care, in the work that you do with young people what do you see as care, or how would you define care?

Shannon:

It's literally like listening to what they actually have to say. Listening to what they want and what their needs are... We then can potentially do something about it and ... actually support that individual and what they want and even they might not know what needs they have, but we can acknowledge what they might be missing and what they might be lacking without them even knowing. And us providing that shows them that they're not alone and that they can come to us with any issues that they have, and we can always be there to try and help them. A lot of these young people ... it's not just their own problems, it's like family problems. So yeah, it isn't just the young people, it's a community thing. And it was a community thing all the time through Covid.

Elisha:

I think what youth work is most especially good at is the relationship part. Not just the team, but also with the young people and the young people who access the youth club. I think the relationship part is what the care part is about. Knowing that regardless of what you do or how they make you feel they're going to come back, because you've invested in that relationship.

Kelly:

You know, there's no other adults that they trust that they willingly go to for support. And I just felt really sharply that we were ideally placed already to do the work. I think that's the beauty about neighbourhood youth work. We are already ideally placed to provide those services because we've done the groundwork. We've known these young people for a while.

When everything was getting back to normal, the young people just really, really struggled [with] their behaviour. We had eyes on them, and we knew they were struggling as well, and we were doing all those extra bits like providing the food parcels and things, but as things came out ... their behaviour just deteriorated so quick, and they seemed angry if I'm totally honest. I think they were angry because now they were expected to go back to school. Now their social workers were visiting again, and all of these things were expected of them, and I think they just felt they couldn't navigate that because they were so emotionally unregulated that they couldn't manage the transition back to normality. What they really need is specialist provision, that particular group.

Shannon:

And then I suppose there's care which is related to that provision of services... So that's 'care for' in a sense. So, one's about emotional work and the other one is 'I care enough about you to be here and to have the garden; and the growing; and the kayaking; and this and that and the other'.

Alison:

You said, they got a lot out of it, and it sounds like you got a lot out of it too. What made the difference in them being able to commit ...Can you think why?

Kelly:

Because I think we were the best thing that they had in their lives to be honest and I know often with youth work you feel sometimes like 'oh It's just a few hours a week, what difference can we make?' And sometimes, you're not seeing the progress, but that was a really intensive period I think because of Covid and because they weren't doing anything else. And because there was a lot of negativity around them and their family and we could be this little gap in the week where we're doing fun things, we're engaging with them, we're feeding them. And we showed them that care and concern.

Shannon:

I think these sessions that we're doing, it's like their little bit of escape once a week. It's their escape from their normality and you escape to someone else's attention, and all that love is on them and the trust is there. It's that they are meaningful, and we do these sessions for them and it's like 'oh well these sessions are for me'. It's of some worth to them. So, they feel... that since the sessions are for them, they are important to us; and we won't just disregard them if they've done something wrong or anything. So for them, I think it is a big part, because when they're at home, they might have been brushed off to the side if there is more important things ... like, you might not get a cuddle one day, but they could walk into a session and like we'd have a laugh and we'd have a joke and ask how the day was. Some kids don't get that if their parents are too busy, but that little... 'How was your day?' 'Are you OK?' [those questions] really can make a difference.

Kelly:

But also, the service element comes in when sometimes we have to be unpopular with young people in order to do the right thing. Young people generally appreciate honesty, and honesty is necessary to build trust, but also to safeguard young people's welfare. So, I kind of see it as like a professional love, professional care...

Alison:

We've talked about how 'care' is really important in youth work and it's actually maybe one of our 'magic ingredients'. How important is it for youth workers to think that the young people they work with care about them?

Elisha:

I think it's a two-way street, ..I care about you and I'm invested in you, and it might take some time for them to care about you back, but it's about building that relationship, and showing them that you care and therefore it's all right to have it back as well ... you're emotionally invested in this person and they are invested in you because they trust you and they share their feelings at the same time. So, it's a two-way relationship of that care.

Kelly:

I think I see it in some respects as service. It's not necessary for young people to care about me back, but inevitably, nine times out of ten it does happen anyway, and it's always lovely when it happens, and I'm always grateful for that.

Shannon:

Maybe the care element ... it's not expected from these young people, but when you have these young people and know that they care about you and they potentially don't have many relationships like that, where they care about your feelings and what you've done, it really does impact you emotionally and it makes you think, aw, although this profession is not well known or its pretty disregarded, it makes you think, well it is a really special career.

Concluding Thoughts

Our reflections on Covid lockdowns highlighted the intensely emotional aspect of youth work which resonates with subsequent debates about Covid and the mental health of young people. The professional 'care' talked about by the workers, also resonates with a strong body of research focussing on the impact of Youth Work from young people's perspectives. The decimation of statutory Youth Work during 12 years of austerity cuts by central Government in the UK has however undermined the efficacy of the profession, and the unique care youth workers provide.

Reference

Ranahan, P. (2018). De/valuing youth work: revealing tensions in professional identity development while enhancing and applying mental health literacy. *Child and Youth Services 39* (2–3), 137–157. 10.1080/0145935X.2018.1475224.

Final Commentary

Chapter 18

Childhood and Care in the Time of Coronavirus, A Commentary

Rachel Rosen

UCL Social Research Institute, UK

Abstract

Far from being 'a great equaliser', the COVID-19 pandemic exacerbated existing inequities and produced new ones. Yet, in the face of the multiple crises which the COVID-19 pandemic amplified, including a crisis of care, novel imaginaries and practices emerged to navigate the instability it wrought. For instance, although children were largely out of focus during the pandemic, when they appeared in discussions it was often along well-worn paths bound up in the chameleon-like figure of the child as the risk and at-risk. Yet by paying close attention to children's own experiences, we can see multiple examples of their care for and about Others. I make the case that this care was radical in the context of Coronavirus, not least because the tropes of the risky or at-risk child threatened to fracture possibilities of intergenerational solidarities necessary for navigating the pandemic and important for addressing widespread injustices.

Keywords: Child carers; child migrants; crises; injustice; practices of presence; solidarity

It is something of an irony that as I sit down to finalise this commentary on childhood and care in the time of Coronavirus, I find myself struggling with Covid-like symptoms. I say 'Covid-like' because there is no longer a standardised testing regime where I live nor is there firm guidance about what to do in the case you think you may have COVID-19. In many ways, the experience of living through Coronavirus, at least in the United Kingdom (UK), seems akin to a nightmare that quickly recedes from consciousness upon waking and, if it does not, public attitudes suggest it is a time best forgotten, if at all possible.

Yet, the ability to forget COVID-19 is not equally distributed, just as the impact of COVID-19 was wildly unequal. Despite the often-cited claim that COVID-19 does not discriminate, the impact of illness, mortality, and numerous quarantines were not the same for all. As multiple studies in diverse contexts have shown, COVID-19 may have been a new virus, but its impacts were stratified because of pre-existing and sedimented inequities. This point is developed in chapters in this volume including Lucy Currie, Sibusisiwe Tendai Sibanda and Athenkosi Mtumtum in Chapter 5; Donald Simpson and Sandra Lydon in Chapter 3; and Clare Matysova in Chapter 9. For instance, poverty increased medical vulnerability to COVID-19 (Blundell et al., 2020) and, relatedly, indigenous people and people of colour in the US (Sidik, 2022) and UK (Apea and Wan, 2021) were more likely to die of COVID-19 than white people. Here, Ruth Wilson-Gilmore's (2007: 28) definition of racism as the 'state-sanctioned and/or extralegal production and exploitation of group-differentiated vulnerability to premature death' rings presciently. It is also well documented that COVID-19 generated new forms of inequity as Black and Brown people in the UK were more likely than White people to be fined during lockdown (Dodd and Gidda, 2020), and it exacerbated existing inequalities as wealth became even more concentrated globally (Oxfam, 2022). These figures shine a cold, but bright light, on the workings of racial capitalism, with its tendencies to differentiate populations for accumulative ends (Bhattacharyya, 2018), at the same time as exemplifying its violences.

In part, the stratified effects of COVID-19 are the result of its emergence in conjunction with another crisis: one of care. Emma Dowling (2021) argues that it is not that people have stopped caring – indeed they have not and cannot, because care is a necessary condition of and for life (Bhattacharya, 2017a). However, she argues, the conditions for caring have become more difficult. This is the case because care is increasingly 'commodified for those who can pay for it and privatized for those who cannot' (Fraser, 2016: 112). Formal care systems have become financialised and sites of profiteering, for instance private equity firms own old age care homes (Horton, 2020) and parts of children's services (Jones, 2019) in the UK. At the same time, the resources of individuals, families, and communities are increasingly stretched as wages stagnate or collapse and others are dispossessed from their means of sustenance by climate change, rentierism, and projects of multinational companies (Katz, 2004), all affecting people's ability to care informally. To say that the care crisis exacerbated, or even amplified, COVID-19's unequal impacts in terms of health and morbidity, but also made possible its financial beneficiaries, is therefore a familiar refrain by now. But another, less rehearsed, argument is that in the UK, as Akwugo Emejulu (2021) argues, it is not just that care has been monetised, but austerity has undermined social rights to such a degree that it seems almost impossible to articulate and make claims on the state for solutions to the twin crises of care and COVID-19. There is a shrinking idea that the state will intervene to help despite the severity of the COVID-19 pandemic or even that the state is capable of doing so. One effect, she intimates, is that the horizons of our collective imaginaries for addressing these crises have also shrunk.

As such, even if it were possible to allow COVID-19 to slowly, but surely, recede from global consciousness, I want to suggest that to do so is not desirable as there is much to learn from this period, including socio-politically. The pandemic was both an unprecedented experience in many people's lifetimes, given its global scale, and it was a moment of 'crisis' that, as with other crises, produced a sense of 'radical uncertainty' (Narotzky and Besnier, 2014). This is not to say that people's lives before COVID-19 were stable and predictable; instability was an everyday reality for those living precarious lives on the margins. Perhaps then we can say that what marked the COVID-19 pandemic was how widespread this uncertainty was and the (new) imaginaries and practices which had to emerge to navigate the instability it wrought (Rosen, 2023b). Part of what makes this collection of chapters so important then is their careful attention to learning from the experience of the COVID-19 pandemic. The attention to childhood here is of particular significance, given that the breadth of children's lives was largely 'out of focus' in responses to COVID-19 (Cortés-Morales et al., 2021: 386). It is not that children were erased from view so much as that when childhood appeared in discussions this tended to follow well-worn paths bound up in the chameleon-like figure of the child as *the* risk and at-risk (Heidbrink, 2014; Smith, 2014).

In countries such as Chile, Columbia, and Spain, for example, children were often the least likely to be allowed out during times of quarantine. This segregation was not simply due to very real fears that those hardest hit by COVID-19, the elderly and people with compromised immune systems, might be infected. Children, and particularly those children deemed as 'Other', were singled out as 'vectors' or carriers of COVID-19. Here, the child was figured as a risk due to a perceived lack of restraint which would lead to the rampant passing of COVID-19 through touch or breath or deficiency in the capacity required to avoid the spread of the virus such as the inability to wear a mask. The risky child was also figured as the embodiment of an unclean, not yet 'civilised' body (Elias, 1978; Leavitt and Power, 1997), exacerbating the virus' spread. Children's sequestration was also related to ideas about what children can, should, and in practice do. For instance, where movement was largely limited to obtaining provisions or engaging in essential work, it was assumed that this was labour carried out by adults. In these cases, the justification for the particularly stringent quarantine of children was effectively based on essentialised assumptions of childhood and made law through the category of age.

The alter-ego of the risky child is that of the precious and 'priceless' (Zelizer, 1994) child-at-risk, for whom the danger of COVID-19 was considered particularly profound (see Chapter 6 by Julie Spray, this volume). Here, risk narratives condensed not so much around the disease itself but around concerns about children's mental health and that their development would be stunted due to time out of schooling. UNICEF, for example, issued a call for global action to 'avert a lost generation' (Unicef, 2020) (see also Chapter 16 by Stephen Crossley, this volume). Calling these 'narratives' of risk is in no way an indication that COVID-19 did not have profound impacts on children, particularly those in already precarious and marginalised positions (echoing the arguments of Alison Ni Charriaghe et al. in Chapter 17 and Catherine Nixon et al., in Chapter 15, this volume). For example, in our research on the Children Caring on the Move project, unaccompanied child migrants who arrived during the early days of the pandemic reported not seeing social workers for months on end. Others were warned about COVID-19 spreading in the shared accommodation where they had been placed by the state, yet they had no possibility of moving elsewhere or staying isolated when they had to share kitchens and bathrooms. In one of my other research projects about destitute families who have no access to mainstream welfare benefits because of their immigration status, children spoke about the impossibilities of doing online schooling, often on the families' only mobile phone in their single room accommodation.

Without seeking to minimize the effects of COVID-19, in what remains of this short commentary, I ask what might happen if we move away from these familiar tropes of childhood and risk to bring the complexity and breadth of children's lives into focus? More specifically – and echoing points raised, in the chapters by Julie Spray in Chapter 6; Tom Disney, Lucy Grimshaw and Judy Thomas in Chapter 11; Fiona Ranson and Cuong Nguyen in Chapter 10 – what can we learn when we consider children not just as risks to care or at-risk recipients of (uncaring) care systems, but themselves as potential car*ers*? In speaking about children's caring practices, I am not using the term in the sense of 'young carer' as it often appears in UK policy – with its hints of family deficit and non-normative child behaviour (Rosen and Newberry, 2018). Nor, am I mobilising the logic that this may be an empirical reality 'over there' but one that is certainly not desirable for 'our' children (Rosen, 2023a), an acceptance of the multiplicity of childhood without attention to its continuing idealisation through Eurocentric norms of racial capitalism (Balagopalan, 2019). In contrast, I draw on the work of care ethicist Joan Tronto (2011) who is instructive in her insistence that care is defined by its reciprocity: everyone provides and receives care. She argues: 'While the typical images of care indicate that those who are able-bodied and adult give care to children... it is also the case that all able-bodied adults receive care from others, and from themselves, every day.... Except for a very few people in states that approach catatonia, all humans engage in caring behaviour toward those around them' (Tronto, 2011: 164). Indeed, historical and contemporary evidence suggests that even very young children have the capacity to, and often do, engage in caring acts for themselves and others (Magazine and Sánchez, 2007; Newberry and Rosen, 2020). Yet, this important point is often lost as care is assumed descriptively and normatively to be an adult activity.

Bringing children's caring practices, or at least their potential, into focus as one way of attending to the breadth of young people's lives during the time of Coronavirus, prompts consideration of questions such as: How is care for and by children shaped by the COVID-19 crisis, and with what affects? What sort of subjectivities, relations, and worlds do children's caring practices bring into being? In what follows, I gesture towards some preliminary responses, drawing particularly on my own research with children and young people with precarious migration status in the UK.

As a starting point, this research suggests that although young people often spend considerable time and energy in family and schooling settings, their lives greatly exceed these institutions in counter distinction to what the popular debate on COVID-19 and the risky/at-risk child often suggested. In my research, young people spoke about delivering food to those – young and old, and often not kin at all – who were scared or unable to leave home due to COVID-19. Others talked about 'holding together' friends who had lost relatives to COVID-19 and had to grieve apart because of closed borders due to COVID-19 and insecure immigration status in the UK's hostile migration regime. Some spoke about providing a sofa or a floor for other young people to stay on, away from the virus that was spreading in their accommodation. Children living with adult family members in conditions of destitution, exacerbated by the pandemic as informal work dried up, spoke about their emotional care for family members, including by trying to protect their mothers from the knowledge of how much they knew about their family's precarity. Many young people spoke about the importance they place on their relationships with other young people, with unaccompanied young people commenting in multiple interviews: 'Friends are like family here'.

Yet, children's caring practices have a spectre-like existence in the UK – 'an absence presence' in professional and public discourses (Rosen et al., 2021). Lack of recognition of this aspect of children's lives certainly impoverishes understandings, and risks flattening complexity to normative understandings of childhood. It represents, at best, a narrow framing of children's sociality. Moreover, this absence of understanding can cause harm rather than helping or caring for children. For instance, in my research with unaccompanied child migrants, we have found that children may be forcibly separated in foster care placements because their care for each other is not recognised. Caring for others may mean their status as a 'child' is contested – because it is not seen as 'what children do', making them subject to suspicion and intensive, hostile age assessments or reduced support in the adult asylum system. Some young people go 'missing' from foster care when trying to reunite with their friends.

More broadly, to explore, deliberate, and understand what must change in order to address the crisis of inequality that lies at the heart of racial capitalism, and which was exacerbated by COVID-19, we need to know which mechanisms are enabling it to survive or take on new forms. Unrecognised care labour, as feminist theorists of social reproduction have long pointed out, is one such mechanism, leading to widespread efforts to mark its value both for, but also against, capital (Bhattacharya, 2017b; Federici, 2014). But children's care labour remains un- or under-valued, despite the fact that our research demonstrates that children with precarious migration status, and others in the UK, are filling system-wide gaps created by the twin crises of care and COVID-19. Young people's care, understood here as a multidimensional practice (Baldassar and Merla, 2014), included providing translation, mentorship, advice, food, financial loans and more for others. This is not just the necessary labour of life, but it often subsidises private, for-profit providers in children's services or enhances their surplus (Rosen, 2023c).

At the same time as care is the site of profiteering and extraction of (under/un-valued) labour, it can simultaneously be understood as 'a radical act', as Emejulu and Bassel (2018: 114) remind us. 'To *care about Others* requires the development of a political imagination that takes seriously the lived experiences of the most marginalized. This caring is radical particularly in the context of the commodified care'. It is also radical, I would suggest, in the context of hostile border regimes that categorise (Crawley and Skleparis, 2017), divide, and differentially in/exclude (Mezzadra and Neilson, 2013) people on the move, creating conditions where competition for deservingness or resentment could take hold. Equally, children's caring for and about Others is radical in the context of Coronavirus where the trope of the risky or at-risk child threatened to fracture intergenerational solidarities (Cortés-Morales et al., 2021).

Returning to COVID-19 crisis then, it is instructive to remember that the term 'crisis' means 'decision', 'choice', and 'judgement' in its ancient Greek roots ('Krísis'). This makes sense if we think about the ways that talk of crisis speaks to a profound sense of rupture and the creativity this requires to navigate. In the instability of crisis, new fields of action, social relations, and subjectivities may emerge or become more important, much as the young people who have been part of my research have demonstrated in relation to caring during the pandemic. This is not to romanticise innovation (Narotzky and Besnier, 2014) or deny the negative impacts of COVID-19, but to recognise that one outcome of the pandemic has been a public deliberation of the questions: Do we really want to get back to 'normal'? Who was 'normal' working for anyway?

In response to these questions, we might think of the enduring and profound, yet entirely everyday acts of care for the Other demonstrated by the children in my research which transcended age, country of origin, and migration status. We might think about the many young people involved in Black Lives Matters protests, caring for each other and caring to make a world were being Black does not mean being 'vulnerable to premature death' even in the face of risks to themselves at protests due to COVID-19 and the disproportionate policing of young people of colour.

Attending to these practices is vital because, as abolitionist scholar Ruth Wilson Gilmore (2023) suggests, to be *against* logics of bordering, profiteering and inequalities which have been brought into sharp relief by the COVID-19 pandemic does not tell us what we are *for*. She proposes that efforts towards the negation of punitive, extractive, and subjugating systems must be accompanied by dreams and practices of presence: 'making something into something else' (Gilmore, 2023: 477). Reciprocal care, mutual aid, conviviality, and horizontal solidarities demonstrated by children as they care for Others (Rosen, 2023b) exemplify Gilmore's (2018) reminder that 'what the world will become already exists in fragments and pieces, experiments and possibilities'. Together with negation, caring practices have the potential to not only contest the causes of the crises we face but change conditions of existence by remaking the world in more equal terms, as David Featherstone (2012) puts it.

Recognising children as (potential) carers, for others and for the world, opens up the possibility of engaging with their insights about the sorts of worlds they imagine and the alternative ways of living they may seek to develop (Rosen, 2023b) as they make where they are into places they wish to be (to paraphrase Gilmore, 2023: 481). There is a lot to learn from how those positioned as children 'decide', 'choose', and care in response to crises. If we learn to look, listen, and value these efforts, imagine how we can galvanise and amplify these practices of presence in response to crises.

References

Apea, V. and Wan, Y. 2021. Yes, there is structural racism in the UK – COVID-19 outcomes prove it. *The Conversation*.

Balagopalan, S. 2019. Childhood, culture, history: redeploying 'multiple childhoods'. In: Spyrou, S., Rosen, R., Cook, D.T. (Eds.), *Reimagining Childhood Studies*. Bloomsbury Press, London, pp. 23–40.

Baldassar, L. and Merla, L. 2014. Introduction: transnational family caregiving through the lens of circulation. In: Baldassar, L., Merla, L. (Eds.), *Transnational Families, Migration and the Circulation of Care: Understanding Mobility and Absence in Family Life*. Routledge, New York, pp. 3–24.

Bhattacharya, T. 2017a. Introduction: mapping social reproduction theory. In: Bhattacharya, T. (Ed.), *Social Reproduction Theory: Remapping Class, Recentering Oppression*. Pluto Press, London, pp. 1–20.

Bhattacharya, T. 2017b. *Social reproduction theory: Remapping Class, Recentering Oppression*. Pluto Press, London.

Bhattacharyya, G. 2018. *Rethinking Racial Capitalism: Questions of Reproduction and Survival*. Rowman & Littlefield International, Ltd, London.

Blundell, R., Costa Dias, M., Joyce, R., Xu, X. 2020. COVID-19 and inequalities. *Fiscal Studies 41* (2), 291–319.

Cortés-Morales, S., Holt, L., Acevedo-Rincón, J., Aitken, S., Ekman Ladru, D., Joelsson, T., Kraftl, P., Murray, L., Tebet, G. 2021. Children living in pandemic times: a geographical, transnational and situated view. *Children's Geographies 20* (4), 381–391.

Crawley, H., Skleparis, D. 2017. Refugees, migrants, neither, both: categorical fetishism and the politics of bounding in Europe's 'migration crisis'. *Journal of Ethnic and Migration Studies 44* (1), 48–64.

Dodd, V., Gidda, M. 2020. *Police in England and Wales Far More Likely to Fine BAME People in Lockdown*. The Guardian.

Dowling, E. 2021. *The Care Crisis: What Caused It and How Can We End It?*. Verso, London.

Elias, N. 1978. *The Civilizing Process*. Blackwell, Oxford.

Emejulu, A. 2021. It's even worse than we imagined. In: *BSA Annual Conference: Austerity Panel (ed BSA)*, online. BSA.

Emejulu, A., Bassel, L. 2018. Austerity and the politics of becoming. *Journal of Communication and Media Studies: Journal of Common Market Studies 56* (S1), 109–119.

Featherstone, D. 2012. *Solidarity : Hidden Histories and Geographies of Internationalism*. London Zed.

Federici, S. 2014. From commoning to debt: financialization, microcredit, and the changing architecture of capital accumulation. *South Atlantic Quarterly 113* (2), 231–244.

Fraser, N. 2016. Contradictions of capital and care. *New Left Review, 100*, 99–117.

Gilmore, R.W. 2007. *Golden Gulag: Prisons, Surplus, Crisis, and Opposition in Globalizing California*. University of California Press, Berkeley and Los Angeles, California.

Gilmore, R.W. 2018. Making abolition geography in California's central valley. *The Funambulist*.

Gilmore, R.W. 2023. *Abolition Geography: Essays Towards Liberation*. Verso, London.

Heidbrink, L. 2014. *Migrant Youth, Transnational Families, and the State: Care and Contested Interests*. University of Pennsylvania Press, Philadelphia.

Horton, A. 2020. Liquid home? Financialisation of the built environment in the UK's "hotel-style" care homes. *Transactions of the Institute of British Geographers 46* (1), 179–192.

Jones, R. 2019. *In Whose Interest? the Privatisation of Child Protection and Social Work*. Policy Press, Bristol.

Katz, C. 2004. *Growing up Global: Economic Restructuring and Children's Everyday Lives*. University of Minnesota Press, Minneapolis, Minn.; London.

Leavitt, R., Power, M.B. 1997. Civilizing bodies: children in day care. In: Tobin, J. (Ed.), *Making a Place for Pleasure in Early Childhood Education*. Yale University Press, New Haven and London, pp. 39–75.

Magazine, R., Sánchez, M.A.R. 2007. Continuity and change in san Pedro Tlalcuapan, Mexico: childhood, social reproduction, and transnational migration. In: Cole, J., Durham, D. (Eds.), *Generations and Globalisation: Youth, Age, and Family in the New World Economy*. University of Indiana Press, Bloomington.

Mezzadra, S., Neilson, B. 2013. *Borders as Method, or, The Multiplication of Labor*. Duke University Press, Durham and London.

Narotzky, S., Besnier, N. 2014. Crisis, value, and hope: rethinking the economy. *Current Anthropology 55* (S9), S4–S16.

Newberry, J., Rosen, R. 2020. Women and children together and apart: Finding the time for social reproduction theory. *Focaal 86*, 112–120.

Oxfam, 2022. Ten richest men double their fortunes in pandemic while incomes of 99 percent of humanity fall. Available at: https://www.oxfam.org/en/press-releases/ten-richest-men-double-their-fortunes-pandemic-while-incomes-99-percent-humanity

Rosen, R. 2023a. Childhood in and through social reproduction theory. In: Balagopalan, S., Wall, J., Wells, K. (Eds.), *Handbook of Theories in Childhood Studies*. Bloomsbury Academic, London, pp. 280–294.

Rosen, R. 2023c. Postponing destitution and deportation through enclosure In: *Children and the Hostile Environment (ed Environment SSAtH)*, online.

Rosen, R. Crafter, S., Meetoo, V., 2021. An absent presence: Separated child migrants' caring practices and the fortified neoliberal state. *Journal of Ethnic and Migration Studies 47* (7), 1649–1666.

Rosen, R. 2023b. Emergent solidarities and children on the move: what's 'crisis' got to do with it? In: Rosen, R., Chase, E., Crafter, S., Glockner, V., Mitra, S. (Eds.), *Crisis for Whom? Critical Global Perspectives on Childhood, Care, and Migration*. UCL Press, London, pp. 20–35.

Rosen, R., Newberry, J. 2018. Love, labour and temporality: reconceptualising social reproduction with women *and* children in the frame. In: Rosen, R., Twamley, K. (Eds.), *Feminism and the Politics of Childhood: Friends or Foes?* UCL Press, London, pp. 117–133.

Sidik, S.M. 2022. How COVID has deepened inequality — in six Stark graphics. *Nature*.

Smith, K.M. 2014. *The Government of childhood: Discourse, Power and subjectivity*. Palgrave Macmillan, London.

Tronto, J.C. 2011. A feminist democratic ethics of care and global care workers: citizenship and responsibilitly. In: Mahon, R., Robinson, F. (Eds.), *Feminist Ethics and Social Policy: Towards a New Global Political Economy of Care*. UBC Press, Vancouver, pp. 162–177.

Unicef, 2020. UNICEF calls for averting a lost generation as COVID-19 threatens to cause irreversible harm to children's education, nutrition and well-being. Available at: https://www.unicef.org/press-releases/unicef-calls-averting-lost-generation-covid-19-threatens-cause-irreversible-harm. (Accessed 28 September 2023)

Zelizer, V. 1994. *Pricing the Priceless Child: The Changing Social Value of Children*. Princeton University Press, Princeton, NJ; Chichester.

Index

Academia, 165–167
Academic scholarship, 5–6
Accommodating care, 174–176
'Active leisure' opportunities, 212
Affect, 7–8
Affect management, 83–84
  children in, 86–89
Alexandra township, 68
Art, 3
Arts-based methods, 146, 149–150
Arts-based participatory methods, 11
Arts-based participatory research, 149
Attentiveness, 167
Austerity, 229

'Babies as perceived mirror of parents' abilities, 113–115
Beveridge on Voluntary Action, 212
Bias, 84
Bioecological theory, 56
British Boxing Board of Control, 211–212
Bronfenbrenner, Urie, 56
'Business models' of ideal motherhood, 107

Canadian study, 29
Capabilities, 123
Capability Approach (CA), 123
Capitalism, 148
Care (*see also* Ethics of care), 2–3, 5, 7–8, 122, 137, 146, 165, 167, 181, 186, 227
  agency, 6–7
  control, 204
  devaluation of, 6
  family and distance, 158
  findings, 125–131
  formal, 2

  informal, 211
  methodology, 149–158
  methodology and research methods, 124–125
  in preschool and a 'new normal', 50–52
  professional love, 12–13
  relational, 13
  school and, 146–148
  school spaces, 154–156
  spaces of, 6–7
  students' experiences of care, 152–154
  walking and movement, 156–158
Care Manifesto, 6
Care-receiving, 166–167
Caregiving, 107, 166
Caring about, 166
  community, 72–74
Caring for, 166
Caring with, 167
Case study approaches, 167–168
Centre for Excellence for Children's Care and Protection (CELCIS), 98–99
Child development, 3, 181
Child migrants, 235–236
Child protection, 12–13
Childcare, 41, 122, 170, 172
Childhood/children, 2–5, 7
  in affect management, 86–89
  experiences of caring for, 169–176
  participation, 193, 196, 199, 203
  policy in UK, 210
  studies, 3, 7, 146–147
  well-being, 25
Children Caring on the Move project, 235–236

Children's Hearings (Scotland) Act (2011), 192
Children's hearings, 192
Children's rights, 22–23
China, 30, 138
Class dynamics, 107
Community sports clubs, 209–210
Competence, 167
Compulsory Supervision Order (CSO), 192
Conviviality, 238
Coping, 75–76
Coping strategies of parents/carers during pandemic, 28–29
Coronavirus (COVID-19), 2–3, 5, 40, 82, 138, 146, 214, 217, 225, 233–234
  and (in) sensitivity to care needs of poor, 43–45
  babies, 107
  care needs of poor and adaptions to practice during, 45–48
  global, 13
  global impacts and inequalities, 13
  inclusion/exclusion criteria, 21
  lockdowns and early care and education balance, 49–50
  methods, 20–21
  national, 20
  pandemic, 20, 55–56, 107, 164
  impact of pandemic on ECEC landscape, 22–23
  parents/carers during pandemic, 27–32
  recommendations, 32–33
  schooling and, 148–149
  virtual hearings, 194
  and window of opportunity for care in preschool, 42
  young children during pandemic, 24–27
Creative making and metaphor, 151
Creative mixed methods qualitative research study, 149–150
Cricket, 209–210
Crisis, 238
Crisis theory (Brammer), 70
Critical Childhood Studies, 7–8
Cross-cultural study, 29

Decision-making, 193
Deficit-based discourse, 42
Dialogical narrative analysis (DNA), 125
Digital learning, 23
Digital space, 196–197
Digital technologies, 106–107
Digitalised care, 167
Discrimination, 84
Display work, 106–107
Distance, 156, 158

Early Childhood Education and Care (ECEC), 22, 40
  impact of pandemic on ECEC landscape, 22–23
Early education, 40
Early Years Foundation Stage (EYFS), 40
Early years settings, 56–61
Education, 3, 181
  during pandemic, 164–165
Educational inequalities, 67
Emotion, 25
Emotional valences, 86
England, 4, 9
ERIC, 20–21
Ethical approval, 150
Ethics of care, 123, 164, 166–167
  context and literature, 164–165
  methodology, 167–176

Family, 3, 5, 158
  tensions, 74–75
Feminist ethics of care, 123
Football, 209–210
Football Association, 211–212
Formal care systems, 234
Foster care, 137
Fraser, Nancy, 2–3, 234

Index

Freewriting, 151
Furlough, 126

Gender, 106
Gender equality, 106, 122
Gender-based violence, 99
General Certificate of Secondary Education (GCSE), 186–187
Geography, 3
Getting It Right For Every Child (GIRFEC), 97
Girls, 146, 149–150
Good mothering, 108
Government policy, 51
Grassroots sports clubs, 209–210, 214, 217
  (de) valuing, 211–214
  'In the Middle of Things', 217–220

Health, 24
Health promotion, 83–84
Health visiting, 98
Health visitors, 10
Hierarchy of Needs Model (Maslow), 70
High school, 186–187
Home, 67–68
Homeschooling, 164–165, 169–170, 172, 176
Hooks, Bell, 12–13, 148
Hope, 10–11
'Hopes and fears for babies' future, 109–111
Horizontal solidarities, 238
Households, 106

Impression management, 114
Inequalities, 6, 238
Informal settlements, 66–67
Initial teacher training (ITT), 185
Institute of Research in Social Sciences (IRISS), 98–99
Interdependency of care, 148

Intergenerational solidarities, 237–238
Invisible in society, 219

Katz, Cindi, 11, 146–147, 234
Key workers, 226

Learning packs, 49
Lockdowns, 3–4, 8–9, 12–13, 67–68, 139, 167, 211, 214, 217
  impacts, 9–10
  measures, 107
  period, 11
  strugglers, 148–149
  survivors, 148–149
  thriver, 148–149
London 2012 Olympic legacy, 213

Māori communities, 87–88
Marylebone Cricket Club, 211–212
Mental health, 9–10, 147–148
Mille Clubs Programme, 213–214
Movement, 156, 158
Mutual aid, 238

National Governing Bodies (NGBs), 210–211
Nature, 5
Near Me (virtual platform), 100
Neglect, 84
New Labour government (1997–2010), 213
New normal, 40, 50, 52
New parents, 107–108
New work routines, 172–174
New Zealand, 82
  children in affect management, 86–89
  children's perspectives, 89–93
  participants and methods, 85–86
Norms, 122

Olympic and Paralympic Legacy Cabinet Committee, 213
Online interaction, 50

Online learning, 30–32
Online peer support groups, 167, 176–177
Online spaces, 107–108
Ontological anxiety, 146–147
Organisational spaces, 148
Othering, 42
Othermothering, 6
Our Hearings, Our Voice (OHOV), 195

Pandemic, 165–167
Pandemic Generation, 84–85
Parental involvement, 23
Parental leave policy, 122–123
Parenthood, 106
    'babies as perceived mirror of parents' abilities, 113–115
    findings, 108–109
    'hopes and fears for babies' future, 109–111
    methodology, 108
    peaceful and oblivious babies, 111–113
Parenting, 10–11, 107
    support group, 164
Parents, 125, 164, 218
    and child conversation, 137
    collaboration between families and ECEC services, 29–30
    coping strategies of parents/carers during pandemic, 28–29
    impact of COVID-19 pandemic, 27–28
    engagement, 29
    online learning, 30–32
    parents/carers during pandemic, 27–32
Peaceful and oblivious babies, 111–113
Peer support group, 167
Personal protective equipment (PPE), 100
Physical activity, 210–211
Policy, 3, 41
Politics of care, 6

Postnatal support, 110–111
Poverty, 41–42, 66–67
    intercorrelations between poverty beliefs and other study measures, 45
Poverty Belief Scale, 44–45
Practices of presence, 238
Practitioners, 42, 44, 55–56
Pre-COVID-19, 40–41
Precarity, 9–10, 219
Preciousness of time, troubling, 127–128
Preschool, 40–42
    care in, 50–52
    COVID-19 and window of opportunity for care in, 42
    findings, 43–50
    and long standing care and education divide, 41
    methodology, 42–43
PRISMA 2020 method, 20–21
Productive work, 128–129
Pseudonymisation, 151
Public health, 3, 83–84
Public sector, 212

Racial capitalism, 6
Racism, 138
Radical uncertainty, 235
Reciprocal care, 238
Refugee, 141
Relationships, 97
Reproductive work, 128–129
Research methods, 124–125
    arts-based, 149
    case study, 168
    comics, 85–86
    participatory research, 149
    systematic review, 27
Resilience, 9–10
Responsibility, 167
Responsiveness, 167
Risk, 12, 210

Rugby, 209–210
Rugby Football Union, 211–212

Safeguarding, 147–148
School (*see also* Preschool), 146, 148
  closures, 67–68
  spaces, 154–156
Schoolification, 41
Schooling and COVID-19, 148–149
Scopus, 20–21
Scotland, 10
Scotland's Children's Hearings System, 192
Scotland's Independent Care Review, 193
Scottish Children's Reporter Administration (SCRA), 192
Scottish Law, 192–193
Secondary school, 181, 185
Self-care, 75–76
Shadow care infrastructures, 209–211, 219
Shared Parental Leave (SPL) policy, 122
Slow breathing, 151
Social advance, 212
Social care and justice, 194
Social constructivist thematic analysis, 125
Social policy, 3
Socially distancing from parents in poverty, 42
Socio-Economic Institute of South Africa (SERI), 66–67
Sociology, 3
Solidarity, 167
South Africa, 66–67
Sport England, 210–211
Sport for All, 212
Sports, 209–210
Sports clubs, 213
Sports Council, 212
'Stay home, save lives', 165
Stereotyping, 84
Stigma, 84

Stjwetla informal settlement, 68
Students' experiences of care, 152–154
Study of Early Education and Development (SEED study), 23
Supportive Group Online, 169–170
Systemic resilience, 24–25
Teaching, 185
  during lockdowns, 181
Teaching assistant (TA), 186
Treasuring time, 125–126
Tronto, Joan, 5–6, 177, 236
Trust, 167

Unaccompanied child migrants, 235–237
UNICEF, 23, 235–236
United Kingdom (UK), 233
United Nations Convention on the Rights of the Child (UNCRC), 97, 192–193

Universal Health Visiting Pathway (UHVP), 98

Value of time with baby, 125–127
Vietnam, 138
Violence against women and girls (VAWG), 99
Virtual hearings
  Covid-19 pandemic and impact, 194
  learning from, 203–205
  negative effects, 196–199
  positive effects, 199–203
  Scotland's Children's Hearings System, 192
  voices of children, 195–196
Virtual learning, 28
Virtual learning environment (VLE), 185
Visibility of parents at work, 129–131
Visible in society, 219
Voices of children, 195–196
Vulnerable girls
  aims of research, 68

248 Index

Alexandra township and Stjwetla informal settlement, 68
caring about community, 72–74
concerns for future, 71–72
coping and self-care, 75–76
data collection, 69–70
family tensions, 74–75
knowledge about virus, 71
lockdown, school closures and home, 67–68
participants, 69
poverty and informal settlements, 66–67
research methodology, 68–76
theoretical framework, 70

Walking, 156–158
Web of Science (WoS), 20–21
Welfare state, 211–212
Well-being, 24, 181–182
WhatsApp, 31–32
Women's motherhood, 106
Work, 164–165
  during pandemic, 169–176
World Health Organisation (WHO), 2

Young children during pandemic, 24–27
  COVID-19, 25–26
  experiences, 24–25
  health and well-being, 24
  outdoor activity, 27
  reading experience, 26–27
  technology, 26
Young people, 3, 5, 225, 236–237
Youth, 3–4
Youth Work, 225–229
Youth Workers, 225
YouTube, 31–32

Zero-covid strategy, 83–84

Printed and bound by CPI Group (UK) Ltd, Croydon, CR0 4YY
19/11/2024

14595298-0002